EXPLORATIONS IN PRACTICAL THEOLOGY

ENCOUNTERING GOD

PRACTICAL THEOLOGY AND THE MISSION TO HEAL

EDITED BY
ROBERT DIXON & MARY EASTHAM

COVENTRY
PRESS

Published in Australia by
Coventry Press
33 Scoresby Road
Bayswater VIC 3153

ISBN 9781922589309

Compilation Copyright © 2023 APTO Inc. (NSW)
Copyright of individual chapters remains with the authors.

All rights reserved. Other than for the purposes and subject to the conditions prescribed under the *Copyright Act*, no part of this publication may be reproduced, stored in a retrieval system, or transmitted in any form or by any means, electronic, mechanical, photocopying, recording or otherwise, without the prior permission of the publisher.

Scripture quotations are from the *New Revised Standard Version Bible*, copyright 1989, Division of Christian Education of the National Council of the Churches of Christ in the United States of America. Used by permission. All rights reserved.

Scripture marked NIV is taken from the Holy Bible, NEW INTERNATIONAL VERSION®, NIV® Copyright © 1973, 1978, 1984, 2011 by Biblica, Inc.® Used by permission. All rights reserved worldwide.

Scripture marked English Standard Version is from The ESV® Bible (The Holy Bible, English Standard Version®), copyright © 2001 by Crossway, a publishing ministry of Good News Publishers. Used by permission. All rights reserved.

Catalogue-in-Publication entry is available from the National Library of Australia
http://catalogue.nla.gov.au

Cover design by Ian James – www.jgd.com.au
Text design by Coventry Press
Set in EB Garamond

Printed in Australia

Table of Contents

Acknowledgments ... 5
Contributors ... 7
Introduction ... 13

Part One   Healing Shattered Relationships   23

Chapter One
    And now! Being Church after the Royal Commission
        Francis Sullivan 25

Chapter Two
    Growing dissatisfaction: Mass attenders' attitudes to
    the sexual abuse crisis in the Catholic Church
        Robert Dixon 33

Chapter Three
    A silent Church lives in darkness: Speaking out
    as response to clerical child sexual assault
    in the Catholic Church
        Christopher Evan Longhurst 53

Chapter Four
    15 March 2019: Remembering the causes of white
    supremacy and racism to be agents of healing
    and justice
        Mary Eastham 70

Chapter Five
    Some Christian attempts at healing with Buddhists
    in Sri Lanka post-independence
        Malcolm Kreltszheim 88

Part Two   Theological Frameworks for Healing   101

Chapter Six
    It was the best of times, it was the worst of times:
    A practical theological reflection in a pandemic
        Rosie Joyce 103

Chapter Seven
    Toward a practical eco-theological approach
    with Christian askesis
        Julie A Hawkins 109

Chapter Eight
　The *habitus*, reflexivity and an Ignatian
　spirituality that does justice
　　　Sandie Cornish 129
Chapter Nine
　What is spiritual health?
　　　Peter Carblis 151
Chapter Ten
　In the beginning was the Word: the place of
　AI technology in the integral approach
　　　Beatrice Green 170

Part Three　Creating Healing Communities　179

Chapter Eleven
　Embracing voices of dissent: Women,
　spiritual authority and the Church
　　　Catherine Lambert 181
Chapter Twelve
　Anxious behaviours at the interface between
　pastors and congregations
　　　Kathy Matuschka 198
Chapter Thirteen
　A possible response to the wicked problem of
　financing the Catholic Church in Australia after
　the sexual abuse crisis
　　　Brendan Long 217
Chapter Fourteen
　Hearing God's voice: The role of revelatory
　experiences in ministry and mission among
　Australian Pentecostals
　　　Tania Harris 236

Table of Contents

Acknowledgments 5
Contributors 7
Introduction 13

Part One   Healing Shattered Relationships   23

Chapter One
And now! Being Church after the Royal Commission
Francis Sullivan 25

Chapter Two
Growing dissatisfaction: Mass attenders' attitudes to
the sexual abuse crisis in the Catholic Church
Robert Dixon 33

Chapter Three
A silent Church lives in darkness: Speaking out
as response to clerical child sexual assault
in the Catholic Church
Christopher Evan Longhurst 53

Chapter Four
15 March 2019: Remembering the causes of white
supremacy and racism to be agents of healing
and justice
Mary Eastham 70

Chapter Five
Some Christian attempts at healing with Buddhists
in Sri Lanka post-independence
Malcolm Kreltszheim 88

Part Two   Theological Frameworks for Healing   101

Chapter Six
It was the best of times, it was the worst of times:
A practical theological reflection in a pandemic
Rosie Joyce 103

Chapter Seven
Toward a practical eco-theological approach
with Christian askesis
Julie A Hawkins 109

Chapter Eight
    The *habitus*, reflexivity and an Ignatian
    spirituality that does justice
        Sandie Cornish 129

Chapter Nine
    What is spiritual health?
        Peter Carblis 151

Chapter Ten
    In the beginning was the Word: the place of
    AI technology in the integral approach
        Beatrice Green 170

Part Three   Creating Healing Communities   179

Chapter Eleven
    Embracing voices of dissent: Women,
    spiritual authority and the Church
        Catherine Lambert 181

Chapter Twelve
    Anxious behaviours at the interface between
    pastors and congregations
        Kathy Matuschka 198

Chapter Thirteen
    A possible response to the wicked problem of
    financing the Catholic Church in Australia after
    the sexual abuse crisis
        Brendan Long 217

Chapter Fourteen
    Hearing God's voice: The role of revelatory
    experiences in ministry and mission among
    Australian Pentecostals
        Tania Harris 236

Acknowledgments

This book is the result of a truly collaborative effort, relying for its very existence on the contributions of many people: the authors, peer reviewers, the Executive of the Association of Practical Theology in Oceania (APTO), the publisher and many others, all of whom provided the support and assistance that my co-editor, Mary Eastham, and I needed in order to produce the book.

It has been a long process, originating in the 2020 APTO conference, a wholly online conference in the first year of the pandemic, when we were all still learning how to manage online conferences. The first achievement of our authors, then, was to record and upload their conference presentations. Their second was to transform those presentations into the chapters that appear in this volume. We are very grateful to them for their patience and persistence in preparing their chapters and through the long and sometimes challenging process of peer review that followed. To all those academics and ministry practitioners who took on the task of peer reviewing a chapter, we acknowledge your efforts and thank you for helping to bring this book to fruition.

The decision to publish a selection of the 2020 conference papers in a book was made by the APTO Executive, under the leadership of the President, Zach Duke, together with Vice-President Jill Gowdie, Secretary Michelle Eastwood (later Julian Kluge), Treasurer Peter Carblis, and members Tracy McEwan, Debra Snoddy and Christopher Longhurst. Former APTO Presidents John F. Collins and Anthony Maher also offered support and encouragement to the project.

We have been extremely fortunate to be able to benefit from the skill, long experience and never-ending encouragement of our publisher, Hugh McGinlay at Coventry Press. This is the second APTO title that Hugh has published after *Faith and the political in a post-secular age*, which was based on the 2015 conference held in Canberra.

Mary Eastham provided me with immense support throughout the entire editorial process. She is the principal author of the Introduction and is responsible for the three-part structure of the book and the order of chapters, the source of the book's dynamic push from crisis to resolution. She also chose peer reviewers for my chapter. I am extremely grateful to her.

Finally, I thank my wife, Cath, who has been a constant source of encouragement and support even when working on 'the book' seemed to have become a permanent fixture in my life.

Robert Dixon
March 2023

> This book is dedicated to the memory of
> Therese D'Orsa
> 1944 – 2023
> Passionate practical theologian and teacher

Contributors

Peter Carblis

Peter has had a varied career in pioneering, leading and governing pastoral ministry in churches and chaplaincy and in education at school, vocational and higher educational levels. He is currently the Churches of Christ in NSW representative on the Civil Chaplaincies Advisory Committee (CCAC) and a member of its Executive. The CCAC has responsibility for the endorsement of Hospital, Corrective Services and Youth Justice Chaplains and the registration of chaplaincy education providers. He is also a member of the executive of the Association for Practical Theology in Oceania (APTO), the Board of Directors of the Australian College of Ministry (ACOM) and the Morling College Academic Board. He holds a PhD in Educating for Emotional Intelligence from Macquarie University, and a second PhD with the Sydney College of Divinity which explores the theological validation of educational outcomes and ministry objectives related to moral and spiritual formation.

Sandie Cornish

Sandie Cornish is a Senior Lecturer in the School of Theology at the Australian Catholic University and a member of the Dicastery for the Promotion of Integral Human Development. She holds a PhD in Practical Theology, a Licentiate in Catholic Social Doctrine and Ethics, a Master of Public Policy, and a Bachelor of Economics. Sandie has worked in faith-based social justice and human rights organisations at the diocesan, national and Asia-Pacific levels where her roles have included organisational leadership, strategic planning, policy analysis and advocacy, social research, mission integration and formation for mission. She was the Director of the Office for Justice, Ecology and Peace of the Australian Catholic Bishops Conference, and one of the periti for the Fifth Plenary Council of the Catholic Church in Australia. Sandie played a significant role in the Bishops' Committee for Justice, Development and Peace's consultations in the 1980s and 1990s.

Robert Dixon

Robert (Bob) Dixon was the Foundation Director of the Australian Catholic Bishops Conference Pastoral Research Office (now the National Centre for Pastoral Research) from 1996 to 2016. He is an Honorary Research Fellow at the University of Divinity and a former Honorary Professor of Australian Catholic University. He served as APTO Treasurer from 2017 to 2021 and was made a Life Member of APTO in 2022. He is the author or co-author of numerous publications and reports about the demography of the Australian Catholic population and aspects of Catholic belief and practice, and has had chapters in two previous APTO publications. Bob has a PhD in sociology from Monash University as well as degrees in science, theology and education. A long-time resident of Melbourne, his interest in Oceania comes from his time in Samoa as a volunteer teacher in the 1970s.

Mary Eastham

A member since 2004, Mary Eastham was appointed an APTO Fellow in 2021. She holds a PhD in Public Theology from the Catholic University of America in Washington DC. From 2011 until 2022, Mary was a member of the New Zealand Catholic Bishops' Committee for Interfaith Relations and chaired the Palmerston North Interfaith Group, which contributed to two national policy documents in 2019: An Interfaith Submission to the Zero Carbon Bill, and the Royal Commission of Inquiry into the Attack on Christchurch Mosques on 15 March 2019. In 2019, Mary was part of a reference group organised by the Office of Ethnic Communities to discuss ways in which Government can work with faith communities and interfaith groups to promote greater social inclusion and to counter racism, religious discrimination and religious intolerance. In 2021–2022, she served on a Working Party organised by the Ministry of Social Development to develop a framework for social cohesion. In 2022, Mary was appointed a Trustee for the Religious Diversity Centre Trust.

Beatrice Green

Beatrice Green is affiliated with Australian Catholic University where she was a sessional lecturer for 20 years. A Life Member of APTO, having served some years as President and Secretary, her publications include *Bede Griffiths' Images of God* (2022), "Wisdom under Fire: Human Vulnerability as the Besieged Heart of the Icon of God" in *Priest, Poet* and *Theologian: Essays in Honour of Anthony Kelly CSsR* (2013), "'I bring a sword': 'My peace I give': experience the binding factor" in *Dreaming a New Earth: Raimon Panikkar and Indigenous Spiritualities* (2012); and "Bridging Difference" in *Catalyst: Pastoral and Socio-Cultural Journal for Melanesia* (2012). She is also, along with Keiti Ann Kanongata'a, contributing editor of the volume *Weaving Theology in Oceania: Culture, Context and Practice* (2020) which arose out of the 2018 APTO conference in Suva, Fiji.

Tania Harris

Tania Harris is a pastor, speaker, author, practical theologian and the founding director of *God Conversations*, a global ministry that equips people to recognise and respond to God's voice. With a diverse history as church planter, pastor and lecturer, Tania ministers across the globe to all traditions and age-groups and is a popular voice on radio and TV. Tania consults with and trains ministers in Spirit-led discipleship and the development of church cultures that facilitate hearing God experiences. Her PhD research, academic publications and books *God Conversations* and *The Church who Hears God's Voice* all aim to equip everyone to recognise the Spirit in the context of their local church. Tania is an ordained minister with the Australian Christian Churches. She makes her home in Sydney, Australia.

Julie Hawkins

Julie Hawkins has recently completed a doctorate in Philosophy/Theology which focused on eco-philosophy, mystical theology, and a deepening of ethics and aesthetics in the Western Tradition. She is currently researching Eco-Theology as an emerging field and an important element in working toward resolutions for Earth's ecological crisis. An earlier PhD developed an analytical framework for Eco-philosophical concepts and ethics in speculative fiction. Julie has studied and worked as a casual academic at the University of New England, and was previously employed as a high school teacher and academic manager. She holds an MLit in Mediaeval Background, and has recently presented at academic conferences on Middle English, Literature, and on the timely ways Speculative Fiction has suggested fresh ethical approaches for living in the 21st century.

Rosie Joyce

Rosie Joyce is a Brigidine Sister whose early years in ministry were spent teaching in primary and secondary schools across Victoria. This included being the principal of four secondary schools. Rosie lectures in canon law at Yarra Theological Union, a Teaching College of the University of Divinity, is a Judge on the Marriage Tribunal for Victoria and Tasmania, and a Judge for the Appeal Tribunal for Australia and New Zealand. She is an adviser on canonical issues and has a particular interest in the governance of church organisations. As a result of this, she is frequently called upon to be a speaker at many seminars dealing with this increasingly important issue. She has been the Provincial Leader of her Congregation and is a past President of *Catholic Religious Australia*, the peak body representing the Congregations of Women and Men Religious in Australia.

Malcolm Kreltszheim

Malcolm Kreltszheim is a PhD (Theology) student at the University of Divinity. Born in Sri Lanka, he completed his initial studies in Architecture in Ceylon in 1970 and emigrated to Melbourne in 1971 to complete his studies. Qualifying as an Architect in 1975, he spent the next 40 years working as an Architect in Melbourne, adding a Bachelor of Arts from Melbourne University in 1985. Following retirement in December 2015, Malcolm joined Pilgrim Theological College, University of Divinity, and received the degree of Master of Theological Studies in March 2019. In December, his proposal for a PhD Thesis titled, *Buddhist Reactions to Christian Missionary Attitudes in the British Colonial Period in Ceylon/Sri Lanka* was accepted and he was awarded a Commonwealth Government scholarship to assist him in that exciting endeavour. Malcolm is married to Neloo (a retired Architect) and they have two adult daughters, Chyonne and Leander.

Catherine Lambert

Catherine completed her doctoral thesis early in 2022, exploring how contemporary women on the edge of the church respond to the beguine mystics of the thirteenth century. With a passion for spiritual direction, she is currently the course co-ordinator for the Dayspring courses in spirituality and spiritual direction. Catherine is also the project administrator for the Spirited Project, researching how families and friends offer spiritual care to loved ones living with dementia. Recently, she has taken co-teaching roles with Pilgrim Theological College and Wellspring. Catherine is the West Australian representative on the Australian Network for Spiritual Direction executive and an elected member of the Australian Ecumenical Council for Spiritual Direction.

Brendan Long

Brendan Long has a PhD from the University of Cambridge, UK, and is a Senior Research Fellow at the Australian Institute for Christianity and Culture at Charles Sturt University. He has worked for over 25 years as a public policy professional, political adviser and in leadership roles for the not-for-profit sector. He has published research on the economic impact of religiosity in Australia in a number of peer reviewed works. He also has published works on the Adam Smith's religious views and economics and theology.

Christopher Evan Longhurst

Christopher Evan Longhurst is a Catholic theologian. He received his doctorate *summa cum laude* from the Pontifical Angelicum University, Rome, in 2009. He researches in clergy sexual abuse within the Catholic Church, with a focus on the theological changes needed to the systems and culture that caused the abuse. Chris is an executive member of APTO and a fellow of the King Abdullah bin Abdulaziz International Centre for Interreligious and Intercultural Dialogue (KAICIID). He has taught at Marymount International Institute in Rome, Al Akhawayn University in Ifrane, Morocco, and Victoria University of Wellington, Aotearoa New Zealand. Currently, he lectures in theology at Te Kupenga Catholic Theological College in Aotearoa New Zealand. Chris is also a core participant in the New Zealand Royal Commission of Inquiry into Abuse in State Care and the Care of Faith-based Institutions, and the founder and National Leader of the New Zealand chapter of the worldwide Survivors Network of those Abused by Priests (SNAP).

Kathy Matuschka

Originally a Physiotherapist, Kathy Matuschka completed a Master of Theological Studies in 2019 which included the Minor Thesis research described in this paper. With a family heritage of Lutheran church workers, Kathy took the plunge from voluntary congregational leadership to paid lay ministry in 2018. She is employed as the Assistant Director for Ministry and Mission for the Lutheran Church of Australia, Queensland District.

Francis Sullivan AO

Francis Sullivan AO was the CEO of the Catholic Church's Truth Justice and Healing Council through the course of the Royal Commission into Child Sexual Abuse. Prior to that he was the Secretary General of the Australian Medical Association and CEO of Catholic Health Australia. He currently is Executive Chair of the Mater Group of hospitals in Queensland, a director of Mercy Health Australia and chairs Catholic Social services Australia.

Introduction

Mary Eastham and Robert Dixon

How can churches contribute to bringing about healing in our troubled world? A prior question: *can* churches contribute to bringing about healing in our troubled world? Has Christianity been a force for good in the world? Is it still today? What about the Catholic Church? Has it completely lost its moral authority?

Practical theologians anguished over questions like these at the 2020 conference of the Association of Practical Theology in Oceania (APTO) whose theme was *Encountering God: Practical Theology and the Mission to Heal*. They may themselves have been 'wounded healers', to use Carl Jung's poignant phrase.

This book contains fourteen chapters that contribute to the broad work of practical theology, drawing upon theological, social, cultural, political and ethical issues within the increasingly complex context of Oceania. Several chapters concern aspects of sexual abuse in the Catholic Church in Australia and Aotearoa New Zealand, while others deal with the impact of COVID-19, terrorist attacks, inter-religious dialogue, the ecological crisis, relationships between pastors and congregations, and the many ways that humanity and the churches must undergo conversion to respond effectively to these challenges.

As Peter Carblis observes in his chapter in this book, healing is at the core of the mission of practical theology. Healing is a holistic process; to purport to offer healing to others, institutionally or individually, involves first of all becoming aware of the existence of their suffering, their woundedness. As we are all wounded to some extent, this is not always easy, although at other times the wounds are obvious and visceral. The route to healing then depends on the discovery of the root causes of the woundedness, followed—where appropriate—by the acceptance of responsibility for any part in causing the wound and a seeking of forgiveness, and finally the discernment of a path to recovery and growth, and the accompanying, with love, patience and persistence, of the wounded person or group along that path.

The chapters in this book have evolved from papers first presented at that December 2020 APTO conference. Originally scheduled to take place in Melbourne in May of that year, it was initially postponed because of COVID-19 and eventually held as a fully online conference, featuring three keynote addresses and 47 presentations by APTO members and other academics, graduate students and ministry practitioners. Two of the three keynote addresses—by Francis Sullivan AO and Dr Rosemary Joyce CSB—are included in this volume. The third—by Dr Ruth Powell, Director of Sydney-based NCLS Research—was not able to be included. In her address, Dr Powell drew on the rich information from the almost 30-year span of the National Church Life Surveys—the largest dataset on local church life in the world—to reflect on how well-equipped churches currently are to carry out their mission to heal.

Twelve chapters in the book have been contributed by authors from among the 47 presenters who responded to the editors' invitation to prepare their conference papers for publication. A further six papers have been published in the online *Journal of Contemporary Ministry*.[1] Apart from the keynote addresses, each of the chapters in the book, the fourth to be published as an outcome of an APTO conference, and the third in the *Explorations in Practical Theology* series[2] was peer reviewed by at least two experts in each author's field. Authors were given an opportunity to consider the feedback from their reviewers and make changes to their chapters.

This book is intended for a wide-ranging audience of academics, practising ministers, church leaders and ordinary Christians who are committed to healing and justice and how they can best be Christian in our broken church and world. It is divided into three sections which analyse the issues named above with reference to the healing and justice traditions of Christianity. The sections are: 'Healing Shattered Relationships', 'Theological Frameworks for Healing' and 'Creating Healing Communities'. Chapters in Part One address the range of shattered relationships caused by the sexual abuse crisis and two horrific instances of terrorist violence. Chapters in Part Two explore the adequacy and appropriateness of traditional Christian resources for healing and justice—communitarian, scriptural and mystical—to the healing task at hand in 21st century Church and society. Drawing further on these traditions, authors in

---

[1] https://www.journalofcontemporaryministry.com/
[2] The other volumes are Anthony Maher (ed.), *:Bridging the Divide Between Faith, Theology and Life*. Explorations in Practical Theology series (Adelaide: ATF Press, 2015); Anthony Maher (ed.), *Faith and the Political in the Post-Secular Age*. Explorations in Practical Theology series (Bayswater: Coventry Press, 2018); Beatrice Green and Keiti Ann Kanongata'a (eds.), *Weaving Theology in Oceania: Culture, Context and Practice* (Newcastle upon Tyne: Cambridge Scholars Publishing, 2020).

Part Three document creative efforts of Christian community that are expressions of healing and hope.

Part One: Healing Shattered Relationships

Part One addresses the range of shattered relationships associated with the scale of sexual abuse within the Catholic Church and two instances of terrorist violence in 2019: the 15 March 2019 attack on the Muslim community in Christchurch, and the bombing of three Christian churches and three luxury hotels in Colombo, Sri Lanka, on Easter Sunday 2019. The sexual abuse scandal is discussed with reference to the venality of the institution, the suffering of victims and survivors, the disillusionment of faithful Catholics, the loss of the moral authority of the Church and the urgent need for reform and renewal within every institutional layer of the Church.

Two authors confront the horror of terrorist violence against people who could not be more vulnerable because they were in sacred places considered to be sanctuaries from the chaos of the outside world. In the New Zealand case, the horrific crime and the violence of the perpetrator are analysed with reference to the 'big picture' of injustice, racism and white supremacy in which European Christians played a major role through the process of colonisation. Contributors challenge Christians engaged in interfaith dialogue to draw on categories within political theology, for example, to be agents of healing and justice in Aotearoa New Zealand. In the case of Sri Lanka, two successful examples of interfaith dialogue are discussed in which, through art, sculpture, drama and liturgy, Christians sought rapprochement with Buddhists. These forms of communication overcame difficulties associated with language.

Chapter One is the impassioned first keynote conference address, delivered by Francis Sullivan AO, the former CEO of the Truth, Justice and Healing Council, the body established by the Australian Catholic Bishops Conference to coordinate the Catholic Church's response to the Royal Commission Into Institutional Responses to Child Sexual Abuse. It is an intensely personal reflection in which the author outlines the full range of reforms needed within the Catholic Church today in order for it to 'speak from a disposition drawn to human suffering and fragility', and thus be able to 'heal divisions, engender relationality, erase factionalism and promote consensus'. He calls for the Catholic Church to 'become a common companion to the underdog, the forgotten and the discarded; a fellow traveller with the outsider and the misunderstood; a soul mate to the confused and abandoned. Most of all ... for a Church less preoccupied with itself, its dogma and its image'.

Chapter Two (Robert Dixon) provides much needed quantitative data to understand how the clergy sexual abuse scandal has affected ordinary Catholics in Australia who still attend Mass. Analysing survey data from 1996 to 2016 reveals that Mass-attending Catholics have become increasingly dissatisfied during that period with the way that the Catholic Church has responded to sexual abuse. He found that, other than age and level of education, demographic factors had little influence over Mass attenders' attitudes to the crisis, and that the most important factors were their frequency of attendance at Mass and their level of involvement in the life of their parish, as well as factors associated with personal faith and spirituality, especially those that tended towards a traditional piety. He concludes that an immediate priority for the Catholic Church in Australia is to begin the work of healing all its members, clergy and lay people, by committing itself to implementing the recommendations of the Royal Commission.

In **Chapter Three**, Christopher Evan Longhurst contends that Catholics have a grave responsibility to speak out against clerical child sexual assault and its cover-up within the Catholic Church. He creatively expands the 'light of the world' metaphor from Matthew 5:14 that Pope Francis used as the title of 2019 procedural rules managing sexual abuse in the Catholic Church, *Vos Estis Lux Mundi* (You Are the Light of the World) by considering the symbolism of light, lamp, lampstand and bowl in relation to the abuse and its cover-up. Longhurst asserts that speaking out is a virtue that brings healing and renewal; that those who speak out are 'the light of the world' for the Church today, and that those who do not, not only live in darkness but also offend against biblical teaching and Catholic Church values. One reviewer noted that this chapter demonstrates why 'addressing the culture of silence in the Church' must also involve addressing 'the passivity, even disengagement, of the Faithful when confronting the abuse scandal'.

Chapter Four (Mary Eastham) analyses the 15 March 2019 terrorist attack against the Muslim community in Christchurch, Aotearoa New Zealand, as a memory of suffering within the deeper memory of suffering—colonisation— which is the cause of the racism and white supremacy of the Australian terrorist who committed this horrific crime. Eastham, a member of the New Zealand Catholic Bishops' Committee for Interfaith Relations at the time of this catastrophe, argues that the Bishops' Committee must deepen its method of interfaith dialogue with reference to Johann Baptist Metz's categories of Memory, Narrative and Solidarity in order to be an agent of healing and justice within the church and society. According to one of the peer reviewers, 'this is a most cogently argued, superbly written and very well developed chapter for a book on Practical Theology ... its insight into [the terror attack] being linked to colonial and evangelising practices of the past ... makes it seminal reading'.

Chapter Five (Malcolm Kreltszheim) contends that the bombing of three Christian churches and three luxury hotels in Colombo, Sri Lanka, on Easter Sunday 2019 that led to the killing of 259 persons by a local Islamic terrorist organisation is symptomatic of the generally anti-Western and anti-Christian sentiments that arose in former European colonies. The author outlines two prime examples of Buddhist-Christian dialogue in Sri Lanka that responded to this anti-Western, anti-Christian sentiment. They are Fr Aloysius Pieris SJ (born 1934) who established the Tulana Research Centre for Encounter and Dialogue in 1974 and the late Sevaka Yohan Devananda (1928-2016), the scion of a wealthy and influential Sinhalese Anglican family who established an ashram in the late 1950s. These examples of outreach were through art, sculpture, drama and liturgy by Christians as they sought rapprochement with the Buddhists. They were initially successful, but have recently regressed, unfortunately again because of Christian arrogance and Buddhist reactions.

Part Two: Theological Frameworks for Healing

Conversion, metanoia, mutation of consciousness, change of heart. These phrases ring throughout the chapters in Part Two, 'Theological Frameworks for Healing', because the authors have personal experience of grace-filled Christian communities through engaging themselves with spiritual disciplines designed to effectuate conversion. The authors understand how absolutely vital is the emergence of a new way of being human in response to the existential threats the human family and the planet now face. We need people formed by spiritual disciplines of compassion and community who will be able to understand what the new paradigm of interdependence is all about and how important it is for the survival of humanity and the planet.

The chapters in Part Two present theological frameworks for healing and justice, methods of thought and behaviour that have emerged from spiritual disciplines of contemplation and meditation. Human beings may not be selfish by nature, but modern Western culture, rooted in the ideology of individualism, has certainly encouraged us to be more concerned about our own individual interests than the wellbeing of others, society or the planet. By cultivating spiritual disciplines of contemplation and meditation, we understand ourselves in relationship with others, nature and the divine, rather than as separate from them. In other words, we experience a conversion that connects us to every living creature. Only this understanding of connection and interdependence will enable us to deal adequately with the effects of pandemics on the international level. Authors speak also of global climate change, and preventing the use of Artificial Intelligence from going rogue.

The second keynote address of the conference appears in **Chapter 6**. Delivered by Rosie Joyce CSB, it was contextualised by the COVID-19 pandemic which paralysed the world from 2020 to 2022. The presence of COVID-19 created dramatic disruptions in everyone's lives caused by national and regional lockdowns. The pandemic forced us to see ourselves in relation to the rest of the world and embrace an ethic of communitarianism as the only way to bring about public health. The author argues that this ethic of communitarianism, which Catholic Social Teaching calls the common good, provides a robust theological critique of the ideology of individualism and a framework of thought and action which promotes wholeness, social healing and social justice, even holiness.

In **Chapter Seven**, Julie Hawkins argues that the ecological crisis is proof that the ideology of individualism has been a colossal failure. She offers a practical eco-theological framework with Christian askesis for addressing separation between humans and the Divine, humans and each other, and humans and nature. This will restore the lost connection that people have with each of these three dimensions of the Real with the sense of a true, profound Reality that undergirds our existence. One of Hawkins' reviewers found the paper to be 'engaging and richly provocative' where 'the broad breadth of knowledge and research supporting the discussion is readily apparent and the arguments come across as impassioned'.

Chapter Eight (Sandie Cornish) explores the efficacy of Ignation spirituality when allied with Catholic Social Teaching. She presents a case study concerned with the interplay between structure and agency. It examines the relevance of *habitus* and reflexivity to an Ignatian approach to social justice. The case study explored the interaction of Catholic Social Teaching and Ignatian spirituality within the praxis of the Jesuit Conference Asia Pacific (JCAP) Social Apostolate Network in relation to vulnerable migrants in Asia in the period from 2008 to 2011. The results point to a link between reflexivity and the capacity to integrate, synthesise and move between these sources of praxis. This secondary analysis places the data in dialogue with Mouzelis' restructuring of Bourdieu's theory of practice.

Chapter Nine (Peter Carblis) provides a New Testament grounded perspective to enrich the practices of spiritual care and spiritual formation. The author answers the questions, 'What is spiritual health?', 'How do conceptions of spiritual health relate to spiritual healing?' and 'What does a spiritually healthy person look like?'. He argues that, in order to fulfil their mission, practical theologians need theologically sound operational definitions of healing and health, noting that these words refer to overlapping concepts that include 'wholeness, soundness of body, freedom from sickness, the process of healing, remedies, well-being, safety, prosperity, spiritual health, moral soundness, and salvation'.

Chapter Ten (Beatrice Green) contends that cultivating the new consciousness to which humanity is being called by the Spirit, and the belief that all of reality is a deeply interconnected dynamic relationship, will be crucially important to ensure that rapidly developing technologies in AI, artificial intelligence, remain a force for good in the world today. She develops her argument with reference to the work of Bede Griffiths, David Bohm, transpersonal psychologist and integral thinker, Ken Wilber, and exponent of Integral Philosophy, Steve McIntosh. Inseparable from these themes, for all four persons, is the emphasis on the vital importance of the practice of contemplation. One of Green's reviewers noted that this chapter is 'a valuable contribution in encouraging people to seriously address the question of Artificial Intelligence'.

Part Three: Creating Healing Communities

Where are signs of life to be found in the Church today? Where do we find healing communities? The chapters in Part Three of this book stress the relationship between freedom and life in the Spirit.

Where women are free to find their inner voice and authority, the life of the Spirit can be found. When Christians experience the Spirit of God, they can interpret times of anxiety and uncertainty as pregnant moments of opportunity to hear the healing voice of God in a new way. A chapter directly related to the challenge laid down in Chapter One proposes a practical, spiritual, healing way to compensate victims and survivors of clergy sexual abuse in the Catholic Church in Australia. Finally, mainstream churches can see the Pentecostal experience in a new light because the direct, unmediated experience of God's voice is a reminder that God's healing Spirit is alive in this world even if it is often hard to see.

Chapter Eleven (Catherine Lambert) outlines the changes that occur in a woman's relationship with the institutional church as she discovers her own spiritual authority and finds her voice. Drawing upon stories from women interviewed from diverse denominational backgrounds across Australia, the author documents women's experiences of their inner authority being challenged or silenced within the institutional church. She also shares common underlying themes woven through the stories that offer insights for how the church can provide a safe, accommodating space for women as they develop spiritually. Her conclusions identify approaches that have brought healing and wholeness to these women during their change in understanding of spiritual authority and make suggestions for how the church could embrace these voices and provide support for women in their faith development.

Kathy Matuschka's study of anxious behaviours in congregations (**Chapter Twelve**) began with her personal experience as a lay leader within a congregation going through an anxious time and noticing that some of the behaviours of leaders—though well-intended—seemed to make matters worse rather than better. In her analysis of material collected from interviews with nine people, including three ordained ministers, who were part of Australian Lutheran congregations, she makes use of Family Systems Theory and Helen Cameron's four voices model of doing practical theology. The chapter extends our horizons about how anxious times present opportunities for growth into the new things that God will do. Anxious times help us let go of what no longer is, or what we thought we had, under our control. One of Matuscka's reviewers wrote that this chapter 'contains excellent insights about issues facing contemporary congregational life. The use of FST [Family Systems Theory] to diagnose perceived issues within the church is a thoughtful methodological approach'.

In **Chapter Thirteen**, Brendan Long makes use of the concept of a 'wicked problem', that is, a problem which increases in complexity with every elusive attempt to solve it, to propose a way of dealing with the 'genuinely wicked problem of church financing which has been potentially made radically worse by the future costs of financing compensation, child safety policies and other redress measures associated with dealing with the fiscal impact of adequately addressing historical sexual abuse in the Catholic Church in Australia'. His proposal—one that draws heavily on Pope Francis' moral theology of economics—is that the wealth-generating sectors in the Church voluntarily redirect some of their revenue to deal with the fiscal crisis caused by the problem of historical sexual abuse in the church.

Chapter Fourteen (Tania Harris) brings to bear the role of revelatory experience in three Pentecostal churches into dialogue with the work of missiologists. The author employs Mark Cartledge's dialectic model and his use of testimonies, Jeff Astley's concept of 'ordinary theology' and David Martin's work on 'rescripting' to reflect on the role of the Holy Spirit in ministry, mission and healing. Missional theology provides a theological framework by which the function of revelatory experience can be understood and responded to in the church setting. It shows that the outcomes of Pentecostal revelatory experience are consistent with the mission of the triune God, demonstrated through the ministry of Jesus and via the revelatory work of the Spirit in the church today. The chapter provides a fitting conclusion to this volume on encountering God through the experience of healing.

Part One

Healing Shattered Relationships

Chapter One

And now! Being Church after the Royal Commission

Francis Sullivan

This chapter is the text of a keynote address to the December 2020 online conference of the Association of Practical Theology in Oceania.

I note the very high calibre audience I virtually stand before this morning and am humbled to give this presentation before people who have put the hard yards into theological study, reflection and concerted action. Your discipline of practical theology is inspiring and such a wonderful contribution in our quest to experience God in daily life.

I can only speak from my journey's experience and it has obviously been profoundly influenced from my time during the Royal Commission into the sexual abuse of children in our Church.

I have lived within the embrace of the Catholic Church all my life. I have been raised in it, married in it, raised children in it, even buried family in it. I have worked in it, prospered because of it, even defended it. There have been many times that I have been proud of it.

From early on in my life, I have seen it as my pathway. I still practice the faith and find personal sustenance in the tradition of my religion. Like everyone else, my life has been marked by ups and downs. I have had to negotiate personal tragedy and been confounded by the inexplicable and the shocking. Most of the time my faith, structured by my Church, has served me well. I have found myself grappling with the deeper questions in my life from the perspective I have learnt through the Church. For most of my life I would have best been described as being a 'contented Catholic'.

These days, I would call myself a 'concerned Catholic'. My time with the clerical sexual abuse scandal changed everything. I was shocked and confronted. I had not understood the degree to which the institution would lie to protect itself; the degree to which it would sacrifice the welfare and wellbeing of defenceless people for the sake of its image; the degree to which the clergy would protect wrong doers from within their ranks even when they were appalled by their actions; the degree to which the bishops and religious leaders would tolerate criminals, belittle victims and obfuscate to the public. In short, I had never imagined how venal the institution could be.

And yet I still had a deep desire to be a part of that living faith community. One where the Gospel means more than words. One where a quest to find God is far bigger than being blindly committed to the institution as if you were joined in some battle to the end. And yet I still had a deep desire to be a part of that living faith community.

This was a significant pivotal moment for me in my faith journey—an awakening. I had to become more adult in my Church. I had to not only grow up, but to wake up. Put simply, I needed to recognise that being a Catholic, being a member of the Church, does not require a rigid compliance to a pre-determined template for living. That being a Catholic means becoming deeply respectful of the diversity of human experience and the dignity of human expression as it is lived out by genuine and sincere people. Holding what can seem at times to be polar opposites or diverse expressions of human nature in a creative embrace is the essence of a Catholic perspective.

I think for a good deal of my adult life I had the assumption that, to be true to my Catholic faith, I somehow needed to place it at odds with the world around me. That to be an authentic Catholic, true to the teachings of the Church, I needed to follow a set of beliefs that often ran in a counter cultural fashion to that of modern life. That the doctrines of the Church required a suspicion of intelligent inquiry, particularly in the technical and social sciences. In short, it seemed to me that the Church asked us to leave our intelligence, reason and critical thought at the door as we entered the chapel. In today's culture I can't see that as a sensible understanding of how God reveals the nature of the Divine in ordinary life.

So my faith journey has taken a deliberate path to actively engage with and search for God in the circumstances and culture in which I live. As St Bonaventure said, 'God is the centre without a circumference'. No need for tribalism, nor for witch hunts to surface the 'true Catholics' from the rest. My experience has leached me of any passion to embrace the style of Catholicism that is like mounting a bulwark against any perceived threats to my religious values or beliefs as if they are immutable and need to be defended to the bitter end.

It is from that basis I want to name some of my concerns and maybe see if you find any resonance for your own circumstances. From the outset, I want to be very clear: it means a lot to me to call myself Catholic and to find ways to be nurtured in the tradition of the Church. I have been patient with the conservatism of the institutional Church; the way it drags the chain on changes that are so obvious to the ordinary person but somehow are anathema to the institution.

I have repeatedly excused the ham-fisted public statements of bishops, even when they embarrass sensible thinking people for their lack of logic or sensitivity. Maybe because I am a male I have been too slow to call out the sexist and homophobic attitudes of bishops and other clergy and spokespeople. I have been too slow as well to join in the rage over the way women are mistreated in the Church, the secret double lives of some clergy and their arrogance in presuming that they can still preach about behavioural and moral standards. Just as expediently, I have been too complicit in bolstering the dominion of the clerical caste and enabling the culture of clericalism to ride roughshod over the interests of the laity and the better natures of the bishops and religious leaders.

That said, these days I find myself angry with the inertia of the institution and its intolerance of differences and the demonising of sincere dissent. My impatience for changes that seem all too obvious, even common-sensical, does corrode my confidence in the Church leadership. I shake my head at the public positions of some bishops. It is embarrassing to be associated with statements that sound homophobic and fail to stand up for vulnerable people out of some misplaced sensitivity of appearing to be too political. I find the inane stridency of loud minority groups trumpeting nasty critiques of their fellow Catholics bordering on the pathological. I find myself beyond lament with the chasm that has emerged between younger generations and the Church.

As a very proud parent of three impressive, socially conscious and compassionate adults, I am thankful for their Catholic education yet remain puzzled over why they, like most other Catholic school graduates, feel no desire to engage formally with the institution. If relevancy is the goal, then I just can't detect the strategy.

In recent times, I wince at the slap downs from some bishops towards groups of practising Catholics articulating the urgency for change. This dismissive episcopal attitude has long been a feature of our Church. It is arrogant and near sighted. It speaks less about leadership and more of a reflection of an institution under threat and out of ideas. And the biggest anxiety I carry is that it increasingly feels like the Church of my upbringing, the Church of my adult life, is no longer keeping pace with my life to the point where becoming homeless is a real possibility.

The recent Church attendance survey demonstrated an accelerated decline in participation by people disillusioned with the way the abuse scandal was handled. Of major note was the rate of fall out in the over

50 aged groups. Nearly 22 per cent of this group's Mass-goers have left regular practice. These once 'rusted on' Catholics have voted with their feet.

I don't think it is overstating the situation when I say that there is a massive dislocation occurring in the Church today. The 'insiders' who can avail themselves of access to decision-makers, influencers and resources navigate their religion very differently from the rest. Those on the periphery struggle to engage with an institution that seems to have a life of its own. Decisions are made well away from the people affected and resources are allocated without any genuine involvement of local communities.

Consultation, even for something as important as the Plenary Council, is at best orchestrated.[1] The selection of delegates has been at the mercy and ideological disposition of local bishops. There has been no open account of the selection process, the criteria used or the individuals involved in the decision-making.

Consultation processes are also manipulated. It is a common feature of the institution that, when processes call for consultation, there is plenty of evidence that they stack the participants and control the numbers when votes are in play. There is equally strong evidence that only some feedback is tolerated. There has been strong anecdotal evidence that too many bishops are wary of the Plenary Council, lukewarm about its prospects and very threatened over the nature of what the laity will call for.

Moreover, even though a major Royal Commission finding for the Church was to instil better accountability and transparency, features the archbishops at the time said were very important in a more functional Church, crucial elements of the Plenary Council process are shrouded in secrecy and the responsiveness of those in charge of the project is anything but accountable to the faith community. It is as if the bishops think that the Plenary Council is theirs to control and theirs to share when and with whom they deem suitable.

Nothing about this cultural cameo of the institution speaks of a contemporary culture where inclusion, participation and mutual respect are hallmarks. Yet we continue to engage and contribute. Concerned Catholic groups and other organised efforts at Church renewal and reform have and continue to put their shoulders to the wheel. Through submissions, discussion forums and public events, these groups keep raising heartfelt concerns about the life of the Church and the needs of

---

1 The Plenary Council, the first in Australia since 1937, was held over two week-long sessions in October 2021 and July 2022. A Plenary Council is the highest form of gathering of the Catholic Church in a particular country and has legislative and governance authority.

ordinary Catholics. These groups have taken to heart the claim from the president of the Bishops Conference, Archbishop Mark Coleridge, in launching the Plenary Council that 'everything is on the table'. That all issues are up for debate, discussion and discernment.

So why the manic control?

Reform groups tell of instances where their efforts are greeted with hostility by some clerics, indifference by prelates and active interference by Church officials. Some Catholic media outlets do not even report on their events. All in a vane attempt to silence, to shut down debate and keep scrutiny at bay. Sadly, the instincts of the institution to control the message, the image and the faithful are still alive and well.

Clearly the attitude of some senior clerics is that democracy has no place in the Church. They pay lip service to the fact that we are all equal as baptised Christians. They are quick to point out that we are not all equal under canon law. The clerics have more institutional power and the laity are regarded as being effectively of a second class. The terms of engagement for the participation of the laity are hard wired in the canon law. The bishop always has the veto vote. There are 'cleric only' zones of influence where clerics administer and adjudicate on their brother clerics.

Community standards of best practice and accountability are alien to the canons when issues of dispute, conflict and probity are at stake. It is effectively a closed shop and the mechanisms to change any of this falls to—you guessed it—the clerics.

The Catholic culture has been too submissive and too compliant for too long. It has not only supported but rewarded this dysfunctional behaviour. Power is never shared, only the burden of administering the Church is shifted to willing lay people. If there was a genuine desire to share governance then lay people would have a vote alongside the clergy in the appointment of parish priests, the selection of bishops, the design and development of pastoral and ministerial initiatives and the formation of priests and other pastors in and for the diocese.

Accountability is never universally adopted. Bishops and clergy are not held to performance assessments, but the employed lay people of the Church almost always are. There are still no hard and fast requirements for priests to retrain, update and keep pace with best practices in pastoral and welfare services. There is still no expectation, let alone obligation, that bishops have high level qualifications in theology and spirituality even though the biggest challenge to the Church in secular times is its capacity to engage intelligently and persuasively.

The scrutiny of lay people by Church authorities is extraordinary. Whether it is about their private lives, the orthodoxy of their beliefs or their propensity to be out spoken and 'difficult', lay people are judged far more harshly than the clergy over similar issues. Yet, despite all this, we remain in the Church and stand ever ready to contribute.

Our current Church context—some of which I have just described—can be best summarised as a state of grief. There is anger, disillusion, despair and a sense of hopelessness. We do see groups turning on each other and bishops reverting to authoritarian styles almost out of desperation. Maybe they, too, are discouraged by the all too obvious decline.

We see Church administrations trying to keep parishes and agencies afloat with overseas clergy who struggle to assimilate into our cultural context. The intransigence over the introduction of married clergy, and even of women deacons, means that Catholics are subjected to liturgical and sacramental services of a quality less than what could be. At the same time, the rapidly declining numbers of Catholics who regularly attend weekend Masses speaks of an irreversible trend unless the teachings of the Church can bring insight and guidance to the lived experiences of their members.

It is from within this context that I admire the efforts of groups like Concerned Catholics Tasmania.[2] In essence, to understand what motivates groupings of Catholics who seek renewal and reform, you need look no further than to their spirituality. They have a vision for an inclusive Church. Open and hospitable. Far from being something new and radical, this understanding of catholicity which seeks unity through diversity rather than one that calls for conformity to a rigid identity is steeped in the tradition of the Church. It is based on the acknowledgment that we are all made in the image of God; that being human is our common cause, not adjusting our God-given nature to comply with some conventional understanding of what constitutes an acceptable human life and behaviour.

This is a vital point. It is fundamentally a pastoral, compassionate approach completely consistent with the teaching of the Church. It calls for an openness to the way human nature is developing and evolving. It is less doctrinaire and more aligned with the commitment Pope Francis calls for—to accompany each other on the journey of becoming human together. For some this may sound like a different orthodoxy from their early years in the Church. It could well be, if you were raised to think that Catholicism was exclusionary and doctrinaire. Yet the richness of the tradition of Catholic social thought is far from being socially conservative

---

2 https://www.concernedcatholicstasmania.org/

and divisive. It forms the basis for a spiritually-inspired movement, motivated to build communities, sustain human development and inspire an appreciation for the Transcendent in daily life. This is a stance very much at the heart of being Catholic. It is what can make Catholicism attractive.

Given that diocesan administrations are preoccupied in the practicalities of their agencies, parishes and clergy, the pastoral strategy of an evolving Church needs a major revamp. Given that there are too few effective Diocesan Pastoral Councils, and where they do exist they struggle to be representative of their faith community, it is left to reform-minded groups to raise the issues that call the Church to its heart, its missionary zeal and purpose.

When this happens, our Church speaks from a disposition drawn to human suffering and fragility, not sinfulness and failure. It calls for the Church to be ever watchful to heal divisions, engender relationality, erase factionalism and promote consensus. It calls for a more mystical approach to the complexities of life, less prone to judgementalism or over-reliance on rules and restrictive practices—more disposed to celebrate life in its quirkiness and beauty than be obsessed with its deviancy from some questionable norm. It calls for a Church more concerned with reaching out to people, addressing their needs, than preaching to them.

This will see the Church becoming a common companion to the underdog, the forgotten and the discarded. A fellow traveller with the outsider and the misunderstood. A soul mate to the confused and abandoned. Most of all, it calls for a Church less preoccupied with itself, its dogma and its image.

A Church where actions speak louder than words, where the poor are no longer homeless, where the young feel at ease, where the elderly are prized for their wisdom, where everyone is encouraged to develop and follow their conscience and where the underside of history finds voice and favour. A Church that inspires us all to be active listeners to the movements of the Spirit, to join the quest in the search for God.

If I could humbly say, it becomes the very task of a practical theologian.

Because I mentioned the upcoming Plenary Council a number of times in my keynote address, the editors kindly invited me to add this brief reflection on the Council's outcome.

Despite the cautious and orchestrated approach adopted throughout the Plenary Council process, some of its resolutions flagged modest changes.

Most notably were decrees to increase the involvement of women in Church decision-making bodies. In effect this only reflects the current practice in other than diocesan entities, namely health care, social services and education organisations. Yet it does indicate that the lack of mutuality between men and women has at least been recognised.

That said, the ingrained conservatism of the institution laboured with any concerted measures to advance the cause of the ordination of women to the diaconate. Likewise, the Plenary Council did nothing to affirm the dignity and inclusion of the LGBTQI+ community. Rather, any explicit acknowledgment of the place of this community within the Church was resisted. Even the language in the documents was devoid of same sex attracted acknowledgment. There was an absence of any considerations of even blessing same sex partnerships or to explicitly develop pastoral programs to better integrate LGBTQI+ people into the life of the faith community.

Apart from supporting the Urulu Statement from the Heart, the Plenary Council was silent on any other major contemporary social issue confronting our nation—an ironic situation given the thrust of the Plenary Council was to promote missionary discipleship!

The Plenary Council demonstrated the timidity characteristic of the Australian bishops over many decades. Any of the flashpoints for the Church with contemporary society—sexuality and inclusion of gender issues—were actively sidelined, even though these issues were repeatedly raised throughout the consultation phases and were consistently raised by younger Catholics as factors that led to their disengagement with the Church. Interested observers could well conclude that the Council's outcomes did not justify the time, resources and heartache of its four-year duration.

Chapter Two

Growing dissatisfaction: Mass attenders' attitudes to the sexual abuse crisis in the Catholic Church

Robert Dixon

Introduction

The sexual abuse crisis has been the defining issue for the Catholic Church for at least the last thirty years, since cases of abuse by clergy and religious began to attract public attention. This is true in numerous countries, including Ireland, the United Kingdom, Germany, France, the United States, New Zealand and Australia. The crisis has given rise to a vast body of literature around the world, in the form of reports of government and Church inquiries, Church responses and academic investigations concerned with the incidence, history and causes of abuse, the psychology of perpetrators, the response of Church leaders, the impact of abuse and of the Church's inadequate response to that abuse on victims/survivors and their families, and calls for changes in governance practices by the Church.[1] Yet relatively little has been written about the views of ordinary Catholics, including Mass-attending Catholics.

In Australia, representative samples of Mass attenders were asked for their views about clergy sexual abuse every five years between 1996 and 2016, first in the 1996 Catholic Church Life Survey (CCLS) and then in the National Church Life Survey (NCLS) (2001–2016). The sexual abuse issue was just one of numerous issues included in the surveys that were designed to inform the Australian bishops and their national and diocesan agencies about Mass-attending Catholics in Australia—their

---

[1] For a comprehensive overview of child sexual abuse in the Catholic Church throughout the world, see Desmond Cahill and Peter Wilkinson, *Child Sexual Abuse in the Catholic Church: An Interpretive Review of the Literature and Public Inquiry Reports* (Melbourne: Centre for Global Research, School of Global, Urban and Social Studies, RMIT University, August 2017). :See also Marie Keenan, *Child Sexual Abuse in the Catholic Church: Gender, Power and Organizational Culture* (New York: Oxford University Press, 2012), and Karen J. Terry, 'Child Sexual Abuse Within the Catholic Church: a Review of Global Perspectives', *International Journal of Comparative and Applied Criminal Justice* 39, no. 2 (2015): 139-154, https://doi.org/10.1080/01924036.2015.1012703

demography, practices, attitudes and beliefs. A report on the sexual abuse questions was prepared by the Pastoral Research Office of the Australian Catholic Bishops Conference (ACBC) after each survey,[2] but this chapter marks the first time that any in-depth investigation of change over time or multivariate analysis of the data has been published.[3] In it, I will investigate how the attitudes of Mass attenders to the sexual abuse crisis have changed as the extent and seriousness of the crisis has grown, and how they vary according to attenders' demographic characteristics, their level of involvement in parish life, and their personal spiritual outlook.

Between the 2011 and 2016 surveys, in response to the deplorable record of many institutions—not only the Catholic Church—the Victorian Government established the Victorian Parliamentary Inquiry into the Handling of Child Abuse by Religious and Other Organisations,[4] and the Australian Government established the Royal Commission into Institutional Responses to Child Sexual Abuse.[5] Both inquiries documented extensive abuse by Catholic clergy, religious and lay persons over many decades. Even though the Royal Commission's 17-volume Final Report, including its 925-page report on the Catholic Church in Book 2 of Volume 16, was not published until December 2017,[6] the extensive media coverage given to the Commission's inquiries throughout its term increased the awareness of ordinary Catholics to the extent of the crisis and very probably affected responses to the survey questions in the 2016 survey. The Victorian Government's inquiry also resulted in intense media scrutiny of clergy sexual abuse in the Catholic Church, especially in the state of Victoria.

---

2 The Pastoral Research Office was renamed the National Centre for Pastoral Research in 2018. The 2016 report can be accessed at https://ncpr.catholic.org.au/wp-content/uploads/2021/02/ACBC-Research-Report-on-the-2016-NCLS-TJHC-Final.pdf

3 Very brief summaries of the 2011 results can be found in Robert Dixon, 'Post-Secularity and Australian Catholics' in *Faith and the Political in the Post-Secular Age*, ed. Anthony Maher (Bayswater, Vic: Coventry Press, 2018), 83, and of the 2016 results in Robert Dixon, 'Australian Catholicism and Globalisation' in *Weaving Theology in Oceania: Culture, Context and Practice*, eds. Beatrice Green and Keiti Ann Kanongata'a (Newcastle upon Tyne: Cambridge Scholars Publishing, 2020), 252.

4 Parliament of Victoria, *Betrayal of Trust: Inquiry into the Handling of Child Abuse by Religious and Other Non-Government Organisations*, (Melbourne: November 2013), https://apo.org.au/node/36348

5 Royal Commission into Institutional Responses to Child Sexual Abuse, https://www.childabuseroyalcommission.gov.au/

6 Royal Commission into Institutional Responses to Child Sexual Abuse, *The Catholic Church*, https://www.childabuseroyalcommission.gov.au/sites/default/files/final_report_-_volume_16_religious_institutions_book_2.pdf. The Final Report from the Royal Commission is the world's most detailed and credible report.

Previous studies

Before examining the survey data, let me look at some other Australian and international studies that have investigated the response of Catholics to the sexual abuse crisis. In their 2013 publication *American Catholics in Transition*, D'Antonio, Dillon and Gautier included results for several questions to do with clergy sexual abuse that had been part of a 2011 nationally representative online survey of adult, self-identified Catholics. They found that most Catholics said that the scandal had had a significant impact on the political credibility of church leaders and had hurt the ability of priests to meet the spiritual and pastoral needs of their parishioners, and that these views were 'prevalent across all generations, with a majority in each saying that the sex abuse issue had negative consequences' for both political credibility and pastoral care.[7] They found little difference in views on these questions between frequent Mass attenders and non-attenders, and between men and women. Only 29 per cent of respondents rated the bishops' handling of the crisis as good or excellent, with 38 per cent rating it as fair and 31 per cent as poor. Weekly attenders were more likely to view the bishops' responses favourably, but even then only 37 per cent rated their performance as good or excellent.[8]

In 2021, the Center for Applied Research in the Apostolate (CARA) carried out an online survey, available in English and Spanish, of 1,050 self-identified Catholics for *America* magazine. The survey primarily concerned reactions to clergy sexual abuse allegations.[9] They found that about one-third of respondents said the sex abuse crisis affected their willingness to speak positively about faith and Catholicism outside of church circles, and a similar proportion said the crisis had made them embarrassed to mention to others that they were Catholic.[10] Only 20 per cent of respondents said they found the US Conference of Catholic Bishops (USCCB) 'very trustworthy', and only 22 per cent said they found Catholic priests 'very trustworthy', in terms of guidance on matters of faith and morals, although this rose to 36 per cent of respondents who considered priests in their own parish to be very trustworthy. There was a marked difference according to frequency of attendance at Mass, with weekly attenders much more likely than those who attended Mass

---

7 William D'Antonio, Michelle Dillon and Mary Gautier, *American Catholics in Transition* (Lanham, MD: Rowman and Littlefield, 2013), 84.
8 D'Antonio, Dillon and Gautier, *American Catholics*, 84.
9 Mark M. Gray, Thomas P. Gaunt and Autumn Gray, *America Magazine National Survey of Adult Catholics: Part 1* (Washington, DC: Center for Applied Research in the Apostolate (CARA), 2021). https://www.americamagazine.org/sites/default/files/attachments/AmericaSpring2021ReportI.pdf
10 Gray, Gaunt and Gray, *America Magazine National Survey*, 19-20.

only occasionally or never to say that the USCCB and Catholic priests were very trustworthy. According to the report, 45 per cent of adult Catholics believed the issue of sexual abuse had hurt the overall reputation of the Church 'a great deal', and 57 per cent believed that the mainstream news media's coverage of the abuse scandal has been 'about right'.[11] Again, these responses varied according to frequency of Mass attendance, with weekly attenders more likely to believe that the media response had been excessive and less likely to believe that the scandal had hurt the Church's reputation a great deal. Forty-five per cent said they 'agree strongly or 'agree somewhat' they had lost trust in what the Catholic Church reported about the issue of sexual abuse.[12]

In 2019, Pew Research published a report of a survey of a nationally representative randomly selected sample of 6,364 American adults about their attitudes to the Catholic Church's response to sexual abuse allegations.[13] They found that just over one-quarter (27 per cent) of the Catholic respondents said that reports of sexual abuse had resulted in their going to Mass less often, and a similar number said they had reduced their financial contribution to the Church. On the other hand, 18 per cent of all Catholics, and 35 per cent of those who attend Mass at least weekly, said they had expressed support or encouragement to the priests in their parish in response to reports of sexual abuse and misconduct.[14]

In a study of the subsample of 1,116 Catholics in the Pew sample, Christina Mancini investigated the extent to which Catholics reported negative and positive actions in response to the scandal, noting that while around half of the Catholics in the sample reported undertaking a specific action as a consequence of the scandal, not all those actions were negative (such as attending Mass less frequently or contributing less financially); some, particularly those who were regular Mass attenders, rejected the largely negative coverage and affirmed their support for the Church as an institution.[15] Overall, she found, socio-demographic factors mattered little in predicting responses to the abuse, with the exception that higher levels of education were correlated with a greater likelihood of reducing one's financial support to the Church and attending Mass

---

11 Gray, Gaunt and Gray, *America Magazine National Survey*, 36.
12 Gray, Gaunt and Gray, *America Magazine National Survey*, 41.
13 Pew Research Center, *Americans See Catholic Clergy Sex Abuse as an Ongoing Problem* (June 2019). The full report and the dataset are available from https://www.pewresearch.org/religion/2019/06/11/americans-see-catholic-clergy-sex-abuse-as-an-ongoing-problem/
14 Pew Research Center, *Catholic Clergy*, 8.
15 Christina Mancini, 'A Test of Faith: Exploring the Attitudes and Experiences of Catholics in the Aftermath of the Church's Child Sexual Abuse Scandal', *Journal of Criminal Justice* 82, (September–October 2022), https://doi.org/10.1016/j.jcrimjus.2022.101933

less frequently.[16] She found instead that views about religion in society, perceptions of institutional sex crime, personal experiences related to the allegations, and confidence in leadership predict the action undertaken by Catholics.[17]

In Canada, according to a 2019 report on a survey by the Angus Reid Institute,[18] 48 per cent of 'practising Catholics'—defined in the report as those who attend Mass at least once a month—said the Catholic Church as a whole had done a good or very good job of addressing the clerical sexual abuse issue, while 52 per cent said it had done a poor or very poor job. 'Occasional' Catholics were more critical—66 per cent said they thought the Church had done a poor or very poor job.[19] The survey also asked what kind of impact the sexual abuse issue and the Church's response to it had had on respondents' overall opinion of the Catholic Church and on their own personal faith and spirituality. Forty-two per cent of practising Catholics said it had weakened their opinion of the Church while a further four per cent said it had ruined their opinion altogether. For occasional Catholics, the corresponding figures were 63 per cent and 14 per cent, and for former Catholics they were 53 per cent and 26 per cent. In relation to personal faith and spirituality, 18 per cent of practising Catholics said the issue had weakened their faith while none said it had ruined it. In contrast, 39 per cent of occasional Catholics said their personal faith had been weakened (and a further 5 per cent said it had been ruined).[20] The abuse itself, and the Church's attempts to cover it up, were two of the most common reasons given by former Catholics for leaving the Church.[21]

A 2007 Australian report examining reasons why Catholics stopped attending Mass found that only interview participants 'who actually knew victims or perpetrators ... stopped attending Mass solely because of the issue of sexual abuse'.[22] According to the report, 22 per cent of infrequently- or non-attending parents of children at Catholic schools

---

16 Mancini, 'Test of Faith', 8.
17 Mancini, 'Test of Faith', 1.
18 Angus Reid Institute, *Crisis of Faith? Even Practicing Catholics Say Church Has Done a Poor Job Handling Sexual Abuse Issue*, (2019), https://angusreid.org/catholic-church-canada/
19 Angus Reid Institute, *Crisis of Faith?*, 16.
20 Angus Reid Institute, *Crisis of Faith?*, 21. No results were given for the impact on the personal faith and spirituality of former Catholics.
21 Angus Reid Institute, *Crisis of Faith?*, 8.
22 Robert Dixon, Sharon Bond, Kath Engebretson, Richard Rymarz, Bryan Cussen and Katherine Wright, *Research Project on Catholics Who Have Stopped Attending Mass: Final report February 2007* (Melbourne: Australian Catholic Bishops Conference, 2007). Available at https://ncpr.catholic.org.au/research-project-on-catholics-who-have-ceased-attending-mass/

gave 'disillusionment with the Church because of revelations of sexual abuse by Church personnel' as one of their reasons for not attending, but only seven per cent gave this as the most important reason. It is likely, given the increased media prominence of the crisis and the impact of the Royal Commission, that in recent years sexual abuse and the Church's response to it would have become a much more significant factor in people ceasing to attend Mass.

Listen to What the Spirit Is Saying, a report by the National Centre for Pastoral Research, sought to identify the common themes emerging from the 17,457 group and individual submissions received during the 'Listening and Dialogue' phase of the three-year process leading to the Australian Church's Plenary Council held in 2021 and 2022.[23] The clergy sexual abuse scandal and the Royal Commission into Institutional Responses to Child Sexual Abuse were discussed in many of the submissions.[24] The report summarised the widely varying and often contradictory opinions by noting that the submissions called for, among other things, repentance by the whole Catholic community, the Church hierarchy to have a greater concern for victims and survivors of clergy sexual abuse, more transparency, accountability and balanced news reporting of the crisis, and the Church to do better in implementing the Royal Commission's recommendations.[25]

The reactions I have been looking at in this chapter have been at the individual level, but around the world the crisis has also resulted in, or at least contributed to, the formation of groups such as Voice of the Faithful in the United States and Catholics for Renewal in Australia.[26]

In summary, these studies have found that many Catholics and former Catholics are critical of the way that bishops have handled the crisis, say they are sometimes embarrassed and ashamed to be Catholic, believe that the Church's capacity to speak on public issues and provide pastoral care and spiritual guidance have been damaged, have diminished trust in priests, bishops and the Catholic Church as an institution, and attend Mass less often and give less to the Church financially because of the sexual abuse crisis. As well, the crisis has resulted in some people leaving the Church entirely. Demographic factors other than level of education

---

23 Trudy Dantis, Paul Bowell, Stephen Reid and Leith Dudfield, *Listen to What the Spirit Is Saying: Final Report for the Plenary Council* (Canberra: Plenary Council 2020 and National Centre for Pastoral Research, 2019). Available at https://ncpr.catholic.org.au/pro-research-projects/plenary-council-2020/
24 *Listen to What the Spirit Is Saying*, 105.
25 *Listen to What the Spirit Is Saying*, 100.
26 William D'Antonio and Anthony Pogorelc, *Voices of the Faithful: Loyal Catholics Striving for Change*, New York: Herder and Herder, 2007). Regarding Catholics for Renewal, see https://www.catholicsforrenewal.org

have been found not to be particularly influential; more important is one's personal religiosity including things like frequency of Mass attendance. Finally, there is a correlation between one's acceptance of reports in the media and their attitude to the Church's response.

Catholics in Australia

During the period covered by this chapter, the Catholic population of Australia rose from 4,799,090 in 1996 to 5,439,267 in 2011, before falling to 5,291,834 in 2016. Despite the increase in numbers between 1996 and 2011, Catholics as a percentage of the Australian population declined from 27.0 per cent in 1996 to 25.3 per cent in 2011 and 22.6 per cent in 2016.[27]

In 2016, nearly a quarter of Australia's Catholics (24.7 per cent) were born overseas, the main countries of birth being the Philippines, Italy, Great Britain, New Zealand and India. About three-quarters of those born overseas (19.7 per cent of all Catholics) were born in non-English-speaking countries. A further 133,528 Catholics were of Aboriginal or Torres Strait Islander origin.[28]

In 1996, the total number of people at Mass in Australia on a typical weekend was about 864,000, or 18 per cent of the total number of Catholics.[29] By 2016, this had fallen to 623,400 (11.8 per cent). During that 20 year period, the percentage of Mass attenders born in non-English-speaking countries rose from about 18 per cent in 1996 to almost 37 per cent in 2016, while the number of attenders born in Australia and in other English-speaking countries almost halved.[30] The figure of 37 per cent born in non-English-speaking countries is actually

---

27 National Centre for Pastoral Research, *Social Profile of the Catholic Community in Australia: Revised Edition*. (Canberra: Australian Catholic Bishops Conference, 2019), 4. The Catholic population further declined between 2016 and 2021, to 5,075,907, just 20 per cent of the Australian population. Available at https://ncpr.catholic.org.au/wp-content/uploads/2019/10/Social-Profile-of-the-Catholic-Community-in-Australia-2016-v2.pdf. See also https://www.abs.gov.au/articles/religious-affiliation-australia
28 *Social Profile*, 5, 17.
29 Robert Dixon, Stephen Reid and Marilyn Chee, *Mass Attendance in Australia: A Critical Moment: A Report Based on the National Count of Attendance, the National Church Life Survey and the Australian Census* (Fitzroy: ACBC Pastoral Research Office, 2013), 4. Available at https://ncpr.catholic.org.au/national-count-of-attendance/
30 Trudy Dantis, Stephen Reid and Marilyn Chee, *The Australian Catholic Mass Attendance Report 2016. A Report Based on the National Count of Attendance, the National Church Life Survey and the National Catholic Census Project* (Canberra: National Centre for Pastoral Research, 2021), i. Available at https://ncpr.catholic.org.au/national-count-of-attendance/. The main overseas English-speaking countries, according to the Australian Bureau of Statistics, are the United Kingdom, the Republic of Ireland, New Zealand, South Africa, Canada and the United States of America.

an undercount, as non-parish migrant Mass centres and parishes of the Eastern Catholic dioceses did not participate in the National Church Life Survey from which this figure is derived.

Data and methods

Including the same questions about the sexual abuse crisis in each of the five-yearly surveys of Mass attenders between 1996 and 2016 resulted in the creation of five comparable datasets. The 1996 CCLS was a parallel survey to the multi-denominational NCLS which had been established by the Anglican Diocese of Sydney and the Uniting Church Board of Mission in New South Wales in 1991. In 2000, the Australian Catholic Bishops Conference became a partner in the NCLS project and, from 2001 until 2016, the questions on the sexual abuse crisis continued to be included in an NCLS questionnaire variant designed for use in Catholic parishes. In 1996, 281 parishes were included in the national random sample; this number was gradually reduced to 193, mainly for cost reasons, by the time of the 2016 survey.[31] Because of adjustments to the percentages of Mass attenders receiving each variant, this reduction in the number of parishes did not adversely affect the number of respondents to these questions (see Table 2). For every survey year, the samples were designed to be statistically representative of all Australian Catholic dioceses and the data analysed in this chapter have been weighted to reflect differing sampling rates for each diocese. The results presented here can, therefore, confidently be regarded as applying, with a high level of probability, to all Mass attenders in Australian parishes.

In each of the survey years, all people aged 15 and over at Mass in a participating parish on the day of the survey were invited to complete one of more than 20 different questionnaire variants during the time usually reserved for the homily. The variant which formed the basis of the report prepared for participating parishes was completed by 67 per cent of respondents in each parish, while the remaining 33 per cent of respondents completed one of the other variants, each dealing with a different topic. Most of these variants were distributed to attenders of all denominations but a small number were designed for use only in Catholic parishes. It was in these specifically Catholic questionnaire variants that the questions on sexual abuse were included.

---

31 In 2016, the Catholic Church in Australia was made up of 1,274 parishes in 28 territorial dioceses, together with 71 parishes in five Australia-wide Eastern Catholic dioceses or eparchies and a further 40 parishes associated with two other non-territorial ordinariates. The parishes in the NCLS sample all came from the 28 territorial dioceses.

In each survey year, respondents were asked, on a five-point Likert scale, whether they agreed or disagreed with five statements on the topic of sexual abuse. The questions and the results are shown in Table 1.[32] In 2016, an additional item was added, at the request of the Truth, Justice and Healing Council, the body set up by the ACBC to coordinate the Catholic Church's response to the Royal Commission. As with the earlier items, it asked whether the respondent agreed or disagreed with the statement.

Table 1: Results for sexual abuse questions 1996 to 2016

Do you agree or disagree?
1. The cases of sexual abuse by priests and religious have damaged* my confidence in Church authorities

	1996 %	2001 %	2006 %	2011 %	2016 %
Strongly agree	20	17	19	21	28
Agree	24	28	29	28	30
Neutral/unsure	12	17	19	20	16
Disagree	29	28	23	21	18
Strongly disagree	15	10	10	10	8
Total	100	100	100	100	100

* The wording of the question in 1996 was 'seriously damaged'

2. My respect for priests and religious has greatly declined as a result of these offences

	1996 %	2001 %	2006 %	2011 %	2016 %
Strongly agree	7	5	9	8	12
Agree	14	15	18	18	24
Neutral/unsure	14	19	19	20	20
Disagree	41	46	38	38	32
Strongly disagree	24	15	16	16	13
Total	100	100	100	100	100

---

32 These five questions were developed by Michael Mason CSsR, who served as project sociologist for the CCLS.

3. The response of church authorities to these incidents has been inadequate and shows a complete failure of responsibility

	1996	2001	2006	2011	2016
	%	%	%	%	%
Strongly agree	26	18	17	22	29
Agree	31	34	32	32	36
Neutral/unsure	21	28	26	27	21
Disagree	17	16	19	15	12
Strongly disagree	6	4	5	4	3
Total	100	100	100	100	100

4. The media have been fair in their coverage of sexual offences by priests and religious

	1996	2001	2006	2011	2016
	%	%	%	%	%
Strongly agree	8	6	7	8	9
Agree	22	29	25	25	25
Neutral/unsure	24	26	29	30	30
Disagree	30	29	27	25	26
Strongly disagree	17	10	12	13	10
Total	100	100	100	100	100

5. The church now seems to be taking appropriate steps in meeting its responsibilities in these cases

	1996	2001	2006	2011	2016
	%	%	%	%	%
Strongly agree	11	9	13	12	13
Agree	42	46	50	44	50
Neutral/unsure	31	32	28	31	27
Disagree	12	11	6	9	7
Strongly disagree	4	2	2	4	3
Total	100	100	100	100	100

6. Church authorities can be trusted when they speak about sexual abuse

	1996 %	2001 %	2006 %	2011 %	2016 %
Strongly agree	–	–	–	–	9
Agree	–	–	–	–	34
Neutral/unsure	–	–	–	–	39
Disagree	–	–	–	–	13
Strongly disagree	–	–	–	–	5
Total	–	–	–	–	100

Data sources: Catholic Church Life Survey 1996 and National Church Life Surveys 2001–2016. Note that column percentages may not add up to 100 due to rounding.

The results for the first four questions are quite strongly correlated, and this is true for all five survey years. I used this fact to make the task of presenting findings based on multiple questions over five surveys more manageable, by combining those first four questions into a single scale, scoring each item from 0 to 4, which I have called the Attitude to Sexual Abuse in the Church scale (ASAC). Items were scored so that 0 indicated the most satisfaction with clergy and the Church in general, and 4 indicated the most dissatisfaction. For example, respondents who strongly agreed that the cases of sexual abuse by priests and religious had damaged their confidence in Church authorities scored 4 on this question. When scores across the four items were aggregated, the total score for a respondent varied between a minimum of 0 and a maximum of 16. Perhaps surprisingly, the fifth question, about whether the Church is now taking appropriate steps to meet its responsibilities, is not strongly correlated with the other four, and its inclusion would weaken the scale's reliability.[33]

The ASAC scale enables us to reduce the mass of information in Table 1 to something more manageable. We can use it to examine what happened in the way people responded to the first four items over the period from 1996 to 2016. As for Questions 5 and 6, which are not included in the ASAC scale, a brief comment will suffice. The results for Question 5 indicate that, in all five survey years, a majority of Mass attenders agreed or strongly agreed that the Church was taking appropriate steps to meet its responsibilities, and that fewer than 20 per

---

33 Scale reliability is a measure of how well the scale consistently represents the concept underlying the items that make it up. Technically known as a 'standardised alpha', its value can be anywhere between 0 (for a scale constructed from items that are completely uncorrelated with each other) to 1 (for a scale where all items are perfectly correlated). For a scale to be considered reliable, the usual rule of thumb is that its value should be above 0.7.

cent in every survey year expressed disagreement with this statement. Nevertheless, around 30 per cent in every survey year said they were unsure, neither agreeing nor disagreeing. The level of agreement rose between 2001 and 2006, only to fall in 2011 and then rise again in 2016, perhaps indicating that attenders believed that the Royal Commission would at last compel the Church to take appropriate steps. In 2016, although only 18 per cent of Mass attenders disagreed that Church authorities can be trusted when they speak about child sexual abuse, only 43 per cent agreed. Just under 40 per cent said they were unsure if Church authorities can be trusted—hardly a vote of confidence.

What does the ASAC scale represent? Higher scores indicate declining respect for priests and religious, damaged confidence in Church authorities, a view that those authorities have been irresponsible, and that the media have been fair. There might not be one single word that encapsulates all these views, but it is clear that people with high scores are dissatisfied with what has been happening in the Church in relation to sexual abuse. A summary of the scale behaviour is shown in Table 2, which displays, for each survey year, the number of people who responded to the survey variant which contained the questions about the sexual abuse crisis, the scale reliability value, the mean value of the ASAC score, and the percentage of respondents scoring between zero and three, and between 13 and 16. Respondents whose scores were in the lower range answered 'strongly disagree' to at least one of the questions, thereby showing support for the Church and the clergy, while respondents who scored in the range 13-16 answered 'strongly agree' to at least one question, indicating that at least one response was highly critical of priests or the Church's response. Over the course of the five survey years, the percentage of attenders registering a moderate ASAC score stayed roughly the same, while the percentage with a low score decreased and the percentage with a high score increased.

Table 2. Attitude to Sexual Abuse in the Church (ASAC) scale behaviour

	1996	2001	2006	2011	2016
Respondents	2,048	1,473	6,850	2,779	2,591
Scale reliability	0.71	0.75	0.77	0.78	0.78
Mean ASAC score (range 0–16)	7.63	8.00	8.15	8.35	9.13
Low (0–3) ASAC score (%)	12.7	9.6	9.4	9.4	7.0
Moderate (4–12) ASAC score (%)	77.1	80.4	77.9	77.1	74.8
High (13–16) ASAC score (%)	10.2	10.0	12.7	13.5	18.2

Results

Variation over time

In Table 2, we see that the mean ASAC score increased in every survey year. In fact, it increased by almost 20 per cent between 1996 and 2016, with about half of the increase occurring between 2011 and 2016. This result is consistent with how the crisis developed during the 1990s and the 2000s, and particularly with the prominence given to the issue in the media during the years of the Victorian Parliamentary Inquiry and the Royal Commission. The percentage scoring zero to three on the ASAC scale (attenders who were largely satisfied with the handling of the sexual abuse crisis) dropped from 12.7 per cent to 9.6 per cent between 1996 and 2001, then stayed roughly the same until there was another substantial fall between 2011 and 2016. Similarly, the percentage scoring between 13 and 16 (those who were most dissatisfied) drifted upwards from 1996 until 2011, but then jumped substantially between 2011 and 2016.

It is important to remember that the total number of Mass-attending Catholics fell during the 20-year period covered by these surveys, and that it is likely that those most disaffected had already stopped attending, and had even ceased to identify as Catholics, by 2016. Had these people stayed, the ASAC score would most likely have increased even more than it did.

Another important thing to note in Table 1 is that, in all survey years, the percentage expressing dissatisfaction with church authorities remained considerably higher than the percentage saying that their respect for priests and religious had declined, even as both percentages increased over time. Given that the surveys were completed by people at Mass, it not surprising that they directed their dissatisfaction towards church authorities rather than towards the man they know and respect who is representative, for them, of clergy in general.

The 2016 results in detail

How do scores on the ASAC scale vary according to the demographic characteristics of respondents? There is a small difference in the mean values of the ASAC score of men and women (9.05 compared to 9.13), but it is not statistically significant.[34] In other words, men and women are no different in their level of satisfaction or dissatisfaction with the Church as measured by the four items included in the ASAC scale. Nor is there

---

34 Statistical significance is usually reported at $p < 0.05$, $p < 0.01$ or $p < 0.001$ level, meaning that there is a probability of less than five in one hundred, one in one hundred, or one in one thousand, respectively, that the result under discussion has arisen by chance. These probabilities are often represented by one, two or three asterisks, again respectively.

any statistically significant difference between respondents according to the type of primary and secondary schools they attended, although this is hardly surprising given that the majority of attenders left school very many years ago.

There is, however, a marked difference in the mean scores of those aged 15 to 34 and older attenders, with younger people being less dissatisfied than their older fellow Mass attenders (7.90 compared to 9.32). Attenders with university degrees have higher mean ASAC scores (9.41) than those with no post-school education (9.17) and those who have a diploma or trade certificate level of education (8.59). Attenders who are separated or divorced (9.71) are also likely to record higher levels of dissatisfaction than those who are married or widowed (9.21) or who have never married (8.46). Statistically significant differences also show up in the three-category birthplace variable, suggesting that Mass attenders who were born in non-English-speaking countries are less dissatisfied than Australian-born attenders, while those who were born overseas in an English-speaking country are more dissatisfied. The differences are small, and would only really be revealing if we took the analysis down to the level of particular countries of birth, an exercise that is beyond the scope of this paper.[35]

Comparing the mean values of the ASAC scale for respondents in different demographic categories provides easy to understand results, but it can also obscure what is going on. For example, is the low mean score for those who have never married due to their never having married (and therefore, in most cases, not having children) or is it that the never-married group is disproportionately young, given that we know that young attenders have lower ASAC scores? This sort of problem can be avoided by using a statistical procedure known as linear regression, a technique that shows the effect of multiple variables acting together.

The results of the regression analysis are shown in Table 3 overleaf. The figures in the table, known as standardised beta coefficients, measure the strength of the effect of each individual independent variable on the dependent variable, the ASAC score: a higher value means a stronger effect. Positive values mean that the ASAC score increases as the standardised beta increases; negative values mean that the ASAC score decreases as the standardised beta increases. At the bottom of each model is a figure called the 'adjusted R^2', an indication of how much of the variation[36] in the ASAC score is explained by each model.

---

35 For an overview of responses by specific countries of birth, see Robert Dixon 'Australian Catholicism in the Third Phase of Globalisation: Demographic Shifts and Unceasing Challenges' in *Asian Pacific Catholicism and Globalization: Historical Perspectives and Contemporary Challenges*, eds. Jose Casanova and Peter C. Phan (Washington DC: Georgetown University Press, 2023).

36 Statistically speaking, the variance.

Table 3. Standardised beta coefficients of various factors in regression of Attitude to Sexual Abuse in the Church (ASAC) score

	Model 1	Model 2	Model 3
Demographic variables			
Male	-0.012	-0.032	-0.054 *
Increasing age (years)	0.109 ***	0.167 ***	0.198 ***
University degree	0.102 ***	0.101 ***	0.080 **
Born in non-English-speaking country	-0.018	0.007	0.071 **
Parish involvement variables			
Frequent attendance		-0.205 ***	-0.138 ***
Diminishing sense of belonging		0.103 ***	0.097 ***
Strong and growing sense of belonging		-0.005	0.057 *
Parish extremely important in my life		-0.095 ***	-0.021
Involved in parish groups		-0.058 *	-0.061 *
Personal spirituality variables			
God the most important reality in my life			-0.092 **
Frequently say the Rosary			-0.088 **
Abortion sometimes justified			0.118 ***
Guided by church teaching but follow my conscience			0.089 ***
Parish meets my spiritual needs			-0.137 ***
Adjusted R^2	0.015	0.096	0.170

* $p < 0.05$; ** $p < 0.01$, *** $p < 0.001$. Positive values indicate that the ASAC score, that is, level of dissatisfaction, increases due to the presence of the factor concerned, whereas negative values indicate that the level of dissatisfaction is lower when that factor is present.

Model 1 shows the impact of the demographic variables on the ASAC score when they are all considered together. The result is not very different from what we would expect on the basis of the earlier bivariate analysis. There is no statistically significant difference between males and females, and the differences for marital status and birthplace have disappeared, but there are differences due to age and having a university education—the fact that they are both positive values means that the ASAC score is likely to be higher among older attenders and those with a university degree, that is, they are more dissatisfied, compared to younger people and those without a university education. The adjusted R^2 for Model 1 is 0.015, which means that Model 1 only explains 1.5 per cent of the variation in scores between respondents. In other words, even though age and level of education do have an effect, a person's demographic characteristics explain very little of the differences in the way they respond to the questions about sexual abuse. What else might explain the differences? Perhaps it is to do with how involved people are in their parish.

Adding a number of parish involvement variables to the analysis results in Model 2. These variables are:

- Frequency of Mass attendance.
- Sense of belonging to the parish.
- Important of the parish in my life.
- Involvement in parish groups.

Other available parish involvement measures, such as whether or not a respondent had a ministry or leadership role in the parish, and how much they contributed to the parish financially, had no influence on the model and so are not included in the final version of Model 2.

Model 2 shows that parish involvement has a statistically significant impact on the ASAC score, and the new model now accounts for 9.6 per cent (adjusted R^2 = 0.096) of the variation between respondents, with age and education also remaining significant. Furthermore, several of the parish involvement variables have a negative value, meaning that attenders who attend Mass more often, who regard the parish as an important part of their lives and who are involved in parish groups are likely to record a lower ASAC score, that is, to be more satisfied, or less dissatisfied, compared to other attenders. Those who reported that their formally strong sense of belonging to their parish was not as strong as it had been in the past were likely to record a higher ASAC score, that is, to be more dissatisfied.

In Model 3, the following set of variables related to personal morality and spirituality has been added.

- Importance of God in my life.
- Frequency of saying the Rosary.
- Attitude to abortion.
- How I make moral decisions.
- The parish is meeting my spiritual needs.

In Model 3, the adjusted R^2 has now risen to 0.170, meaning that the model explains 17 per cent of the variation in the way people respond. All of these variables are either strongly ($p < 0.001$) or moderately ($p < 0.01$) statistically significant. Three of them are negative, indicating that those who see God as being the most important reality in their lives, who say the Rosary frequently, and whose spiritual needs are being met by their parish are generally more satisfied with the Church in relation to clergy sexual abuse than those who do not share these attributes. On the other hand, those who believe that abortion can sometimes be justified and who say they follow their conscience in making moral decisions are likely to be more dissatisfied than those who say that abortion is always wrong and those who make their moral decisions by always following the teachings of the Church. Of the demographic variables, age and education still have an impact on the ASAC score but are now joined by sex and birthplace; men are a little less likely than women to be dissatisfied with the Church in relation to sexual abuse, and attenders born in non-English speaking countries a little more likely to be dissatisfied. Among the parish involvement variables, the importance of the parish in a person's life no longer has any impact on the ASAC score, but those with a strong and growing sense of belonging to their parish are a little more likely to be dissatisfied with the Church, perhaps because they see what has happened as a form of betrayal after their many years of faithful service.

This analysis has shown that demographic variables on their own account for very little of the variation in Mass attenders' attitudes to sexual abuse by clergy and religious and to the Church's handling of the issue. Measures of a person's involvement in their parish and their personal spirituality have more explanatory power; those with higher levels of involvement and who follow traditional Catholic spiritual practices and moral teachings of the Church are likely to be more satisfied with the situation than those who do not. Yet Model 3 still only explains 17 per cent of the variation in responses. What accounts for the other 83 per cent? Mostly it is due to factors that have not been measured in the survey, including whether or not the respondent has had any close experience of abuse, either through being a victim/survivor of abuse or knowing someone who has been abused, or through knowing a priest or religious who is known to have been an abuser.

Discussion and conclusion

In this chapter, we have seen that, among Mass attenders in Australia, the level of dissatisfaction around the clergy sexual abuse crisis increased between 1996 and 2016, and especially during the last five years of that period, most probably as a result of the extensive media coverage of the Church's failings that emerged during the Victorian Parliamentary Inquiry and the Royal Commission into Institutional Responses to Child Sexual Abuse. In all survey years, older attenders and those with a university education were more likely to be dissatisfied than younger and less well-educated attenders. The reasons for these differences cannot be identified from the survey data, but it is possible that older attenders have felt a greater sense of betrayal, shame and anger after decades of belonging and faithful service to their Church, whereas younger attenders—those in the 15-34 age range—tend to be more ready to defend the Church and to see it in a positive light. With regard to educational level, it is possible that university-educated attenders are better informed about the crisis and also that they expect better from their Church in terms of standards of governance.

Despite the impact of age and education, my analysis showed that demographic factors accounted for very little of the variation in Mass attenders' responses. Far more influential were attenders' frequency of attendance at Mass and their level of involvement in the life of their parish, as well as factors associated with personal faith and spirituality, especially those that tended towards a traditional piety marked by frequent saying of the Rosary, strong opposition to abortion, and always following the Church's teachings in making moral decisions. Attenders with this type of faith and spirituality were less likely than others to express dissatisfaction about priests and the Church, which accords with Mancini's finding that 'for very devout Catholics, reports of inaction on behalf of the Church did not shake their confidence in the institution'.[37]

We saw in our brief look at the international literature on Catholics' response to the clergy sexual abuse scandal that Catholics who attend Mass infrequently or not at all are more likely to take a negative view and to take actions such as ceasing to attend Mass, contributing less to the

---

37 Mancini, 'Test of Faith', 3.

Church financially or even leaving the Church altogether, and that even regular Mass attenders are likely to 'lean negative' in their attitudes, as D'Antonio and his colleagues put it. We are not able to tell from the survey data whether attenders with a high level of dissatisfaction have reduced their frequency of attendance at Mass or their financial contribution to their parish, although we do know that Mass attendances across Australia have been falling steadily for decades, and it is highly likely that some of this decrease in the period under consideration has been due to anger at the crimes committed by priests and dissatisfaction with the Church's response. The level of disidentification by Catholics in the Australian Census has also increased in recent years.[38]

This paper has reported on how Mass attenders have responded to questions about the clergy sexual abuse crisis every five years from 1996 to 2016. Unfortunately, we do not know how attenders would have responded in 2021. The questions were not asked, as the ACBC had by that time withdrawn as a partner in NCLS, meaning that while Catholic parishes could still participate in the survey, it was no longer possible to include Catholic-specific variants like those that included the sex abuse questions in earlier years. Even if the questions had been asked, it is likely that the different impact of COVID-19 on church attendances in the different states of Australia would have made the results difficult to compare with those from previous years.

The sexual abuse crisis has done enormous damage, most especially to victims and survivors, but also to the reputation of the Catholic Church and its capacity to influence public debates about social policy and to deliver pastoral services. The damage to ordinary Catholics has largely been overlooked. As we have seen in this chapter, even many of the most loyal Catholics—those who are at Mass on Sundays—have lost respect for priests and are highly dissatisfied with the Church's response. They are angry, ashamed, disillusioned and dismayed. They feel betrayed and they no longer trust their bishops. As Lakeland noted as long ago as 2004, 'the total inadequacy of the institutional response ... highlights a structural weakness in the church whose ramifications go far beyond this single issue'.[39] The theme of the 2020 APTO conference was 'Practical theology and the mission to heal'. In the case of the Catholic Church in Australia, an immediate priority must be to attend to the work of healing all its members, clergy and lay people. A good place to begin would be by the

---

38 Dixon, 'Australian Catholicism and Globalisation', 242.
39 Paul Lakeland, *The Liberation of the Laity: In Search of an Accountable Church* (New York: Continuum, 2004), 189.

bishops committing themselves to implementing the recommendations of the Royal Commission.[40]

Data sources

Michael Mason and Robert Dixon 1996. [computer file], 1996 Catholic Church Life Survey (version F). Canberra: National Centre for Pastoral Research.

Keith Castle, Ruth Powell, Sam Sterland and Robert Dixon. 2001. [computer file], 2001 NCLS Attender Surveys – Catholic (version X). Sydney: NCLS Research.

Ruth Powell, Sam Sterland and Robert Dixon. 2006. [computer file], 2006 National Church Life Survey: 2006 NCLS Attender Surveys – Catholic (version W). Sydney: NCLS Research.

Ruth Powell, Miriam Pepper, Nicole Hancock, Sam Sterland and Robert Dixon. 2011. [computer file], 2011 NCLS Attender Surveys – Catholic (version S3). Sydney: NCLS Research.

Ruth Powell, Miriam Pepper, Nicole Hancock, Sam Sterland and Robert Dixon. 2016. [computer file], 2016 NCLS Attender Surveys – Catholic (version S3). Sydney: NCLS Research.

---

40 The Second Session of the Plenary Council, held in July 2022, committed the Catholic Church in Australia to doing whatever possible to 'promote healing for those so gravely harmed and to make the Church a truly safe place for everyone' without making any commitment to implement specific recommendations. https://plenarycouncil.catholic.org.au/wp-content/uploads/2022/07/FINAL-Decree-2-Choosing-Repentance-Seeking-Healing.pdf

Chapter Three

A silent Church lives in darkness: Speaking out as response to clerical child sexual assault in the Catholic Church

Christopher Evan Longhurst

Introduction

Fundamental biblical values and official Catholic Church doctrine establish that Catholics have a duty to speak out when confronted with wrongdoing. Based on that teaching, this chapter contends that Catholics have a grave responsibility under pain of sin to speak out against clerical child sexual assault and its cover-up within the Catholic Church. After some commendations on speaking out, the reflective method is used to expand the 'light of the world' metaphor from Matthew 5:14 in relation to clerical and religious child sexual assault in the Catholic Church and used by Pope Francis to title his 2019 procedural rules managing sexual abuse in the Catholic Church, *Vos Estis Lux Mundi* (You Are the Light of the World).[1] Addressing the question of who is this light of the world today, this chapter asserts that speaking out is a virtue that brings healing and renewal; that those who speak out are 'the light of the world' for the Church today, and that those who do not, not only live in darkness but also offend against biblical teaching and Catholic Church values.

---

1 Pope Francis, *Vos Estis Lux Mundi* ('You are the Light of the World'), Apostolic Letter issued *Motu Proprio*, Vatican City, Libreria Editrice Vaticana, 9 May 2019. This document was originally enacted for a three-year trial period that ended on 1 June 2022. Its effectiveness has been assessed and it has been established as permanent law in the Catholic Church despite criticisms remaining. Anne Barrett Doyle, co-director of BishopAccountability.org published 'Francis' clergy abuse law, "Vos Estis," isn't working. Here's how to fix it' (*National Catholic Reporter*, 22 May 2022), https://www.ncronline.org/news/accountability/francis-clergy-abuse-law-vos-estis-isnt-working-heres-how-fix-it

1. Speaking out

If ever there were a test of Catholic moral consciousness, it would be the response to children sexually assaulted by clergy and religious. Given that Catholics are commonly known to publicly protest social justice issues, when they remain silent about their priests sexually assaulting children and their bishops covering it up on a systemic scale, then society must ask why. Surely there is no virtue in such a silence and cover-up. The opposite response—speaking out and exposing the abuse—can be described as simply not remaining silent in the face of this wrongdoing. Such action comprises educating oneself on the relevant issues and being vocal to uncover the crimes and misconduct. The purpose is to break the silence and concealment around institutional abuse, and to empower victims and survivors to tell their stories so that they may heal and society may be a safer place for all.

Regarding the characteristics of speaking out, this action can be seen as a good habit akin to the Greek idea of *parrēsia*, the virtue allied to courage by which one dares to speak up. The term *parrēsia* denotes speaking candidly and with courage[2] and can signify asking forgiveness for speaking openly and truthfully when the speech is challenging or not welcomed. It is a form of open and honest speech towards someone in authority who needs to know the facts so as to properly fulfil their duty. The Christian scriptures contain several examples.[3] When the high priest questioned Jesus about his teaching, Jesus replied, 'I have spoken openly to the world ..., I said nothing in secret' (John 18:20). However, Jesus was not popular for speaking out publicly against the hypocrisy of the pharisees. He exhibited the virtue of *parrēsia* when he called his religious leaders 'hypocrites', 'serpents', 'whited sepulchres', 'false prophets', 'blind guides', 'ravening wolves' and 'a generation of vipers'. He showed that speaking out can make one unpopular in certain circles.

Speaking out can also be seen as a form of blessing. The word 'benediction' which means blessing comes from the Latin *bene* meaning 'well' and *dícere* meaning 'to say'. In the Roman Catholic liturgy when the Eucharistic assembly is invited to pray the Lord's Prayer, the celebrant leads with '*audémus dícere*' ('we dare to say'). Daring to speak up against abuse and injustice blesses the world because it exposes the truth in order

---

2 See Blue Letter Bible Lexicon, Strong's G3954 – *parrēsia*. https://www.blueletterbible.org/lang/lexicon/lexicon.cfm?t=kjv&strongs=g3954

3 The Greek word παρρησία (*parrēsia*) occurs 32 times in 31 verses in the Greek concordance of the New American Standard Bible.

to prevent further harm. This blessed speaking may be understood as a kind of dutiful public lament that aims to bring the truth into a broader social conversation, thereby inspiring change.[4] As such it has the power to heal broken relationships and guard against deception and concealment.

Speaking out may be seen as a form of 'bearing witness'. In Catholicism, witness is an act of justice that establishes the truth or makes truth known.[5] This is an important aspect of the Christian mission to the extent that Christians are impelled 'to act as witnesses of the Gospel and of the obligations that flow from it'.[6] Such witness is a transmission of faith and morals through both words and deeds. According to Brian Clites, a specialist on clergy sexual assault within the Catholic Church, Catholics 'must bear witness to the Catholic experiences of abuse that [survivors] have suffered'.[7] Christians are obliged to acknowledge how this abuse has damaged the witness of the Church. Such witness is borne by all members of the Church, as Jesus required his followers to be involved in his ministry (John 9:4). To bear witness, Christians are required to recognise within their communities where abuse occurred and work to make the necessary changes to stop it.

Regarding the purpose of speaking out, Brian Devlin, whistleblowing priest in the case of disgraced Cardinal O'Brien of Scotland, commented on the motivation of those who speak out. He identified the whistle-blower's purpose as 'to prevent the further abuse of power by men at the head of a Church that claims to be holy'.[8] However, this motivation appears more institution-focused than people-focused. The interim report of New Zealand's Royal Commission of Inquiry into Abuse in Care, *He Purapura Ora, he Māra Tipu: From Redress to Puretumu Torowhānui* noted that a key motivation of survivors to speak out was to prevent further abuse.[9] Similarly, the survivor-support group SNAP

---

4 See Christopher Longhurst, 'Theologies of Lament, Listening and Healing: Responses to the Institutional Crisis of Clerical Child Sexual Abuse', *Catholic Thinking, WelCom* (1 April 2019), https://www.wn.catholic.org.nz/adw_welcom/catholic-thinking-theologies-of-lament-listening-and-healing/.
5 See Catholic Church, *Catechism of the Catholic Church* (hereafter CCC), second edition (Vatican City: Libreria Editrice Vaticana, 2012), n. 2472.
6 CCC 2472.
7 Brian J. Clites, 'Breaking Our Silence: A Primer for Research on Clergy Sexual Abuse', *American Catholic Studies Newsletter* 47, no. 2 (2020): 16.
8 Brian Devlin, 'Minding the Church: How Should the Hierarchy Respond to Whistle-blowers?' *Commonweal* (20 October 2021), https:// www.commonwealmagazine.org/minding-church?
9 Abuse In Care Royal Commission of Inquiry, *He Purapura Ora, he Māra Tipu: From Redress to Puretumu Torowhānui* 1 (December 2021), 201.

(Survivors Network of those Abused by Priests) advocates speaking out to protect children and adults at risk, hold predators to account, and raise community awareness.[10]

Devlin equated the motivation behind speaking out with the ancient principles of righting wrongs and truth-telling. 'When those are the real motivations, then whistleblowing must be seen as an ethical action, no matter how uncomfortable it makes the wider organization'.[11] He concluded that the Church's default position 'must be to support whistle-blowers rather than to impugn their motives'.[12]

> Whistle-blowers in the Catholic Church must never be punished for following their prophetic calling. Bishops—and those they choose to appoint to senior positions—who try to punish whistle-blowers must be investigated by the Holy See and subject to formal due process.[13]

In this sense, speaking out is also a form of honesty. Honesty builds trust, especially when combined with good judgment and empathy. When a call to speak out against injustice is made in a faith-based context, then the obligation on believers to do so is particularly acute, with the risk of being accused of hypocrisy for failing to do so.

A few other basic reasons to speak out are to advocate for the oppressed, to help restore the injustice by holding offenders to account, to support those affected in their healing process and to improve institutions by driving accountability in the public eye. One may think that remaining silent avoids having to be involved in the issue. However, when it comes to actions that are categorically wrong or intrinsically evil such as the rape of a child,[14] because silence is still an active form of communication, then the silence itself becomes wrong.

Why not speak up? Perceptions that speaking up may lead to more problems, or hurt another person, or seem unkind or unwise can be real. However, the following sections looks at why remaining silent is ultimately not an option for a Catholic when it comes to speaking out against wrongdoing based on Catholic Church teaching and biblical values.

---

10 See SNAP Mission Statement, https://www.snapnetwork.org/about.
11 Devlin, 'Minding the Church'.
12 Devlin, 'Minding the Church'.
13 Devlin, 'Minding the Church'.
14 CCC n. 2356. '[Rape] is always an intrinsically evil act. Graver still is the rape of children committed by parents (incest) or those responsible for the education of the children entrusted to them.'

The Catholic requirement to speak out

According to Catholic social teaching, human dignity is maintained only when human rights are protected and human responsibilities are met.[15] Safeguarding all members of society and speaking the truth are essential to this achievement. According to Catholic Church teaching, all members of society are obliged to meet the demands of justice and charity and 'to honour and bear witness to the truth',[16] which includes not only religious truth but 'truth as uprightness in human action and speech' as well.[17] The eighth commandment forbids misrepresenting the truth in human relationships.[18]

In cases of clerical child sexual abuse, speaking out can serve as a corrective to the sinful silence that enabled abuse and sought to prevent people from discovering the truth that ought to be known. Different kinds of sinful silence exist, such as that of victims silenced by their abusers and those who covered for the abusers, and the silence of those who knew and never spoke up. While silencing is a sin of commission, keeping silent amounts to a sin of omission because it perverts the course of justice by preventing knowledge of the abuse, thereby preventing the crimes from being exposed and eradicated, thus risking furthering abuse. This has occurred when perpetrators were moved by church officials from school to school and from parish to parish, where they continued to abuse, while the truth was hidden from those who had a right to know so as to take the measures necessary to prevent further harm.[19]

In relation to 'showing oneself true in deeds and truthful in words',[20] speaking out against crimes and their cover-up would fall under the moral virtue of justice to the extent that truth-telling is giving what is due in speech. The corollary is that lying or denying the truth to those who have a right to know it is wrong. It follows that for Catholics to live in the light, they must be truthful to one another: 'If we claim to have fellowship with [Jesus] and yet walk in darkness, we lie and do not live out the truth' (1 John 1:6, NIV).

---

15 CCC n. 1930.
16 See CCC n. 2495 and CCC n. 2467.
17 CCC n. 2468.
18 CCC n. 2464.
19 See reports such as New Zealand's Royal Commission of Inquiry into Abuse in Care's *He Purapura Ora, he Māra Tipu, From Redress to Puretumu Torowhānui*; Australia's Royal Commission into Institutional Responses to Child Sexual Abuse; England and Wales IICSA Report; Pennsylvania Report in the USA, and Ireland's Murphy Report, amongst others. See also the original Spotlight report in *The Boston Globe*, 'Church allowed abuse by priest for years', 6 January 2002.
20 CCC n. 2505.

Official Catholic teaching states that 'society has a right to information based on truth, freedom, justice, and solidarity'.[21] Given the requirement for all members of society to meet the demands of justice and charity, how much more are Christians obliged to meet those demands? Therefore, when witnessing wrongdoing, the Catholic's failure to speak up or any attempt to deny the truth becomes sinful because there is a duty to tell the truth, as the aforesaid scriptures and Church teachings affirm.

When the truth is unpleasant, some may argue that it is better not to reveal it. However, amongst the themes of Catholic Social Teaching is the principle of the life and dignity of the human person. Reflecting on the crime of clerical sexual abuse, Pope Francis admitted that abuse is killing: 'As a priest, I have to help people grow and save them. If I abuse, I kill them'.[22] Not only does Catholicism teach that human life is sacred and the dignity of the human person is the foundation of a moral vision for society,[23] but slaying the innocent and the righteous is prohibited by the fifth commandment (Exodus 23:7). Clerical sexual abuse is gravely contrary to the dignity of the human person.

There is also the principle of the common good for which the truth of certain crimes must not be kept hidden. When not knowing the truth causes the crimes to continue, then the lack of knowledge is itself bad because it prevents the crimes from being stopped. This is why some truths must not be hidden. In such cases, article 2488 of the Catholic Catechism which states that 'the right to the communication of the truth is not unconditional' does not apply. The communication of the truth of clerical and religious child sexual assault is not conditional if such communication would prevent more children from being harmed. It is also the reason why hiding the crime constitutes a perversion of the course of justice.

Article 2489 of the Catholic Catechism states that 'the duty to avoid scandal often commands strict discretion. No one is bound to reveal the truth to someone who does not have the right to know it.'[24] However, when it comes to clerical and religious child sexual abuse, this teaching is unsuitable because there is no duty to avoid scandal here. On the contrary,

---

21 CCC n. 2494.
22 Kathleen N. Hattrup, 'Pope: For Priests, to Abuse is to Kill', *Aleteia* (8 July 2022), https://aleteia.org/2022/07/08/we-have-to-fight-against-every-single-case-says-pope-francis-on-abuse/.
23 'Seven Themes of Catholic Social Teaching', (Washington, DC: United States Conference of Catholic Bishops), https://www.usccb.org/beliefs-and-teachings/what-we-believe/catholic-social-teaching/seven-themes-of-catholic-social-teaching; 'Human Dignity: Te Mana o te Tangata' (Caritas Aotearoa New Zealand), https://www.caritas.org.nz/catholic-social-teaching/human-dignity.
24 CCC n. 2489.

'scandal is an attitude or behaviour which leads another to do evil'.[25] The evil is the abuse and the cover-up itself. For the Christian community to stand by and let such abuse continue to happen is scandalous, as such failure keeps society unsafe by enabling abusers to reoffend. According to Mary Demuth, American author and artist, 'ministries that cover up sexual abuse are not ministries at all. Their silence allows evil to thrive'.[26] Such behaviour amounts to perverting the course of justice and allowing the abuse to continue. When the issue involves the sexual abuse of children by priests, then the duty to be charitable and tell the truth applies all the more, and with utmost caution, because the issue effects the faith and lives of many.

Biblical teaching

From a biblical viewpoint, society as a whole, and religious people in particular, are obliged to defend the rights of the poor and needy and promote the common good. Proverbs 31: 9 states, 'Speak out, judge righteously, defend the rights of the poor and needy'. Isaiah 1:17 says, 'learn to do good; seek justice, rescue the oppressed'.

The Bible also instructs believers to speak out and not remain silent in the face of oppression and victimisation. Paul ordered the Ephesians to 'take no part in the unfruitful works of darkness, but instead expose them' (5:11). According to Leviticus: 'If anyone sins because they do not speak up when they hear a public charge to testify regarding something they have seen or learned about, they will be held responsible' (5:1, NIV). Jesus' sternest words of condemnation were levelled against those who abuse the vulnerable: 'If any of you put a stumbling block before one of these little ones who believe in me, it would be better for you if a great millstone were fastened around your neck and you were drowned in the depth of the sea' (Matthew 18:6). These biblical passages clearly oblige Christians to speak out when confronted with abuse.

Further, according to official Church teaching, Catholics have a social duty to 'act as witnesses of the Gospel and of the obligations that flow from it'.[27] From the Catholic perspective, speaking out falls under the umbrella of social justice to the extent that such action is intended to create a safe society for all. This is true to the extent that speaking out

---

25 CCC n. 2284.
26 Mary Demuth, 'When We Neglect the Millstone We Cast Stones at Survivors' (11 December 2018), https://www.marydemuth.com/millstone/.
27 CCC n. 2472.

leads to reduced corruption by meeting the demands of telling the truth to those who have a need or right to know it. Vaclav Havel stated 'when anyone steps out of the system and tells the truth, lives the truth, that person enables everyone else to peer behind the curtain too. That person has shown everyone that it is possible to live within the truth'.[28] This teaching calls on all Catholics, clerics and lay, to speak out.

Therefore, Catholics who knew about the abuse of children by priests and religious and did not condemn it or failed to report it, were guilty not only of ignoring the suffering and pain of victims, but also of passively contributing to that wrongdoing according to biblical standards, by failing to do what the Bible commands them to do. In this sense, they betrayed the common good which cannot be achieved without particular concern for the most vulnerable members of society, including children.

Unacceptable responses

Based on Catholic moral and biblical teaching, there seem to be two major kinds of response to clerical child sexual abuse that are unacceptable. One is to do nothing, which includes remaining silent, and the other is to deny the abuse or try to cover it up. Regarding the first response, to do nothing risks perverting the course of justice by failing to ensure that justice is attained. Shay Cullen, an Irish Columban missionary, asserted that not reporting abusive clergy was a major part of the problem.[29] Such a failure to report not only signifies indifference towards the abuse. Cullen claimed that 'the silence of bishops and other priests makes them accessories to the crimes'.[30] According to Cullen, remaining silent in the face of such abuse makes one an accomplice as it allows the abuse to be perpetuated.[31]

---

28 Václav Havel and Paul Wilson, 'The Power of the Powerless', *International Journal of Politics* 15, no. 3/4 (1985): 23–96.

29 Shay Cullen, 'Catholic Leaders Have to be Defenders of Children', *The Manila Times* (14 November 2021), https://www.manilatimes.net/2021/11/14/opinion/columns/catholic-leaders-have-to-be-defenders-of-children/1822129.

30 Cullen, 'Catholic Leaders'. See also National Domestic Violence Hotline, 'Why Didn't You Say Anything?' (Austin, Texas), https://www.thehotline.org/resources/why-didnt-you-say-anything/; and Survivors Network of those Abused by Priests (SNAP) in Aotearoa New Zealand, 'Closing Statement to the Royal Commission of Inquiry into Abuse in Care', at Faith-based Redress Hearing, Phase 2 (29 March 2020), https://www.abuseincare.org.nz/assets/Uploads/Closing-statement-from-SNAP-for-Faith-based-Redress-hearing.pdf.

31 Cullen, 'Catholic leaders'. This silent complicity has been articulated by various other researchers as well. See Florian Wettstein, Silence as Complicity: Elements of a Corporate Duty to Speak Out Against the Violation of Human Rights, *Business Ethics Quarterly* 22, no. 1 (January 2012): 37-61.

He explained how the light of Christ is diminished by those who remain silent.[32]

Further, Cullen claimed that 'the culture of silence is the shield of the abusers'.[33] It seems that for those in positions of authority, to keep silent or not to advocate speaking out is a dereliction of duty. Pope Francis talked about how in the Church this duty fell, above all, on bishops.[34] Commenting on the official response from Catholic bishops in New Zealand, David Tombs, of the University of Otago, publicly asserted that the Catholic Church's response to historic sexual abuse had been 'a failure of the church's moral leadership ... ethically wrong and a failure to witness to the Gospel'.[35]

It seems reasonable to concede that when Catholics do not speak out, their silence transforms into what has been called an evil silence by the absence of the witness that is due. The betrayal of witnessing becomes sinful given the biblical command to speak up. Devlin acknowledged that 'many of the faithful now recognize the internal machinations of the hierarchy and its tendency to suppress damaging revelations as akin to the omerta of organized crime gangs'.[36] Commenting on the degree to which Church officials tolerated abuse, Devlin claimed that their 'icy silence' was 'intended to intimidate, to put victims and whistle-blowers in their place'.[37] However if 'outside the Church such failure to respond would be completely unacceptable' and amount to 'piling further abuse onto people who have already been traumatized' as Devlin contended,[38] then how much truer must this be for those inside the Church given the Church's teaching?[39]

While doing nothing is a passively wrong response, the other kind of response, denial and cover-up, is actively wrong. Such action is a sin of commission which constitutes a violation of God's moral law in the Ten Commandments. In some cases, it could also be an act of criminality

---

32 Shay Cullen, 'Days of Darkness and Light for the Catholic Church', *Union of Catholic Asian News* (15 October 2021), https://www.ucanews.com/news/days-of-darkness-and-light-for-the-catholic-church/94561#.
33 Cullen, 'Catholic Leaders'.
34 Francis, *Vos Estis Lux Mundi*, Introduction.
35 Chris Morris, 'Church Attacked for Silence', *Otago Daily Times*, 13 October 2018, https://www.odt.co.nz/news/dunedin/insight/church-attacked-silence.
36 Devlin, 'Minding the Church'.
37 Devlin, 'Minding the Church'.
38 Devlin, 'Minding the Church'.
39 CCC n. 2495 and CCC n. 2467.

through perverting the course of justice.⁴⁰ Obviously, to deny credible complaints or to purposefully conceal abuse or fail to report it amounts to contributing to that wrongdoing.

While psychology experts have explained some legitimate reasons for denial of abuse, the denial still causes a lot of harm.⁴¹ When done on purpose, such denial is sinful and tantamount to cover-up. Catholic Church leaders have frequently been charged with routinely concealing child abuse offences.⁴² Such concealment, failure to respond, and refusal to take effective action constitute entirely unacceptable responses.

2. Giving light to the world

In the biblical verse used by Pope Francis to title his procedural rules to manage the crimes of sexual abuse in the Catholic Church (Matthew 5:14), Jesus referred to his faithful followers as 'the light of the world'. The pericope continues:

> A town built on a hill cannot be hidden. Neither do people light a lamp and put it under a bowl. Instead, they put it on its stand, and it gives light to everyone in the house (Matthew 5:14-15 NIV).

---

40 In criminal law, an omission would constitute an *actus reus* and give rise to liability when the law imposes a duty to act and the defendant is in breach of that duty. In Australia, concealing a child abuse offence is a crime under section 316A(1) of the Crimes Act 1900.

41 Darlene Lancer, 'Are You Overlooking or Rationalizing Abuse? That's Denial!' *Psychology Today* (1 December 2019).

42 For example, the Final Report of Australia's Royal Commission into Institutional Responses to Child Sexual Abuse documented thirty case studies on religious institutions. They revealed that 'many religious leaders knew of allegations of child sexual abuse yet failed to take effective action. Some ignored allegations and did not respond at all ... Some concealed abuse and shielded perpetrators from accountability. Institutional reputations and individual perpetrators were prioritised over the needs of victims and their families'. Royal Commission into Institutional Responses to Child Sexual Abuse, 'Final Report', 16, Religious institutions, https://www.childabuseroyalcommission.gov.au/religious-institutions. At hearings conducted by the New Zealand Royal Commission of Inquiry into Historical Abuse in State Care and in the Care of Faith-based Institutions, victims and survivors of abuse in New Zealand's Catholic Church accused Catholic church leaders of covering up sexual abuse. See Abuse in Care - Royal Commission of Inquiry, Faith-based Redress hearing - Phase One, Nov/Dec 2020, and Phase Two (15-29 March), https://www.abuseincare.org.nz/our-inquiries/state-and-faith-based-redress/faith-based-redress-hearings-phases-1-and-3/. See also SNAP Opening Statement, 22 March 2020, and Closing Statement, 29 March 2020. https://www.abuseincare.org.nz/assets/Uploads/Closing-statement-from-SNAP-for-Faith-based-Redress-hearing.pdf.

The following briefly expands the metaphorical significances of light, lamp and lampstand, bowl, and darkness in relation to clerical child sexual abuse.

Metaphorical significances of light (phōs)

With regard to the metaphorical significances of light, the Hebrew word for light (*aur*) in the First Testament reveals one of God's first creative works (Genesis 1:3). This indicates something that is of God's self, that God is light. In the Second Testament, Jesus echoed this sentiment when he claimed to be 'the light of the world' (John 8:12).

In biblical history, light counters darkness and chaos (Exodus 10:23). The term light is also used symbolically to represent life (Psalms 56:13), salvation (Isaiah 9:2) and the commandments (Proverbs 6:23). In Christian theology, light symbolises the mechanism that removes the darkness of ignorance and falsehood.[43] Thus, it contains a moral dimension, symbolising goodness in contrast to the darkness associated with evil deeds.[44]

The Greek word for light (*phōs*) in the Second Testament describes Jesus not as a physical light but the illumination of a spiritually dark world. Again, Jesus referred to himself as 'the light of the world' and stated that 'whoever follows me will never walk in darkness but will have the light of life' (John 8:12).

This light is seen by believers in God's truth and actions reproduced in those who are honest and upright. In this sense, light possesses both an intellectual-knowledge basis and a moral-action basis. The light is both truth telling and good deeds. These intellectual and moral dimensions of 'being' light and 'transmitting' light serve to counter darkness.

The moral action basis of light as goodness is explicated in the Second Testament. God's people are told to 'live as children of light, for the fruit of the light is found in all that is good and right and true' (Ephesians 5:8-9). It also warns us to 'take no part in the unfruitful works of darkness, but instead expose them' (Ephesians 5:11).

The agency of the darkness is those who prevent the light of truth from shining forth. The act of speaking out, as light-giving, would have the opposite effect. It would help restore the credibility and effectiveness

---

43 See Michael J. Wilkins, *Baker's Evangelical Dictionary of Biblical Theology*, Walter A. Elwell, ed. (Grand Rapids, Michigan: Baker Books 1996), at 'Light'.
44 Genesis 1:4 states 'God saw that the light was good'.

of the Church's authentic mission by providing the antidote to the cover-up and silence.

Metaphorical significances of lamp (lychnon) and lampstand (lychnian)

The Bible uses the terms lamp (*lychnon*) and light (*phōs*) synonymously.[45] Considering the lamp, Jesus said, 'a city on a hill cannot be hidden, nor do people light a lamp and put it under a bowl'.[46] In Jewish homes of biblical times, lamps were partially closed clay reservoirs.[47] They had a hole on top to pour in oil and a spout at one end into which a wick of flax or cotton was placed. They were relatively small vessels and gave off only modest light. This is why they were placed on a lampstand, to emit maximum light.

Jesus advised his followers to put the lamp on a stand (Matthew 5:15). In practical terms, the lampstand is simply the instrument enabling the light to reach its maximum emission in order to provide light for everyone in the house. Since Jewish homes in Jesus' times were relatively small and usually single roomed, a lamp on a stand would transmit light to everyone in the house. Otherwise, the lamp was carried around the house to find one's way during the night.[48]

In the context of clerical child sexual abuse, the lamp, like the light-bearer, could be any person who shines the light of truth despite how unpleasant or distressing that truth may be. Such emitting of light could be the voices of the faithful speaking out and reporting abuse by lodging complaints with relative civil and ecclesiastical authorities. Other ways of emitting light could be actions such as reaching out to victims and survivors through available means such as announcements in church bulletins, parish notices and media advertisements, as well as giving support for therapy, drug and alcohol rehabilitation, job training and the like.

Lamps could also be such movements as the LOUD Fence,[49] tying colourful ribbons to fences at churches or schools to show solidarity with victims and survivors of abuse. They could also be intentional

---

45 Fred H. Wight, *Manners And Customs of Bible Lands* (Chicago: Moody Press, 1953), 29.
46 Matthew 5:15.
47 See Robert H. Smith, 'The Household Lamps of Palestine in New Testament Times', *The Biblical Archaeologist* 29, no. 1 (February 1966): 1-27.
48 Smith, 'The Household Lamps of Palestine in New Testament Times'.
49 The Loud Fence movement began in Australia in 2015, at St Alipius Boys' School in Ballarat, a site of abuse. The movement aims to raise awareness of clerical and religious child sexual abuse.

peer-support groups and restorative justice processes. These would all be lamps figuratively because they emit God's light for the afflicted.

The lampstand, as a metaphor for any device that permits more effective speaking out and therefore more light transmission, could be non-euphemistic speech, public speech, or big and bold notices, prominent places in church bulletins offering support for victims and survivors. They could be constant media advertisements to raise awareness and authentic safeguarding programs.

Lampstands are also the relentless voices of survivors and their advocates crying out for justice. These are the vehicles that allow God's light to shine more effectively in speech and in action. The key idea here is that light is transmitted in the best possible way and not concealed, and a lampstand would facilitate that process.

Metaphorical significances of bowl (modion)

With regard to the metaphorical significances of bowls, to extinguish the light, lamps were placed under a bowl or a bushel. Therefore, the bowl in verse 15 represents the device used to extinguish the light. Luke associated a bowl with a secret place when he said, 'No one lights a lamp and puts it in a place where it will be hidden, or under a bowl' (Luke 11:33, NIV).

In relation to clerical child sexual abuse, bowls are what cause the darkness. In the first instance, this is the abuse itself, the greatest bowl. In the second instance, bowls are factors such as denial and the cover-up of abuse. These include Christians who cover up or deny the abuse within their communities. It also includes Christians who remain silent in the face of such crimes.

Bowls are especially Church leaders who place institutional reputation or finances before truth and justice, confounding the Church through a false sense of loyalty with something other than its members.[50] Bowls are also occurrences of institutional betrayal such as punishment for reporting abuse or maltreatment for speaking out.

A bowl is also the crafting of inauthentic redress schemes that fail to provide honest accountability or fair compensation for the abuse. Bowls

---

50 Vaughan Leslie, a New Zealand Catholic priest, explained how misguided actions by church leaders within New Zealand and overseas has fuelled the abuse scandal. Leslie asserted that the Catholic hierarchy's 'misguided protectionism' had occurred 'at the expense of truth and justice'. Chris Morris, 'Alexandra's priest speaks out', *Otago Daily Times*, 15 October 2018, https://www.odt.co.nz/regions/central-otago/alexandra\%E2\%80\%99s-priest-speaks-out.

are also victim silencing and victim blaming, gaslighting and secondary trauma triggers. Other bowls include the unwarranted shame inflicted upon victims by perpetrators and those who enable perpetrators by shielding them.

Significance of darkness (skotia)

With respect to the metaphorical significances of *darkness*, in the Bible darkness is presented in contrast to light or as the absence of light. The scriptural claim that 'God separated the light from the darkness' (Genesis 1:4, NIV) implies an opposition or estrangement between light and darkness. This contrast has stimulated a metaphorical distinction between good and evil. In Christian theology, light represents what is good and true while *skotia* (darkness), as used in John 8:12, is associated with wrongdoing and the subsequent misery of a life lived in darkness.

As light is the symbol of God's truth and goodness, darkness compares to falsehood and wrongdoing. While the good walk and work in the light, the wicked walk and work in darkness.[51] The implication here is that those who do not follow in Jesus' footsteps to speak the truth and perform good deeds live in darkness.

In relation to clerical child sexual abuse, priests and religious who abused children under their care, and those who enabled them, including bishops and congregational leaders who covered up their crimes, as well as the faithful who have kept silent, metaphorically live in darkness. Hiding the abuse in a culture of silence and denial is the epitome of darkness. Pope Benedict XVI acknowledged that clerical child sexual abuse has 'obscured the light of the Gospel to a degree that not even centuries of persecution succeeded in doing'.[52] Those who deny the abuse or keep silent contribute to that obscurity. They are like those who hide the lamp under a bowl rather than putting it on its stand to give light to everyone in God's household. They thereby cause others to live in darkness and the darkness to persist.

3. Minimally acceptable response

According to both social standards and biblical teaching, speaking out must be the lowest possible level of a morally acceptable response to

---

51 See Psalms 82:5; Proverbs 2:13; John 3:19; Romans 13:12.
52 Benedict XVI, *Pastoral Letter to the Catholics of Ireland* (Vatican City: Libreria Editrice Vaticana, 2010).

child sexual abuse because justice is the rock bottom of the moral life. To descend below that level would imply that injustice is being tolerated.

Catholics are obliged to act when faced with injustice otherwise they sin. According to the Bible, they may not do nothing in the face of unjust occurrences. James says, 'if anyone, then, knows the good they ought to do and does not do it, it is sin for them' (4:17, NIV). While doing nothing in the face of criminal activity may not constitute a crime under most nations' statutory law, it is manifestly wrong according to biblical and Church teaching.[53] According to New Zealand legislation, hiding a crime by concealing or destroying a document is in fact a felony. But this has repeatedly occurred in the history of church responses to clerical child sexual abuse.[54]

4. Let your light shine

Jesus told his disciples to 'let your light shine before others, that they may see your good deeds' (Matthew 5:16, NIV). This verse emphasises what Jesus called his followers to do. In this sense, the pericope concerns discipleship-action. It informs of a purpose for transmitting light, one that requires good actions. This instruction cannot be a prescription of believing alone, such as the light of Christian doctrine, but rather the light of truth in action.

When faced with knowledge of abuse, the counterforce is to 'let your light shine'. From the biblical perspective, knowing about the crimes of clerical child sexual assault and abhorring them would not be enough. The Christian is obliged to act, to speak out in the face of injustice, to expose such crimes by shining the light of truth on them.

While good deeds serve as a counterforce to the abuse—as indirect exposure of the darkness in order to eradicate it—speaking out or direct speech against the abuse and reporting it to law enforcement officials becomes a very good deed. The implication here is that all instances of child sexual abuse by clergy and religious are times to speak out.

---

53 Perverting the course of justice is an offence committed when a person prevents justice from being served on themselves or on another party. Statutory versions of the offence exist in Commonwealth countries. A similar concept, obstruction of justice, exists in United States law.

54 See article 71 of the New Zealand Crimes Act 1961 which deals with being an accessory after the fact, and articles 257-260 which deal with altering, concealing, destroying, or reproducing documents with intent to deceive, https://www.legislation.govt.nz/act/public/1961/0043/latest/whole.html#DLM330458. See also the evidence before the Abuse in Care Royal Commission of Inquiry at the Faith-based redress hearing – Phase Two, 29 March 2021, https://www.abuseincare.org.nz/library/v/224/closing-addresses-all-core-participants-at-faith-based-redress-hearing-phase-2.

Otherwise, Catholics, according to their own teachings, will eventually be held to account for failing to do so. This is supported by aforementioned biblical passages that oblige Christians to not remain silent but to speak up when faced with injustice. By corollary, those who speak up are significant players in being that 'light of the world'. Those who do not speak out, by their own standards, have also disobeyed God.

The peculiarity of speaking out is that revealing the dark truth dispels the darkness. Conversely, hiding that truth destroys the light. This choice of passage used by Pope Francis in relation to the issue of reporting clerical child sexual abuse implies that speaking out against the abuse is a good action. This is the aptness of Pope Francis's application of Mathew 5:14 to such a repulsive reality as clerical child sexual abuse in *Vos Estis Lux Mundi*. The Pope reaffirmed how true discipleship results in actions necessary to counter wrongdoing. Such actions would therefore be not hiding the truth, despite how dark that truth is, but bringing it into the light for all to see so as to eradicate it. In other words, exposing the dark truth becomes a good act. It enables the light to shine.

In sum, to live in the light, Catholics are required to destroy the darkness directly by speaking out against what causes it, and indirectly by living good lives. Those who fail to do so, silent Catholics, cause the darkness to endure; however, those who speak out shine the light of truth to uncover the abuse so that victims and survivors and the wider community may heal. They live in the light and give light to the world.

Conclusion

The culture and systems of the Catholic Church that allowed clerical and religious child sexual abuse and its cover-up to occur have produced a darkness inside the Church, exacerbated by those who remain silent. This paper has demonstrated that remaining silent in the face of clerical child sexual abuse is wrong according to both biblical and official Catholic Church teaching. Failing to speak out leads to communal darkness but speaking out against this abuse and its cover-up gives light for everyone. It is, therefore, the Catholic's duty based on biblical and Church teaching to speak out and defend the rights of all victims of such crimes.

An analysis of the metaphorical significances of Matthew 5:14-15 has shown that the light symbolises the truth uncovering the abuse and its cover-up, and the good works performed in countering the abuse. The lamp represents the voice that speaks out. Such speaking out is an act of justice for the common good. It is the virtue of bold and honest speech that serves to break the evil silence, a form of public witness, and a blessing for society. The lampstand is any mechanism that empowers the voice that speaks out. The bowl symbolises the concealment and denial of the abuse, along with the silence of the people of God. The darkness symbolises the abuse itself along with its cover-up.

Chapter Four

15 March 2019: Remembering the causes of white supremacy and racism to be agents of healing and justice

Mary Eastham

Part One: 'They Are Us'

Probably everyone in New Zealand can remember where they were when they heard the news that a lone gunman had entered Al Noor and Linwood Mosques in Christchurch and murdered 51 men, women and children on their knees at prayer. About 1:40 pm, a Channel 1 News Special Report began to document the tragedy, and New Zealanders learned that the perpetrator was an Australian-born white supremacist.

When given the news, Prime Minister Jacinda Ardern wrote the phrase 'They are us' on a piece of A4 paper. Her response was an immediate expression of empathy, unity and solidarity, and became the clarion call for the nation's response to one of the most heinous crimes in its history.[1] A special radio NZ memorial, *They Are Us*, provided a more intimate look into the lives of the people lost in this tragedy.[2] 'They' were 46 men, ranging in age from 16 to 77, well-educated, middle-class professionals. 'They' were scientists, engineers, medical doctors, university professors, owners of businesses and restaurants, hardworking students. Four women were murdered: two were in their 60s; one was 44; the youngest was 25. 'They' were educators and students. The mother of a three-year-old boy shot amidst the mayhem had a heart

---

1 Another heinous crime was the murder of 2,100 Maori killed by the Crown over the course of the Land Wars.
2 Radio New Zealand, *They Are Us. A memorial to the victims of the 15 March 2019 Christchurch terror attacks. Kia kaha, kia kotahi ra. As-salaam alaikum. Our strength is our unity*, March 2019, https://shorthand.radionz.co.nz/they-are-us/index.html.

attack and died when her son did not survive his injuries. The death toll, therefore, was actually 52. 'They' came from: Abu Dhabi, Afghanistan, Bangladesh, Fiji, India, Indonesia, Jordan, Kuwait, Palestine, Pakistan, Saudi Arabia, Somalia, Syria, United Arab Emirates. One woman was a Pakeha New Zealand convert to Islam, which she described as a 'religion which gave her peace'.[3]

Then there are those who survived the attack—40 counts of attempted murder, 32 widows, many of them very young, and many orphans. 'They' were people just like us, expecting to be safe in their place of worship. The heartfelt 'they' expressed by Prime Minister Jacinda Ardern affirmed our common humanity and common heartache.

But is the Prime Minister's response 'aspirational' or descriptive of the social reality in this country?

Pleas for protection against threats from the alt-right not taken seriously by government

In countless media interviews following the attack, Anjum Rahman, media spokesperson for the Islamic Women's Council of New Zealand (IWCNZ) and member of the Waikato Interfaith Council, expressed outrage at the failure of the New Zealand Security Intelligence Service (NZSIS) to take seriously threats of violence towards the Muslim community caused by Islamophobia.[4] In 'We warned you. We begged. We pleaded and now we demand accountability',[5] Ms. Rahman documented the five year effort of IWCNZ to persuade government to take seriously threats against the Muslim community, particularly Muslim women, because wearing the *hijab* made them visible targets for hate speech and other forms of physical and verbal discrimination. From 2014 to 2019, *five* years before the 15 March terrorist attack, IWCNZ approached no less than *seven* different government agencies to report how Islamophobia

---

3 This statement was attributed to Linda Armstrong.
4 In the 2019 Queen's Birthday Honours, Anjum Rahman was appointed a Member of the New Zealand Order of Merit for services to ethnic communities and women. In 2020, she was shortlisted for New Zealander of the Year. Ms Rahman was born in India and her family moved to New Zealand from Canada in 1972 when she was five years old, after her father completed a PhD and was offered a post-doctoral position at the Ministry of Agriculture and Fisheries in Hamilton. She became a naturalised New Zealand citizen in 1976.
5 Anjum Rahman, 'We warned you. We begged. We pleaded and now we demand accountability', *The Spinoff*, 17 March 2019, https://thespinoff.co.nz/society/17-03-2019/we-warned-you-we-begged-we-pleaded-and-now-we-demand-accountability/

and the increasing vitriol of alt-right groups was 'terrorising' them. These meetings included:

- October 2016 meeting with the New Zealand Security Intelligence Service at their request to present the concerns of IWCNZ.

- December 2016 meeting with then Race Relations Commissioner Dame Susan Devoy who afterwards championed their cause for as long as she held the position.

- January 2017 meeting with the Department of Prime Minister and Cabinet explaining their concerns.

- March 2017 meeting with the Human Rights Commission and State Services Commission on the impacts of discrimination on their community, what was needed from government, how they could support their communities, and how their suggestions would benefit all minority communities and New Zealand.

- August 2017 meeting with the Department of Internal Affairs (DIA) in Hamilton and the Office of Ethnic Communities over the next few months. IWCNZ insisted that action was needed at the national level to respond effectively to the rising vitriol of the alt-right against their community, but DIA told them that programs would be made available in Waikato only.

- In January 2018, meeting with two ministers from the new government. This would have been Jacinda Ardern's Coalition government.

- In February 2018, IWCNZ asked the Security Intelligence Service why they could justify spending so much money ($7 million[6]) on surveilling the Muslim community, but nothing on programs to prevent violence against them.

To understand the urgency behind IWCNZ's efforts, recall that in 2014 terrorist organisations like ISIS controlled large portions of

---

6 See David Williams, 'Five Frustrating Years and Eight Awful Months', 9 December 2019. https://www.newsroom.co.nz/five-frustrating-years-and-eight-awful-months. Here Aliya Denzeisen, National Coordinator of IWCNZ, tells us that "Prime Minister John Key announced the Government would introduce new laws to deal with New Zealanders recruited by terrorist groups like ISIS. Changes included powers to suspend or cancel passports, and warrantless surveillance. The Security Intelligence Service also got a $7 million boost."

Iraq and Syria. Because the media often uncritically linked words like 'Muslim', 'terrorist', 'Islamic extremism', 'jihad', etc.,[7]. Muslims in New Zealand, who had always been good citizens, were unwittingly connected with the extremism of groups like ISIS. Consider, therefore, how then Prime Minister John Key's cavalier remark about 'Jihadi brides'[8] in 2014 would have intensified the fears of Muslim women about threats to their personal safety.

Reports of hate speech and hate crime against Muslims not documented by police

That police ignored reports of hate speech and hate crime against the Muslim community was a major concern IWCNZ shared with government. In a religiously pluralist democracy where the civil rights of all citizens are supposed to be protected by law, how could the police ignore reports of hate speech and hate crime against vulnerable Muslim women by white supremacist groups? The document, *It Happened Here: Reports of race and religious hate crime in New Zealand 2004-2012*, published by the Human Rights Commission in June 2019, provides an answer:

> The Christchurch shootings have re-ignited public debate about hate crime and hate speech, but there is little information available about the extent of racially and religiously motivated crime in New Zealand. Police do not collect this data, despite calls from the New Zealand Human Rights Commission since 2004, recommendations from the United Nations Committee on the Elimination of Racial Discrimination in 2007 and 2017, and from the United Nations Human Rights Council in 2009. Shortly after the Council made its recommendation in 2009, the Government of the day agreed with the recommendation but said it was not a priority. The recommendation has never been actioned.[9]

---

7 Khairiah A. Rahman, 'Policy Brief on the Role of the Media: Building Cultural Understanding and Countering Violent Extremism,' *He Whenua Taurikura—New Zealand's Hui on Countering Terrorism and Violent Extremism*, June 2021, 2.
8 See Williams, 'Five Frustrating Years'. It is a proven fact that there were no Jihadi brides from New Zealand; they all came from Australia.
9 Paul Hunt, *It Happened Here: Reports of Race and Religious Hate Crime in New Zealand 2004-2012* (Human Rights Commission, *Te Kahui Tika Tangata*), June 2019, 1.

It is significant that reports of hate speech and hate crime recorded in this milestone document were taken from the annual reports of Race Relations Commissioner, Joris de Bres (2002-2013) born in South Africa, and Dame Susan Devoy (2013-2018). They documented that, in 2005, a Muslim woman in Blenheim was verbally abused for wearing the *hijab*, accused of being a terrorist, and told to go home, even though she had lived in New Zealand for fifteen years. They documented that, in 2006, a West Auckland Muslim woman was shot at in a bus stop from a passing car.[10]

'They are us'? The failure of police to collect this data against a truly vulnerable community in New Zealand, plus the failure of government to hear the cry for protection of the IWCNZ, might suggest that racism and white supremacy are so embedded in this country that neither police nor government could see the incidents cited above as the precursor to the tragedy that took place on 15 March 2019.[11]

This is 'US'

In 'The connection between white supremacy and colonisation', the late Dr Moana Jackson situated the terrorist violence of the Christchurch killer within the terrorism of colonisation. The common threads are the 'shared ideas and history that still lurk in the shadows of every country that has been colonized',[12] and thus he rejected the often-heard description of the Christchurch terrorist as a 'lone wolf psychopath'. What are these ideas? That 'so-called white people in Europe were inherently superior to everyone else' and thus have the right to conquer and dispossess the indigenous people in their historical campaign to civilise the world.

Dr Jackson used the phrase 'social amnesia' to describe the 'collective forgetting' that enables non- Maori to live in a colonised country without acknowledging the ongoing pain caused by colonisation, a phrase echoed by human rights lawyer, Daniel Kleinsman in 'Anzac discomfort after Christchurch'.[13] Here, Kleinsman, a member of the New Zealand

---

10 Hunt, *It Happened Here*, 3- 4.
11 Bryce Edwards, 'Political Roundup: How Intolerant is New Zealand?' *New Zealand Herald*, 4 April 2019.
12 Moana Jackson, 'The connection between white supremacy and colonisation', *E-Tangata*, 24 March 2019. https://e-tangata.co.nz/comment-and-analysis/the-connection-between-white-supremacy/. Dr. Jackson passed away on 31 March 2022.
13 Daniel Kleinsman, 'Anzac Discomfort After Christchurch', *Eureka Street*, 29, No 8 (18 April 2019), https://www.eurekastreet.com.au/article/anzac-discomfort-after-christchurch

Bishops' Committee for Interfaith Relations, suggests that the very phrase 'They are us' reflects the white supremacy of the dominant culture:

> Evidently, when we say: 'They are us', we mean that our common identity is dictated by a particular (white) norm; that 'they' are only 'us' when we say so, and to the extent that they conform; that sameness is more important than difference, and that some lives are more important than others...
>
> Here in Aotearoa New Zealand, while we honour those who lost their lives abroad, we forget the Maori lives lost while *defending their own land* against the Crown. This social amnesia, as Moana Jackson calls it, enables us to forget the past, to forget the history of colonisation and the violent alienation of Maori land, and to say in response to the Christchurch massacres, 'This is not us'.
>
> This is us, and we will not be one until we acknowledge it and embrace, rather than eliminate, difference. We can no longer presume to know who 'we' are, or what defines 'us'. Genuine and enduring peace requires trust and relationships of understanding that recognise and rectify injustice, prevent the perpetuation of hatred, and ensure an outcome that values the lives and identities of all.

Response of the Bishops' Committee for Interfaith Relations to the terrorist attack

The New Zealand Catholic Bishops' Committee for Interfaith Relations (NZCBCIF) was established in 2009 to further understanding, mutual respect and dialogue between the members of the Catholic Church and members of other faiths, and to work with other faiths for the common good.[14] As a member of that committee from 2011 to 2022, I can affirm that it aims to affirm our common humanity as children of God through four streams of interfaith dialogue: religious experience, life, action and theological exchange. These methods have enabled us to establish deep interpersonal relationships of trust and friendship. Immediately after the Christchurch tragedy, the Bishops' Committee reached out to the Muslim community and organised multi-faith vigils which brought together people from all walks of life to express our love for the Muslim community, our grief and our sorrow. We also established support groups

---

14 See *Promoting Interfaith Relations in Aotearoa New Zealand (Te Whakatairanga i te Nohotahitanga o ngā Whakapono i Aotearoa)*. These guidelines were adapted, with permission, from the 2007 Guidelines of the Archdiocese of Melbourne, Australia. A revised edition of the NZ guidelines was published October 2018.

of practical action. These are clearly examples of the dialogue of religious experience, life and action.

However, there was no interfaith critique of the causes of the terrorist attack, even though this conversation was raging throughout civil society. Since liberation theology makes important theological links between colonisation, Christianity and white supremacy, I felt morally obliged to at least name this connection in a public statement at the Islamic Centre on 22 March:

> Thank you for inviting me to speak today. I come in great sadness and with a huge sense of responsibility. Catholics in New Zealand and the rest of the world are 20 days into the Holy Season of Lent, a period of 40 days of fasting and penance in preparation for the crucifixion of Jesus of Nazareth and the Resurrection of the Christ at Easter. I'm wearing today the colour purple because this is the liturgical colour for the season of Lent. Purple can symbolise pain, suffering, and therefore mourning and penitence. Besides mourning the precious loss of life in Christchurch and the incredible harm inflicted on the Muslim community, I am in mourning because Christianity played a role in the colonisation of New Zealand, and, thus, there is a direct unmistakeable connection between colonisation, Christianity and the ideology of white supremacy. This is because the English and Europeans who colonised New Zealand believed they were the superior people and theirs was the superior religion. This we know is not true. And I am hopeful that the liberating elements within Christianity will join forces with other liberating elements within New Zealand to defeat the horrific evil of white supremacy. Catholics are committed to this goal.

NZCBCIF defines the dialogue of theological exchange as the process whereby 'dialogue partners seek to deepen their understanding of their respective religious traditions and to appreciate each other's spiritual beliefs and values.'[15] This definition would seem to permit a critical engagement with practices which actively discriminated against people from other religions and cultures. However, a consensus appears to exist that 'divisive' conversations in which participants critically acknowledge those dark moments in their religious histories might breach the kind of trust on which interfaith friendships have been formed.

Nevertheless, if Catholics regard 15 March 2019 as one of the darkest moments in New Zealand history, then every institution in civil society,

---

15 *Promoting Interfaith Relations in Aotearoa New Zealand*, October 2018, 8.

including the Catholic Church, is morally obligated to scrutinise their past for evidence of injustice, unless the 'this is us' to which Daniel Kleinsman refers above does not include Catholics. But it does, because colonisation is part of the Catholic story.

Part Two: Healing the Church and society through memory, narrative and solidarity

The political theology of Johann Baptist Metz provides the categories to deepen the dialogue of theological exchange, which is the depth dimension of interfaith dialogue. This is because *suffering* is the fundamental theological category in political theology. Metz's theology emerged from his reflection on the horrific suffering inflicted on six million Jews, homosexuals, the Romani people and the disabled by the technocratic systems of Nazi Germany fuelled by a particular ideology of white supremacy. Metz believed the phrase 'dangerous memory of suffering' to be the only appropriate category for theological reflection to rework the whole of Christian theology in light of the suffering inflicted on innocent people in the Holocaust.

To call 15 March 2019 a 'dangerous memory of suffering' is to capture the shock and horror of this event, so that it becomes forever a vehicle for spiritual and moral transformation in the New Zealand psyche. It also allows us to situate this most vicious manifestation of racism and white supremacy within the colonial story of racism and white supremacy which is part of our Catholic story. We do this out of sense of grief and moral awareness. In *The Emergent Church: The Future of Christianity in a Postbourgeois World*, Metz expresses the grief and moral awareness with which German Catholics have had to confront their complicity in Auschwitz:

> Auschwitz concerns us all. Indeed what makes Auschwitz unfathomable is not only the executioners and their assistants, not only the apotheosis of evil revealed in these, and not only the silence of God. Unfathomable, and sometimes even more disturbing, is the silence of men: the silence of all those who looked on or looked away and thereby handed over these people in its peril of death to an unutterable loneliness. I say this not with contempt but with grief. Nor am I saying it in order to revive again the dubious notion of a collective guilt. I am making a plea here for what I would like to call a moral awareness of tradition. A moral awareness means that we can only mourn history and win

from it standards for our own action when we neither deny the defeats present within it nor gloss over its catastrophes. Having an awareness of history ... means ... that there is at least *one* authority that we should never reject or despise—the authority of those who suffer.[16]

Metz's critique of bourgeois Christianity[17] is another important dimension of political theology which is directly applicable to the Catholic Church in New Zealand. The Enlightenment process of secularisation pushed the Church to the margins of society to be concerned with the private lives of believers. This was an effort to rid the public square of the divisive religious meanings that nearly destroyed European society in the religious wars of the Reformation. But in the process, Christianity became a middle class institution and 'an endorsement and reinforcement for ... those with secure possessions, the people in this world who already have abundant prospects and a rich future.'[18] It lost the prophetic voice of the Gospel of Jesus of Nazareth who reached out to those marginalised by powerful elites in society: religious and political.

Political theology retrieves the prophetic voice of Jesus' message so that Christian faith is defined by Metz as 'a solidaristic hope in the God of Jesus as the God of the living and the dead, who calls all to be subjects in God's presence'.[19] The Church is those disciples of Jesus, who are:

> the public witness and bearer of a dangerous memory of freedom in the 'systems' of our emancipatory society. This thesis is based on *memoria* as the fundamental way that Christian faith is expressed, and on the central and specific significance of freedom in this faith. It is in faith that Christians actualise the *memoria passionis, mortis, et resurrectionis Jesu Christi*. They faithfully remember the testament of his love, in which God's dominion among men and women appeared precisely in the fact that the dominion that human beings exercise over one another began to be pulled down, that Jesus declared himself to be on the side of the invisible ones, those who are rejected and oppressed, and in

---

16 Johann Baptist Metz, *The Emergent Church: The Future of Christianity in a Postbourgeois World* (New York: The Crossroad Publishing Company, 1981), 17-18.
17 See Metz, *The Emergent Church*, Chapter 1, 1-16.
18 Metz, *The Emergent Church*, 2.
19 Johann Baptist Metz, *Faith in History and Society: Toward a Practical Fundamental Theology* (New York, Herder and Herder, 2007), 81.

so doing announced to them God's dominion as the liberating power of an unconditional love.[20]

That Jesus declared himself to be on the side of 'the invisible ones, those who are rejected and oppressed' calls the Church, and therefore the Bishops' Committee, which represent the healing presence of Christ to all faith communities in New Zealand, to be in solidarity with the marginalised. We must be agents of healing who understand the causes of the 'dominion that human beings exercise over one another' in order to participate with Christ in pulling them down. Applied to the 15 March terrorist attack, this mission obliges us to look at colonisation and evangelisation as the source of white supremacy in New Zealand, and New Zealand immigration policy as an expression of white supremacy. For Catholics to understand their story as a dangerous memory of suffering is a necessary first step in developing a liberating praxis that walks alongside *Tangata Whenua* as signatories of *Te Tiriti*, Muslims and other marginalised groups in Aotearoa New Zealand.

Colonisation and evangelisation as a dangerous memory of suffering

The terrorist from Grafton, Australia, entitled his manifesto, 'The Great Replacement'. The title plagiarised the book by Renaud Camus considered the father of the global alt-right anti-immigration conspiracy theory of 'genocide by substitution'. Quoting Lara Bullens, "great replacement theory purports that an elitist group is colluding against white French and European people to eventually replace them with non-Europeans from Africa and the Middle East, the majority of whom are Muslim. Renaud Camus often refers to this as 'genocide by substitution'."[21] To paraphrase Douglas Pratt, the Christchurch terrorist's manifesto endorsed this theory, and used social media to 'let the world know that no place on earth was safe from white supremacists' whose mission was to purge their nations from the Muslim invaders.[22]

These ideas—as grotesque as they are—stem from the language and history of colonisation and evangelisation, which legitimated religiously that

---

20 Metz, *Faith in History and Society*, 88-89.
21 Lara Bullens, How France's 'great replacement' theory conquered the global far right, 08/11/2021. https://www.france24.com/en/europe/20211108-how-the-french-great-replacement-theory-conquered-the-far-right
22 See Douglas Pratt, 'The Christchurch Mosque Massacre: Terror and Hope', *The Journal for the Academic Study of Religion*, 33, No 3 (2020), 273-275.

one group of people —Europeans and their religion, Christianity—were superior to all other races and religions. To call colonisation and evangelisation a 'memory of suffering' is to signal that distortions of the Gospel message of Jesus occurred within our history, and these distortions inflicted pain and suffering on innocent people. To acknowledge this fact does not minimise the good that was achieved in proclaiming the Gospel of Jesus Christ. But it does signal that a collective remembering of the pain of colonisation is an important first moment toward healing and reconciliation. Ours is a story in which light and dark elements intermingle.

The Church came to New Zealand first as a missionary Church to the Maori people in 1838, and then as an Irish settler Church in the 19th and 20th centuries.[23] As a missionary Church, Catholics 'earthed the Gospel'[24] within the spirituality of the Maori people and, thus, many Maori embraced Christianity. Bishop Jean-Baptiste François Pompallier urged his priests to build Catholic belief around Māori customs. The missionaries set up a printing press, and printed books in the Māori language.

The mission of the Sisters of Compassion, founded by Suzanne Aubert (1835-1926), is a significant expression of how the gospel was earthed to serve the Maori people in Hiruhārama or Jerusalem, which nestles in a valley beside the flowing waters of the Whanganui River. The houses in the small settlement are clustered around the *Patiarero Marae*. Here the Sisters of Compassion came into being, and have served the local community ever since. The Sisters are privileged to have the status of *tangata whenua* (people of the land).

As a settler Church, however, Catholics were also part of the colonisation process which dispossessed and marginalised the indigenous Maori people. The work of two scholars of Irish Catholic background is particularly useful to lifting the veil of 'social amnesia' in the Catholic story of colonisation.

In 'Best we forget: decolonising a settler family's history',[25] Richard

---

23 See Rory Sweetman, 'Catholic Church - First Catholic Missionaries', *Te Ara - the Encyclopedia of New Zealand*, http://www.TeAra.govt.nz/en/artwork/29277/catholic-church-wellington-1840s
24 Gerald A. Arbuckle, *Earthing the Gospel: An Inculturation Handbook for Pastoral Workers* (Sydney: St. Paul Publications, 1990).
25 Richard Shaw, 'Best We Forget: Decolonising a Settler Family's History', paper written for International Symposium, Settler Responsibilities Towards Decolonisation, February 9-11, 2021. See also Richard Shaw, *The Forgotten Coast* (Massey University Press, 2021), and Shaw, 'Truth Hidden By Silence', *Tui Motu InterIsland*, No 270 (May 2022), 6-7.

Shaw, of Irish Catholic heritage, lifts the veil of the social amnesia of his great grandfather's acquisition of three family farms as a result of his participation in the invasion of Parihaka on 5 November 1881. His great grandfather was a member of the Armed Constabulary's No. 3 Company, a force of 1,500 men who invaded Parihaka on 5 November 1881, occupied Parihaka until 1884, and eventually acquired land that used to belong to the people of Parihaka.

New Zealanders will recognise immediately the significance of Parihaka. The resistance of Maori at Parihaka to the brutal acquisition of Maori land by the colonisers is a story of non-violent passive resistance. This story of how his great grandparents acquired the three family farms that became the foundation for the family's wealth for three generations, was never told in family gatherings. Rather, Shaw heard the familiar story of how hard-working Irish immigrants, themselves victims of English colonisation and oppression, dedicated themselves to their families and communities to make a better life. That his great grandfather used the same violence against the Maori people that the English used against his family in Ireland was never told. For Shaw, telling his family's story as a 'dangerous memory of suffering' is a necessary first step in participating in the process of decolonisation.

How could Catholics participate in this plunder? In *Healing our History*, Robert Consedine, himself of Irish Catholic background, documents the papal religious and moral legitimation of colonisation during the European 'age of discovery'. What European explorers had discovered, of course, was the existence of indigenous cultures in lands rich with natural resources, which they could conquer and exploit.

In 1537, Pope Paul III's (1534- 49) *Sublimus Deus* subordinated aboriginal religions to the evangelising mission of the Church, so that the interests of the Church and colonising powers remained paramount. Consedine tells us that:

> The majority of missionaries (Catholic and those of other Christian denominations) had a culture-bound theology in which evangelisation was synonymous with civilisation. Missionaries and colonial administrators were in the business of exporting European culture and religion to other parts of the globe.[26]

The Treaty of *Waitangi, te Tiriti o Waitangi*, was signed in 1840. For Maori, it was an agreement between two groups of people who saw themselves as equal partners, each with duties and obligations to the

---

26 Robert and Joanna Consedine, *Healing our History: The Challenge of the Treaty of Waitangi* (Auckland: Penguin Books, 2005), 68.

other. However, despite a legal agreement about how Maori land was to be purchased by land agents appointed by the Queen, the acquisition of Maori land by the Anglo-Celtic settlers is a story of plunder and shame, as Richard Shaw's story tells us.

The white supremacy and racism at the heart of New Zealand's colonial history is reflected in the White New Zealand Immigration Policy that was passed in 1899, which explicitly discriminated against Chinese and favoured European immigrants. David C. Atkinson uses the phrase 'racial anxiety' to describe the sentiment held by many New Zealanders, and links this with the terrorist attack against the Muslim community because many Muslim immigrants are people of colour. Atkinson wrote:

> Friday's attack demonstrates that such anxieties are not far from the forefront in New Zealand and Australian life. Unconscionable acts of violence are the inevitable result of relentless anti-immigrant invective—invective that lives in both the past and the present.[27]

Metz' category of narrative designates a liberating story of discipleship which obliges those who understand the story of the sufferers to participate in a new story of belonging based on forgiveness and accountability as the basis of social justice. This picks up Metz' point that the whole purpose in seeing our story as a dangerous memory of suffering is to 'win from it standards for our own action when we neither deny the defeats present within it nor gloss over its catastrophes'.

Narrative: decolonisation and social cohesion as a liberating praxis: A New Story of Belonging

The 'New Story of Belonging' in Aotearoa New Zealand is based on what *te Tiriti* envisioned as the right relationship between the indigenous Maori people and those they welcomed to this land. It must be restored in the process of decolonisation, which Moana Jackson defines as an 'ethics of restoration':

> ... restoring values, restoring the sense of justice and harmony that the Treaty of Waitangi envisaged, restoring for Māori the sense

---

27 David C. Atkinson, 'It's Time for Australia and New Zealand to Confront Their White Nationalist Histories', *The Washington Post* (16 March 2019), https://www.washingtonpost.com/opinions/2019/03/15/its-time-australia-new-zealand-confront-their-white-nationalist-histories/. David C. Atkinson is an associate professor of history at Purdue University.

of self-determination that is 'of the people, by the people, for the people'.[28]

This vision is completely compatible with the liberating praxis underpinning the new story of Christian discipleship in 21st century Aotearoa New Zealand. Applied to the power imbalances between Maori and Pakeha, restoring right relationships requires both forgiveness and accountability. Efforts have been initiated by Maori, through, for example, Matthew Tukaki, Executive Director of the New Zealand Māori Council, to request a formal apology from the Church about its role in the confiscation of Maori land and colonisation. In a Radio New Zealand interview on 22 January 2020, in which Tukaki addressed issues of historic racism associated with the arrival of James Cook in New Zealand on 8 October 1769,[29] he commented that Pope Alexander VI's Doctrine of Discovery was used in the case of 'Wi Parata vs The Bishop of Wellington case of 1877', to declare the Treaty of Waitangi 'a simple nullity'.[30] Tukaki also said that the NZ Catholic Bishops Conference was consulting over the matter of an official apology before releasing a definitive statement.

Furthermore, the method of parallel workshops which Robert Consedine proposes in *Healing our History* could well be an indispensable resource in grounding interfaith groups with the bi-cultural vision of *te Tiriti*. Within Interfaith Councils, Maori Anglicans, Maori Baha'i, Maori Catholics and Maori Muslims could be encouraged by members of the Bishops' Committee to lead these workshops utilising Consedine's method, or developing their own. In line with Metz's insistence that 'authority belongs to those who have suffered', they have the first word in the conversation.

---

28 Kennedy Warne, 'The Hope for Change: Imagining Decolonisation Here and Now', *E-Tangata* (16 May 2021), https://e-tangata.co.nz/comment-and-analysis/the-hope-for-change-imagining-decolonisation-here-and-now/.

29 Radio New Zealand, "Catholic Church called on to apologise for colonial land confiscations", 22 January 2020, https://www.rnz.co.nz/news/national/407887/catholic-church-called-on-to-apologise-for-colonial-land-confiscations.

30 'In 1848 the Anglican Bishop of NZ made an agreement with Ngati Toa to put a piece of land in Porirua aside for educational purposes. This land was supposedly held under native title. Governor George Grey issued a crown grant to the Bishop in 1850, without Ngati Toa's consent, to build a school. Wi Parata, a Maori MP and chief, took the case to the Supreme Court to try and recover the entrusted land for his tribe. He petitioned the court for the return of the land to its original Maori owners as the promised school had never been built therefore the grant had never been fulfilled meaning native title had never been extinguished.' Emily Tyler, 3.5. *Wi Parata v Bishop of Wellington* (1877), https://quizlet.com/75453867/35-wi-parata-v-bishop-of-wellington-1877-flash-cards/.

When Pakeha participate in Consedine's method of parallel workshops, they begin to understand that two very different spiritual and anthropological worldviews underpinned te Tiriti and, therefore, Pakeha must come to understand *Te Ao Maori* as a precondition for understanding what Maori chiefs believed they were signing, because what the English called 'sovereignty' had no direct translation in Te Reo Maori. This is the basis for Jackson's 'ethics of restoration'.

According to Metz, when Catholics understand the Easter message of salvation as a liberating praxis, they might come to see decolonisation as an opportunity to create a new story of reconciliation between those who have been exploited and those who now wish to walk alongside them as brothers and sisters in the mutual quest for justice. Then we might give witness to Mary's song of praise and justice in the Magnificat:

> He has mercy on those who fear him
> in every generation.
> He has shown the strength of his arm,
> he has scattered the proud in their conceit.
> He has cast down the mighty from their thrones,
> and has lifted up the lowly.
> He has filled the hungry with good things,
> and the rich he has sent away empty.
> He has come to the help of his servant Israel
> for he has remembered his promise of mercy,
> the promise he made to our fathers,
> to Abraham and his children forever. (Luke: 1:46-55)

Conclusion: solidarity: a new story where everybody belongs

There is a sense in which 15 March 2019 changed New Zealand forever. The advocacy of the Islamic Women's Council of New Zealand was prophetic in alerting government to the ugly presence of Islamophobia in a religiously pluralist, multi-ethnic democracy. Government had guaranteed both the freedom of religion and the right for faith communities and their members to safety[31] and, yet, Islamophobia and hostility towards Muslims had manifested itself in hate speech and hate crimes towards Muslim women, a truly vulnerable segment of society. Furthermore, even after 15 March 2019, IWCNZ continued to sound the alarm that Islamophobia had actually increased.[32] Their advocacy obliged government to see the

---

31 *Religious Diversity in Aotearoa New Zealand, Statement on Religious Diversity* (Human Rights Commission, Third Edition, July 2019), 8-9.
32 Pratt, *The Christchurch Mosque Massacre*, 278.

face of the Muslim community, and in many ways, the *Report of the Royal Commission of Inquiry into the Terrorist Attack on Christchurch Mosques on 15 March 2019* was a response to the concerns they themselves raised in 2016 when they first met with the New Zealand Security Intelligence Service. The Maori title of the report, Kō tō tātou kāinga tēnei, which means 'This is our home', expresses the government's aspiration to create a country in which a genuine solidarity exists for all.[33] Not 'They' nor 'Us' but 'WE'. This country belongs to everyone and it is a multi-ethnic democracy on a bi-cultural foundation.

This 'mission' requires a concerted effort to address the causes of Islamophobia and to promote solutions to transform it. Metz's category of solidarity is useful here, which he defines as:

> a category of assistance, of supporting and encouraging the subject in the face of that which threatens him or her most acutely and in the face of his or her suffering, ... not over people's heads and not detouring around their painful sense of nonidentity.[34]

Since a liberating praxis obliges Catholics and, thus, the Bishops' Committee, to privilege the perspective of those who suffer, we must work alongside our Muslim brothers and sisters to end the negative stereotyping of Muslims in the media. In Part One of this paper, I referred to IWCNZ's efforts to point out the harmful effect on the local Muslim community of international reporting of terrorist violence overseas. The Report of the Royal Commission addressed the impact of this biased reporting:

> The media often perpetuates ... stereotypes by disseminating or providing a platform for racists and xenophobic speech. The Special Rapporteur would also like to highlight that media bias is a particularly problematic phenomenon in a counterterrorism context. The disproportionate coverage of certain types of terrorism, the use of certain terminology or images and the overall framing of news stories about terrorism distorts public perception. A recent study examined the domestic media coverage of terrorist attacks that occurred in one North American country during the period 2011–2015. The study found that attacks by

---

33 *Ko tō tātou kāinga tēnei Report: Royal Commission of Inquiry into the terrorist attack on Christchurch masjidain on 15 March 2019*. Ko tō tātou kāinga tēnei is a comprehensive response to the Royal Commission's Terms of Reference. The report was presented to the Governor-General on 26 November 2020. The Minister of Internal Affairs presented the report to Parliament on 8 December 2020.
34 Metz, *Faith in History and Society*, 208.

Muslim perpetrators, particularly foreign-born Muslims, received 4.5 times more coverage than other attacks. Only a small proportion of attacks were perpetrated by Muslims (12.4 per cent) or foreign-born Muslims (5 per cent). Yet, these attacks received 44 per cent and 32 per cent of the news coverage, respectively. Research also found that an attack is more likely to be considered an act of terrorism when carried out by a Muslim. By contrast, threats posed by right-wing violence are often underestimated and not considered to be terrorism.[35]

The Bishops' Committee and thus Interfaith Councils end this negative stereotyping of Islam first by telling the real story about Islam. In every dialogue of religious experience, theological exchange, dialogue of life and action, members of faith communities speak for themselves by their words and action. And thus we know the Muslim community as people of intense piety as we worship with them, as people of incredible generosity and hospitality as we join them in celebrations of Eid al Fitr, and as communities of service who reach out to those in need in our community.

Consider the heroic story of Farid and Husna, humbling as it is inspirational. Farid Ahmed, who lived in New Zealand for over 30 years, became a paraplegic when a drunk driver ran him over on a street in Christchurch. He survived, but was confined to a wheelchair. Nevertheless, Farid became a Senior Leader at the Deans Avenue Mosque in Christchurch and worked as a homeopath.

On 15 March, Farid and his wife, Husna, were praying when the terrorist burst into the mosque and shot Husna as she was going back into the mosque to look for her vulnerable husband after she had already led other women and children to safety. She died. Remarkably, Farid forgave the man who murdered her, and afterwards, wrote a book about her selflessness, bravery and courage in *Husna's Story: My wife, the Christchurch massacre & my journey to forgiveness*.[36]

To dispel ignorance about Islam, let us tell this story again and again. Let us also tell the story about the generosity of the Manawatu

---

35 *Ko tō tātou kāinga tēnei Report: Royal Commission of Inquiry into the terrorist attack on Christchurch masjidain on 15 March 2019*. See Part 9: Social Cohesion and Embracing Diversity, Introduction 1.35, footnote 20 from United Nations Report of the Special Rapporteur on contemporary forms of racism, racial discrimination, xenophobia and related intolerance (2017) A/72/287 https://digitallibrary.un.org/record/1304009?ln=en.

36 Farid Ahmed, *Husna's Story: My Wife, the Christchurch Massacre & My Journey to Forgiveness* (New Zealand: Allen & Unwin 2021).

Muslim Association's 'Helping Hands' project during lockdown in 2020, in which the Muslim community in Palmerston North prepared and delivered 5,000 serves of food (pre-packed hot dinners) for the wider (non-Muslim) community and organisations already helping the most needy. This was done during Ramadan when the country was in lockdown.

The Bishops' Committee could share countless stories about how the Muslim community enriches us and the broader society by giving witness to the highest ideals of Islam. But the word limitations of this paper prevent further discussion.

Nor can I address the 'painful nonidentity' of the terrorist, who is after all a human being who committed the most horrific crime. But he was not born a killer. What were the forces that shaped him to be a cold- blooded murderer of innocent men, women and children on their knees at prayer? Douglas Pratt's article[37] provides important insights into the terrorist's motives and is, therefore, an important resource for interfaith groups who walk alongside the Muslim community and all ethnic communities to transform religious and cultural prejudice into acceptance of diversity as a spiritual, cultural, social and political strength.

---

37 Pratt, *The Christchurch Mosque Massacre.*

Chapter Five

Some Christian attempts at healing with Buddhists in Sri Lanka post-independence[1]

Malcolm Kreltszheim

The bombing of three Christian churches and three luxury hotels in Colombo, Sri Lanka, on Easter Sunday 2019 that led to the killing of 259 persons by a local Islamic terrorist organisation not only sent shockwaves around that island, but was also symptomatic of generally anti-Western and anti-Christian sentiments that arose in former European colonies. These sentiments are part of the ongoing Buddhist reaction to the attitude of the Protestant missionaries who came to the island during the British colonial period (1796-1948) to continue that negative attitude to Buddhism demonstrated by the Portuguese (Roman Catholic) and Dutch (Reformed Church) before them in the period 1505-1796.

Most missionaries were quite open in their contemptuous attitude to the Buddhists. This attitude was rooted in the Christian/British belief that they were culturally and socially superior to the Buddhists, who were uneducated Idolators, Heathens and Devil Worshippers and that their *Sangha* (priesthood) was corrupt and showed a distrust and ignorance of the true Buddhist philosophies and traditions. The charge of being 'uneducated' was levelled despite the fact that many of the missionaries learnt Pali from Buddhist monks. Rev. Daniel Gogerly, for example, learnt Pali in order to write *Kristiyani Prajnapti*, which strongly challenged and ridiculed the Buddha's teaching. A further example was the two young Buddhist monks from Dodanduwa in the south of the island, who accompanied retiring Chief Justice Sir Alexander Johnston to England in 1819. There they were hosted for two years by Dr Adam Clarke, a Wesleyan educator, and baptised as 'Adam' and 'Alexander' at Liverpool's

---

1 This paper draws on my nascent Doctor of Philosophy Thesis at Pilgrim Theological College, University of Divinity; the writings of Dr Elizabeth Harris, Department of Theology and Religion, Honorary Fellow, Edward Cadbury Centre, University of Birmingham, who maintains a special research interest in the Theravada tradition of Buddhism and who spent seven years in Sri Lanka (1986-1993); and Fr Aloysius Pieris SJ, Founder/Director of the Tulana Research Centre for Encounter and Dialogue, Kelaniya, Sri Lanka.

Brunswick Chapel. Dr Clarke was convinced that, 'These men cannot be treated as common heathens: they are both philosophers'.[2]

My more recent research has shown that the ongoing hostilities between Buddhists and Christians also relate to a deeper reason, that being the misunderstandings and misinterpretations based on the translations— from English to Sinhala and Sinhala to English—of five important historical debates on key principles of Buddhism and Christianity between leading representatives of the two faiths. The debates began in 1865 and culminated in what has become famously known as the 'Panadura Debate' of 1873, in which the Buddhists were led by Ven Mohottiwatte Gunanada Thera, a powerful preacher and leader, and the Christians by Rev. David De Silva, a Wesleyan Methodist Minister.

The Panadura Debate was attended by an audience estimated to have been between five thousand and seven thousand persons, most of them Buddhists. Addressing the crowd in the vernacular Sinhala, the points made by the Buddhist clerics were well understood. However, the Christian leaders made the mistake of using Pali and Sanskrit—classical languages not understood by a significant majority of the crowd, and even by themselves in some instances—in their arguments. This error provided an opportunity for their opponents to expose and exploit mistakes in translation of the ancient Buddhist texts by the Christians.

In his response to the first talk of Rev. David de Silva, Ven Mohottiwatte Gunanada,

> took a swipe at Rev de Silva's command of the Pali language, suggesting that someone who makes elementary mistakes in it cannot be expected to have a good understanding of abstruse metaphysics described in it ... He then accused Christian missionaries of being deceptive on account of their use of various local deities names for the Christian God, like in Calcutta the Hindu god Ishwara and in Ceylon Dewiyanvahanse.[3]

And in his response to the second talk of Rev. David de Silva,

> He continued by asking why de Silva had made no comment about the (mis)translation of 'jealous' in the Sinhalese Bible, and why the Biblical God is referred to as 'jealous'. He continued in this vein, asking what de Silva's level of competence in Pali was when he repeats the others' grammatical errors without bothering to correct them. And despite de Silva's praise of the honesty

---

2 RF Young and GPV Somaratna. *Vain Debates. The Buddhist-Christian Controversies of Nineteenth-Century Ceylon* (De Nobili Research Library Volume XXIII, Vienna, 1996), 58.
3 Ranjith Daluwatte, Archivist. Panadura Wadaya, *Summary of the Great Debate*. (www.dhammikaweb.com/?p=11931).

of Bible translators, the rearrangements of parts of it suggests something suspicious about Bible translators.[4]

The Panadura Debate has been celebrated by the Buddhists as a watershed in their fightback against the missionaries, for it was published in print and widely circulated internationally, including in the United States, where it came to the attention of the leading Theosophist Colonel Henry Steel Olcott. Olcott came to the island shortly afterwards to establish a branch of the society and begin a renaissance in the study and propagation of Buddhism.

In addition to the people mentioned in footnote 1 above, I am indebted to several primary sources, including books and tracts written by the early missionaries, commentaries on these publications by nineteenth and twentieth century scholars, the writings of British colonial administrators and visitors to the island, missionary magazines and the Missionary Registers. Here are two examples from Missionary Registers which, though an initiative of the Church Missionary Society, included reports from all the missionary societies scattered across the world:

> Mr Benjamin Clough [one of the earliest Wesleyan missionaries] whose return from Ceylon ... has furnished the Society with the following account of the awful superstition of Devil Worship which prevails in that island. It is more full and particular than any which has before appeared; and should awaken earnest prayer for the deliverance of people, held under such debasing and cruel bondage.
> In Ceylon, there are Five Systems, at least, of Heathen Idolatry—Brahminism, Buddhism, Capoism, Baliism and Yakadurism. A minute description of these different forms of idolatry, the nature and tendency of the ceremonies connected with them, and the demoralizing effects which they severally have upon the native inhabitants, would excite the deepest sympathies on behalf of these benighted Heathens ...
> The ESTABLISHED Heathenism of the island is Buddhism. Buddhu was an atheist, in the most absolute sense of the word: his writings, or more properly the writings of his learned followers, which are very voluminous, exhibit a most complete and sophistical system of atheism. In these writings, the eternity of matter is asserted—the existence of a Creator is unequivocally denied ... They are truly left in the state described by the Apostle—*without God in the world*. They have no 'Universal Father', ... the world has no moral or righteous Governor; and,

---

4 Ranjith Daluwatte, *Summary of the Great Debate*.

consequently, no final Judge! So that, strange and affecting as the statement may appear, yet it is an awful fact, that, in every part of the world where Buddhism has established its atheistic influence, the inhabitants are left to the uncontrolled dominion of the Devil![5]

And from a CMS Missionary at the Baddagame Station (South of Colombo) who challenges a stranger he meets on the road:

'My friend,' I said, 'you are a Sinner against God, the Creator and Governor of all things: you have broken His Laws, and are condemned to suffer in Hell for your sins: do not think that you can ... obtain salvation by making images, and presenting offerings to them and to the Priests that attend them. If you have no better way of salvation than this, your soul will be lost ... My friend! two religions are before you—a true and a false Religion. It is your duty to examine them both; and if you find that you are ignorant, as you certainly are, you should pray God, to enlighten your understanding, and to lead you into the right way.'[6]

Notwithstanding the tremendous sacrifices that many missionaries *did* make to convert the Buddhists in the most trying of circumstances (heat, isolation, loneliness, sickness, death of loved ones and their commitment to establishing an effective education system that continues to this day), their contemptuous attitude led to a significant backlash by the Buddhists from the mid-19th century that continues to reverberate to this day, as evidenced by the rise of Sinhalese-Buddhist institutions and political, cultural, economic power and influence at the expense of Christian and Western institutions. This was especially so after the General Elections of 1956, when a strongly Sinhalese-Buddhist nationalist government under Mr S.W.R.D. Bandaranaike was swept into power promising to make Sinhala the first language of the country, relegating Tamil and English to second languages and leading to violent race riots in 1958. A decade later, many of the Christian schools were nationalised by the government.

History has shown that memories, especially bad ones, are extremely difficult to erase. Stories of the missionaries' hostility has been kept alive by generations of Buddhists through word of mouth, teaching in

---
5 Wesley Missionary Society, 'Account of the Devil Worship of Ceylon', *Missionary Register for MDCCCXXIII containing the Principal Missionary Transactions of the Various Institutions for Propagating the Gospel with the Proceedings at Large of the Church Missionary Society* (London: LB Seeley and Son, 169 Fleet Street, January 1823), 551.
6 Baddagame: General View of Station', *Missionary Register for MDCCCXXIX containing the Principal Missionary Transactions of the Various Institutions for Propagating the Gospel with the Proceedings at Large of the Church Missionary Society* (London: LB Seeley and Son, 169 Fleet Street, August 1829), 376.

Buddhist schools and Sunday schools, and a multitude of magazine, tracts, pamphlets and newspaper articles, books and speeches by prominent Buddhist leaders, including members of the Sangha and politicians.[7]

Certainly, honest attempts have been made by many Christians to offer the hand of healing and understanding to Buddhists. This paper offers two interesting examples of outreach by two leading Christian traditions—the Roman Catholics and the Anglicans—in a practical, theological endeavour to heal rifts in a small country in which Buddhists make up more than 70 per cent of the population. A third cleric, Fr Michael Rodrigo OMI, paid with his life at the hands of rebels in 1987 (although many now believe that he was killed by government forces). It is recognition by some Christians of the critical mistakes made by the British missionaries in their attempts to convert the overwhelmingly Buddhist majority in the island and who sought to establish the superiority of Christianity by learning Pali and Sanskrit, the languages of the ancient Buddhist scriptures, in order to attack sacred Buddhist principles. These examples of outreach were through art, sculpture, drama and liturgy by Christians as they sought rapprochement with the Buddhists. They were initially successful but have recently regressed, unfortunately again because of Christian arrogance and the perceived attempts at 'forced conversions' by fundamentalist Christians.

This paper will consider two prime examples by Fr Aloysius Pieris SJ (born 1934), who established the Tulana Research Centre for Encounter and Dialogue in 1974, and the late Sevaka Yohan Devananda (1928-2016), the scion of a wealthy and influential Sinhalese Anglican family who established an ashram in the late 1950s.

1. Fr Aloysius Pieris SJ and the Tulana Research Centre for Encounter and Dialogue

Fr Aloysius Pieris SJ was the first Roman Catholic priest to gain a doctorate in Buddhist Studies from a Sri Lankan university. Fr Pieris recounts many interesting anecdotes from his student days in his paper to the Jesuit Symposium held in Goa, India, in July 2018, two of which I include below.

In the first, he recounts that when he wrote his L.Ph thesis on Buddhism in 1958, 'my mentor ... tried hard to convince me that my negatively critical approach towards Buddhism was not Christian; my

---

[7] Amongst the earliest tracts published (in 1862) included Ven Hikkaduwe Sri Sumangala Maha Nayaka Thera's *Sudarsanaya* from Galle and a series titled *Durlabdhi Vinodaniya* by Ven Mohottiwatte Gunananda Thera in Kotahena. Both attacked Gogerly's *Kristiyani Prajnapti*.

insensitivity frustrated him'.[8] In the second, he writes that, following his Superior's instructions, he enrolled himself at London University to undertake PhD studies.[9] On his way to London, however, he was taken to meet a famous Buddhologist in Belgium who demanded, 'How can/dare you compare what you know with what you do not know? You must forget your Christianity and immerse yourself into Buddhism and write something from within it. Leave comparative studies to the end of your life!'

One of Fr Pieris' first attempts at outreach was through the insertion into the Catholic Mass of readings from the Buddhist Pali Canon for the three lessons, the Introit and the inter-lectionary Psalm.[10] This early attempt to assert liturgically that both Buddhism and Christianity anticipated a time when compassion and righteousness would reign was controversial among Christians, but received a positive response from the Buddhists. He continued to write marriage liturgies for mixed-faith couples and, in his teaching of candidates for priesthood, developed a contemplative Mass which drew on his own experience of practising satipatthana (mindfulness meditation).[11] Elizabeth Harris, who worked as his assistant during part of her tenure in Sri Lanka, writes that it was a form of liturgy, this time by a Buddhist, which led Fr Pieris to what is considered to be his most innovative approach to Christian-Buddhist dialogue and healing—inviting Buddhists to interpret Christianity for him through art.

The outcome of Fr Pieris' initiative has been a series of art and sculpture by Buddhist artists on Christian themes, some of which are on display at Tulana (see the photographs in Figure 1). These include a mural, Jesus washing the disciples' feet; Pieta Lanka, a sculpture which portrays Mary shaped as Mother Lanka; a baked clay mural, Jesus conversing with the priests in the Jerusalem Temple, together with Jewish leaders, gods of other faiths and several Greek philosophers; and Jesus and the Samaritan Woman at Jacob's Well (John 4:5-42). Restrictions of space prevent me from discussing further details of these works, but the point I am making is that they were all Christian themes executed by Buddhist artists.

---

8 Fr Aloysius Pieris SJ, 'Jesuit-Buddhist Dialogue in Sri Lanka: From its Origins to the Present Times'. (A revised and updated version of a paper originally written at the request of the Xavier Centre of Historical Research, Goa (India) and presented at the Jesuit Symposium held on July 12-13, 2018.)

9 His topic was a comparative study of *mindfulness* in the Bible and Buddhist Scriptures.

10 Elizabeth Harris, 'Art, Liturgy and the Transformation of Memory: Christian Rapprochement with Buddhists in Post-Independence Sri Lanka'. *Religions of South Asia*, 10, no 1 (2017), 66.

11 Harris, 'Art, Liturgy and the Transformation of Memory', 50-78.

Fr Pieris is proud that Tulana is a venue for Buddhists and Christians to meet, not only for academic research and study, but also for religious experience and spiritual guidance. It is a place for gathering, encouraging inter-faith and inter-ethnic encounters, engaging in what he terms *trans-ecclesial ecumenism*.

Figure 1: Art and Sculpture at Tulana

1. **PIETA LANKA** 1989 by Kingsley Gunatileke

2. **JESUS WASHING THE FEET OF HIS DISCIPLES** (based on the Gospel of JOHN 13:1-20) by Ven. Uttarananda Thera

3. **THE TULANA MURAL** (based on the Gospel of LUKE 2:41-52) by Kingsley Gunatileke

4. **JESUS AND THE SAMARITAN WOMAN AT JACOB'S WELL** – The Water of Life (based on the Gospel of JOHN 4:5-42) by Kingsley Gunatileke

Photos reproduced with kind permission of Father Aloysius Pieris, Tulana Research Centre for Encounter and Dialogue

Sevaka Yohan Devananda and the *Devasaranámaya* (*Monastic Garden of God's Refuge*).

Yohan Devananda (formerly John Cooray) was born into a wealthy Sinhalese family and was ordained an Anglican priest in 1957. In that year, he established an ashram in the hill country of Sri Lanka. Three years later, he moved the ashram to a larger property at Ibbagamuwa, near Kurunegala, the capital of the North-Western Province of Sri Lanka. It was at this stage that he changed his name to Devananda and adopted the prefix, 'Sevaka' (Servant), dropping the title 'Reverend'.[12]

Named *Devasaranarámaya* (Monastic Garden of God's Refuge), the ashram was at first a predominantly Anglican, male community that sought to live in harmony with its overwhelmingly Buddhist neighbours. It emphasised meditation and prayer, study, celibacy, manual labour, vegetarianism and the holding of possessions in common. The members of the ashram were also encouraged to visit the surrounding villages and attend Buddhist *viharés*. However, Devananda soon went much further, sharing in rituals such as offering alms at *Wesak* (the day commemorating the birth, enlightenment and death of the Buddha) and encouraging others to follow his example. In 1964, one of two Christian families invited the monks of the *viharé* and members of the *arámaya*[13] to a *dané* (alms-giving) at the ashram. The other Christian family did the same the following year and in the same year a Buddhist family brought a *dané* to the ashram in memory of a deceased relative.

When the ashram completed its tenth anniversary in 1967, around 150 people were present, of whom only around a third were Christians. The rest were Buddhists. The main speaker was the Methodist Minister Rev. Lynn de Silva, but two *bhikkhus* (Buddhist priests) also spoke, and Buddhist and Christian children sang verses from their respective traditions.[14] These shining examples of trans-ecclesial ecumenism showed that, within the relatively short period of ten years, a strong bond had developed between the two traditions, primarily as a result of the Christian community showing a willingness to reach out to the Buddhists and adopt some of their practices so that they were 'visibly in harmony with Buddhist practices'.[15]

In time, however, the ashram came to reflect the other pressing needs of the villagers of *Ibbagamuwa*, which were political representation and

---

12 Harris, 'Art, Liturgy and the Transformation of Memory', 56.
13 One of the meanings of the Pali word *arama* (Sinhala: aramaya) is a garden donated to a monastic community.
14 Harris, 'Art, Liturgy and the Transformation of Memory', 57.
15 Harris, 'Art, Liturgy and the Transformation of Memory', 57.

economic issues, dropping the suffix of *'arámaya'I* from its name and becoming a multi-faith community committed to furthering the social justice concerns of the community. It began to support trade union activity and campaigned for land reform, founding organisations such as a women's multi-faith community. In reflection of this changed ethos, the New World Liturgy was developed. While the structure of the liturgy was based on the Christian Eucharist, it deliberately drew on other religions and Marxism. Harris includes the following extracts from the liturgy:

> Leader: We honour
> the Hindu sages
> for their earnest seeking
> of the ultimate reality
> and for their experience
> of the divine powers.
>
> Response: We honour
> the Buddha
> for showing us
> the power
> of a liberated and awakened mind
> and the necessity
> of self-control and discipline.
>
> Leader continues: We honour
> Jesus Christ
> for showing us
> the power
> of self-sacrificing love
> and the joy
> of serving one another.

Stanzas followed, honouring the Prophet Mohammed, Karl Marx and saints and martyrs of all religions. There followed a period of silence in which they took responsibility for sin and evil in the world and a commitment made for different kinds of change, including the struggle for liberation.[16]

> Go now, monks,
> and wander
> for the good of the people
> for the happiness of the people
> out of compassion
> for the world (the Buddha)

---

16 Harris, 'Art, Liturgy and the Transformation of Memory', 58.

The Spirit of the Lord
has been given to me;
he has sent me
to bring good news to the poor
to proclaim freedom to the prisoners
to the blind new sight
to the oppressed liberation
(Jesus in the Nazareth synagogue, reading from the scroll of Isaiah. Luke 4:18)

The true revolutionary is guided by a great feeling of love (Che Guevara).[17]

In Harris' view, the New World Liturgy tightened the bonds between Christians and Buddhists and extended relationships to Buddhist monks and people of other faiths who were known to be committed to socialism, human rights and political change in the country. After this, Devananda was regularly seen at public events with members of the Buddhist priesthood.

The initiatives of Fr Aloysius Pieris and Sevaka Yohan Devananda and others such as Rev. Lynn de Silva and the late Fr Michael Rodrigo OMI did much to heal and cement good relations between Christians and Buddhists in post-independence Sri Lanka. Genuine attempts were made to repair the damage caused by the Christian missionaries, especially during the British colonial period.

Unfortunately, however, various events and disturbances in Sri Lanka over the past decade have contributed to a watering-down or regression in these important links that had been forged between the traditions. These include:

a) The rise of a political party led by militant Buddhist monks. Draft anti-conversion bills (in contravention of international covenants) were presented to Parliament in 2004 and 2009, calling for an end to people being forced to convert from one religion to another under duress or when enticed by money or economic advantages (as often happened during colonial times). Most Sri Lankan Buddhists welcomed the anti-conversion bill. A young university student claimed that 'we must rid ourselves of all those who convert [others], priests and pastors who destroy our Buddhist-Sinhalese culture. Christians are living in this land peacefully because of the great

---

17 Harris, 'Art, Liturgy and the Transformation of Memory', 59.

Buddhism ... Otherwise they would have washed out long ago'.[18] Another, a Buddhist businessman, agreed with the student, stating that 'there is no place for many religions, many ethnic groups or many cultures. This is the only purely Buddhist and Sinhalese country in the world'.[19]

These two comments underscore the most egregious error that the European—and particularly the Protestant missionaries—made, that for over 2,300 years the Sinhalese- Buddhists had claimed Sri Lanka as their own land and they were not going to be challenged or bullied by any Western power that chose to denigrate the teachings of the Buddha and steal that coveted position under any circumstances.[20] The country has failed to build an inclusive society due to successive governments' (and voters') insistence on Sinhala-Buddhist supremacy, and this has resulted in the ethnocratic nature of the state and its institutions as protectors of the Sinhalese-Buddhist community at the expense of minorities.

b) Renewed competition between religions at the levels of space and sound. At Ibbagamuwa, for example, Harris reports of a discussion she had with a current leader at Devasarana in a fieldwork interview in 2012, who told her:

> You have four mosques in the neighbourhood ... and at 4.45[am]or 4.40[am] you will hear the Call to Prayer. And each mosque has its special way of doing this. As soon as this is over, you have the Pirit chanting from the local temple ... and recently the Catholic Church has begun a perpetual novena on a Wednesday evening. And then again you hear the singing of the Marian hymns and the Mass being celebrated. So there is this continual bombardment and it does not serve devotional purposes.[21]

---

18 Melani Manel Perera, 'Anti-Conversion Bill: Minorities Fear Restrictions on Religious Freedoms'. https://www.asianews.it/news-en/Anti-conversion-bill:-minorities-fear-restrictions-on-religious-freedom-14360.html
19 Perera, 'Anti-Conversion Bill'.
20 According to the *Mahavamsa* or 'Great Chronicle' of Ceylon, the island was visited by the Buddha on at least three occasions. As he lay dying in the state of *parinibbana* c.543 BCE, his instructions to the great god Sakka that 'in Lanka O lord of gods will my religion be established', are regularly used by Buddhists to justify their claim that Sri Lanka is pre-eminent among Buddhist countries throughout the world and the leader of Theravada Buddhism, the original form of Buddhism preached by the Buddha.
21 Harris, 'Art, Liturgy and the Transformation of Memory', 58.

The interviewee's belief was that this was a recent development, following the renewal of Sinhalese nationalism and the push for the all-out defeat of the Tamil rebels in the North.

c) Church insensitivity and intransigence. One example is of Devasarana following the passing of its leader, Sevaka Yohan Devananda. Two months after his passing, priests of the Anglican Church demanded ownership of the land. The land had been given in Trust to the Diocese by the late Bishop de Mel (Devananda's uncle). The Anglican Church unlawfully took produce from the property, posted a security guard and locked its gates. An initiative to commence an agricultural university, intended to educate farmers on organic farming and organic agriculture and funded by the Germans, was stopped by the local bishop and trees that had been planted to make organic fertiliser cut down. When the Archbishop of Canterbury visited Sri Lanka in 2019, he was presented with a petition in the form of an Open Letter by a Buddhist who had attended the ashram, calling upon him to intervene in the dispute.[22]

Conclusion

Christians account for just seven per cent, of whom approximately 80 per cent are Roman Catholics, in a majority Sinhalese-Buddhist country. Important advances made in Buddhist-Christian relations since independence in 1948 are now being destroyed and may eventually lead, sadly, to violence, loss of human rights and even greater suppression and disenfranchisement of Christians.

Let me close with what I believe to be a very perceptive comment (especially in the context of healing) by Professor Asanga Tilakaratne of the Postgraduate Institute of Pali and Buddhist Studies (University of Kelaniya), Colombo. In his review of Young and Somaratna's *Vain Debates*, he writes:

> The lesson to be learned from *Vain Debates*, is that, old or new, subtle or gross, both inter-religious controversies and controversies over inter-religious controversies contribute little to inter-religious under- standing, which is worth trying.[23]

---

22 Sunanda Deshapriya, '"Devasaranaya"' and Devasarana Development Centre founded at Ibbagamuwa by "Sevaka" Yohan Devananda Facing Huge Problems from Anglican Bishop of Kurunegala and Church Leaders: An Open Letter to the Archbishop of Canterbury Seeking Justice', 4 August 2019.
23 Asanga Tilakaratne, *Journal of the Royal Asiatic Society of Sri Lanka* 43 (1998), 97–109. http://www.jstor.org/stable/23732444.

Part Two

Theological Frameworks for Healing

Chapter Six

It was the best of times, it was the worst of times: A practical theological reflection in a pandemic

Rosie Joyce

> *It was the best of times, it was the worst of times, it was the age of wisdom, it was the age of foolishness, it was the epoch of belief, it was the epoch of incredulity, it was the season of light, it was the season of darkness, it was the spring of hope, it was the winter of despair.*[1]

Such was the way Charles Dickens described the sentiment and condition of Europe in the mid-19th century on the eve of the French Revolution. For Dickens, it was the best of times because there was change in the air and this change promised an end to the tyranny of the nobility, and would give rise to the freedom of the common people. But it was also going to be the worst of times because a lot of sacrifice had to be made by these people to achieve this freedom; were they up to it?

Twelve months ago, it was beyond our comprehension to think that for at least some of this year the wearing of masks would be mandated; that we could be fined up to $5,000 for being more than five kilometres from our home; that we were not to leave our homes for more than one hour a day; that we would be suffering from social isolation and forbidden to visit family or friends or have them visit us in our own homes; that we would be forbidden to have our weekly times of worship and community gatherings! What is the message for us in suddenly having restrictions placed on how we live our personal lives and having to adapt to such regulations, and what is there for us to learn from having our satisfied lives quickly and completely turned upside down?

When the first lockdown was announced, the reaction of many was to do all that was possible to minimise any inconvenience and there was an immediate emptying of supermarket shelves! The stockpiling of goods

---

[1] Charles Dickens, *A Tale of Two Cities*.

like toilet paper had begun, and too bad about the needs of our neighbour! Was this a reaction of our best selves? Was this the image we wished to portray to our neighbour and to the world? Perhaps it was symptomatic that we were attempting to ensure that our lives would not be changed or inconvenienced in any way by a virus!

In his recent encyclical, *Fratelli Tutti: On Fraternity and Social Friendship*, Pope Francis reminds us that the pandemic has exposed our false securities and the existing inequalities in our neighbourhoods, while at the same time spurring 'a fragmentation that made it more difficult to resolve problems that affect us all'. He wrote:

> Anyone who thinks that the only lesson to be learned was the need to improve what we were already doing, or to refine existing systems and regulations, is denying reality ... The pain, uncertainty and fear, and the realisation of our own limitations, brought on by the pandemic have only made it all the more urgent that we rethink our styles of life, our relationships, the organisation of our societies and, above all, the meaning of our existence.[2]

Pope Francis calls on Christians to back policies that promote justice and the common good and he reaffirmed a link between religious faith and human dignity. Along with his call for an unconditional rejection of war, capital punishment and excessive wealth, it is a call to our better selves to have an astute reading of the signs of the times and, as one commentator reminds us, it is the simple virtues like love, compassion, kindness and openness to the stranger that are the essential ingredients to the healing of our common woes.[3]

Pope Francis was far from being the first to challenge us to be prepared to make sacrifices for the 'common good'. Almost three decades ago, when referring to the situation in America, a Newsweek columnist wrote that 'we face a choice between a society where people accept modest sacrifices for a common good or a more contentious society where groups selfishly protect their own benefits'.[4]

Nor is this idea of making sacrifices for the common good a twenty-first century invention. Rather, it can be found in the writings of

---

2 Pope Francis, *Fratelli Tutti: On Fraternity and Social Friendship*, 2020, nn. 7, 33.
3 Joseph Sinasac, 'New Encyclical on Human Fraternity: The Pope's "Cri de Coeur"', *La Croix* (6 October 2020) https://international.la-croix.com/news/religion/new-encyclical-on-human-fraternity-the-popes-cri-de-coeur/13130
4 Samuelson, Robert J. 'How Our American Dream Unraveled'. *Newsweek* (1 March 1992), https://www.newsweek.com/how-our-american-dream-unraveled-195900.

Plato, Aristotle and other early philosophers. For Plato (428–348 BCE), the best political order was that which promoted social harmony and an environment of cooperation and friendship among different social groups, with each benefiting from and adding to the common good. Aristotle's (384–322 BCE) view that the common good was constituted in the good of individuals led to the classical definition that referred to it as 'a good proper to, and attainable only by, the community, yet individually shared by its members'.[5]

Before we examine in detail the implications of what we take on if we make the principle of the common good as a way of life whereby we put the interests of the community before our own comfortable lifestyle and our abundance of goods and opportunities, let us look closely at the diametrically opposed concept of individualism.

The notion of individualism can be described as the practice of being independent and self-reliant. Many countries in the western world, including our own, are described as having an individualist culture which celebrates and promotes individualism and wealth over the common good. Do you identify your country as having characteristics where being dependent upon others is considered shameful or embarrassing, where independence is highly valued, where the rights of the individual are paramount, and where being unique and standing out is highly valued? If this is the case, we are called to have a new understanding of our rightful place on this earth and the responsibility each of us has to contribute to the common good.

It goes without saying that the rights of the individual must be respected as valid and we salute those individuals who, as agents of change, have fought over the centuries for the rights of workers and minority groups. This is not what individualism is! Neither is the example of Debbie Wardley, who fought to become the first woman to gain employment as an airline pilot in Australia. Debbie first applied to Ansett Airlines in 1976 and was rejected for no other reason than she was a woman. Though highly criticised for what was termed as pursuing her own selfish dreams rather than the good and safety of the general community, Debbie spent the next two years applying to enter the training program. Her applications continued to be rejected during which time ten of her fellow male flying instructors were accepted into the training program. It required a landmark legal battle in the Sex Discrimination Commission before Ansett was ordered to employ

---

5 Louis Dupré, 'The Common Good and the Open Society', *The Review of Politics* 55, no. 4 (1993), 687-712.

her as a pilot. Ansett rejected the initial ruling and appealed in the Supreme Court, then the High Court, where the final appeal was dismissed in 1980. What factors were present which prevented the Australian community from seeing this discrimination in its midst and not supporting Debbie in her pursuit of justice?

While this case happened forty years ago, it is more than relevant today in these COVID-19 times where there is discrimination and, when this is occurring, some in the community continue to have 'the worst of times'. So often, when an individual is fighting for her rights, she is representing a group who have been denied theirs. So while Debbie was an individual fighting for her rights, she was also doing this for the common good! Each of us is called to 'go and do likewise' both in our own personal lives and by supporting those groups which stand with the less privileged. A message for us all at this COVID-19 time is to go beyond 'the epoch of incredibility' in order to 'see' the types of discrimination in our midst and to actively do something about it.

It is not infrequent that the rights of the individual are at odds with the common good and, while it is important that we value and protect the rights of all individuals, no right is absolute. As in the case of the Melbourne lock-down experienced recently, we are reminded that we live in a community where the good of the community can override the rights of the individual. What is totally rejected is the attitude of superiority and the misuse of power which follows from a mindset where one cannot see beyond one's claim to prestige. This is another aspect of individualism. We want a world where it is the best of times for all peoples, not just for some. This demands justice for all.

Having considered the experience of Debbie Wardley and the too-often inability of the general community to see discrimination in its midst and to question accepted practices, the experience of COVID-19 challenges us all to think in a new communitarian way where all are considered equal. Furthermore, this pandemic has created in us an understanding and awareness of the interdependence of communities, the necessity of connections and the fragility of human beings left to themselves. We are being challenged to develop and promote a collectivist culture where characteristics such as self-sacrifice, consideration of the common good, generosity and caring for the neighbour become our chosen values as opposed to a culture of preserving my perceived rights and privileges or my country's perceived rights and privileges, regardless of whether any person or thing is being discriminated against. We are called to recognise that the rights of the individual to personal possessions and community resources must be balanced with the needs of the disadvantaged and dispossessed.

So where does this lead us to if we take to heart the lesson that this pandemic has brought to light? What does it mean for each of us personally and for us as a community that cares about each other? The common good is reached when we work together to improve the wellbeing of all people in our society and the wider world. It is reached when all members of society have access to those things we consider necessary for a decent living and the rights of the individual to personal possessions and community resources are balanced with the needs of the disadvantaged and dispossessed. How easy or difficult is it for us to put the considerations of the other before our own? We are reminded of the words of Jesus that 'those who find their life will lose it, and those who lose their life for my sake will find it'.[6]

Establishing and maintaining the common good requires the continued ongoing efforts of a community where altruism is valued over individualism, where the neighbour is known and cared for and where the disadvantaged are no longer disadvantaged! It is an increasing awareness that not all peoples have it as easy as we do and often it is the discomfort that this understanding gives us which leads us to action personally, communally and globally. We are reminded of the words of William Deane, a former Governor General of Australia (1996-2001), who used his position to 'mirror' to Australians their responsibilities to each other and to their country. In 1998 he gave us this challenge:

> It is my firm belief that the ultimate test of our worth as a democratic nation is how we treat our most disadvantaged. And by 'we' I refer to all of us, as members of the community.[7]

Finally, the pandemic is a timely reminder that we belong to a global community and are economically, socially, and politically interdependent. What happens in one corner of the world inevitably affects everywhere else, and the pandemic has reminded us of this. How quickly COVID-19 spread across the world! It has reminded us that we have to treat each major local problem as a global concern from the moment it begins. Universal responsibility is the key to human survival. It is the foundation for world peace, the equitable use of natural resources, and the proper

---

6 Matthew 10:39.
7 Sir William Deane at the Opening of the Mission Australia National Conference, Newcastle, 2 February 1998.

care of the environment. It requires the efforts of us all to contribute to the common good for all peoples. As the Dalai Lama has reminded us:

> The necessity for cooperation can only strengthen humankind because it helps us recognise that the most secure foundation for the new world order is not simply broader political and economic alliances, but rather each individual's genuine practice of love and compassion. For a better, happier, more stable and civilized future, each of us must develop a sincere, warm-hearted feeling of brotherhood and sisterhood.[8]

In this time of pandemic, we are called to a new way where it can be the best of times for our earth and for all peoples. We are challenged to live a spirituality which takes to heart the message of Jesus: 'Just as you did it to one of the least of these who are members of my family, you did it to me'.[9]

---

8 Dalai Lama, 'The Global Community and the Need for Universal Responsibility', *International Journal of Peace Studies* 7, no. 1, (Spring/Summer 2002), 1-14.
9 Matthew 25:40.

Chapter Seven

Toward a practical eco-theological approach with Christian askesis[1]

Julie A Hawkins

> There is now developing a profound mystique of the natural world. Beyond the technical comprehension of what is happening and the directions in which we need to change, we now experience the deep mysteries of existence through the wonders of the world around us.
> (Thomas Berry, from *The Great Work*[2]

1. Introduction

The quotation from Thomas Berry offers an idea to help inspire us all as we work on finding solutions to the ecological crises we are now negotiating. He suggests we turn toward the 'mystique of the natural world', and experience 'the deep mysteries of existence through the wonders of the world around us'. This type of contemplative attention to Nature would help to open a deep sense of awe within our hearts as a species, and this in turn would help us to re-engage respectfully with the natural world. In this paper, I will discuss this approach to resolving part of the Human-in-relation-to-Nature problem, and suggest that dualistic human behaviour patterns have been one factor that has been driving the increasing imbalance in Earth's Ecosphere. Rather than experiencing our world as a Whole-Earth, our civilisation's overly material-based strategy has seemed to separate humankind from Nature; this has led to a further sense of separation and, for many of us, even from our own inner lives. This has increased the difficulty of rediscovering a spiritual communion with the Divine. However, Berry suggests a re-engagement with the mystical core of our being, which he says can be awakened by the experience of 'the deep mysteries of existence through the wonders of

---

1 This paper is inspired by the author's late mother and young granddaughter.
2 Thomas Berry, *The Great Work: Our Way into the Future* (New York: Three Rivers Press, 1999), 200-201.

the world around us'. This is a path that many mystics have followed, and it is alluded to, advised, and expressed in beautiful poetic verse in the Scriptures. In order to approach these 'deep mysteries', humankind will need to transition into a less dualistic style of living on Earth. Eco-theology can help to facilitate this transition.

In writing about an eco-theological approach, we may consider how best to help guide humanity into a culture of greater respect for life and Nature.[3] If it is dualistic human behaviour patterns that have led to some of our species' unconscionable actions against the natural world, there is also an urgent need to offer help in altering this behaviour. There are two points to consider here: one is to encourage the aspiration to overcome blocks to living by the example that Jesus provided, and which St Paul advised the early Church to follow; the other is to encourage the inspirational sense of awe as an experience that may allow access to a more profound level of consciousness, one that can connect with an inner discovery of the Divine, as well as with the deep mystique of Nature in the 'outer' world. The ability to shift our behaviour away from dualising habits can help enable access to this deeper spiritual consciousness, which Berry suggests will help humanity to move beyond the old view.

2. Some definitions: duality and nonduality

2.1 Duality

Before proceeding, it will be helpful to provide some definition of what is meant by 'dualistic behaviour', and suggest alternatives for it. Behaviour depends upon states of mind, and a dualistic state of mind is likely to lead to dualising behaviour. The term 'duality' originates with the Latin 'dual' from 'dualitas', which means having a quality of 'two-ness' rather than oneness. Therefore, using 'duality' as a term to describe a state of human consciousness identifies a mental state with a tendency toward twoness, dividedness, or division. We might wonder what has been divided? Since 'duality' indicates a process of division, it can only be that a oneness has been divided, a prior non-duality, an undivided state of being or of mind. Such a state of mind would experience the world as whole, and would not perceive any need to divide it. The kind of separation we tend to experience from the world, is one in which we feel as if we are not fully

---

[3] The word 'nature' is capitalised when speaking of it as if as a proper name. The same is applied to Earth, and World. At other times when the words are used in their more conventional sense, lower case is used.

engaged or included, but perceive the world more as observers. In this sense, we feel separated from Nature, we might rarely visit natural areas, our minds might tend to be focused on tasks we have to complete, and we might not feel that our species is really a participant in Nature, in the same way that 'other' species are. Thus we come from a subject-objectifying perspective, which, by this subtle distancing effect, allows us to utilise parts of the natural world for our own benefit, regardless of whether these acts damage or destroy ecosystems and put the ecosphere out of balance, endangering its survival. This type of dualistic behaviour is not that of all individuals, but it is the effect of the actions of entire nations and the modern civilisation as a whole.

2.2 A nondual approach to living on Earth

A nondual approach would not commit such acts of separating oneself from the world through a layer of conceptual projections. It would, however, still recognise the constituents of which the whole is composed. For example, air is composed of mainly oxygen and nitrogen, and it is not beneficial to introduce toxins into that mixture. Our human bodies are composed of flesh, blood and water, and of limbs, the trunk and the head, and it is not beneficial to remove any of these. Similarly, Earth is composed of ecological features, including expanses of land, bodies of water, atmosphere, fire, ice, and life as living vegetation and creatures. The health of the whole-Earth, as of the air and the body, depends on balance in its composition. Yet humankind, in its industrious approach to producing new objects for people to own, interferes with the equilibrium of each organism and the interconnectedness of all organisms as a collective whole, and Earth itself as a whole-world. In a conceptual sense, a dualistic state of mind has a tendency to divide things not so much into categories as into pairs of opposites, such as good/bad, possible/impossible, bearable/unbearable. It might then view the various components that compose the air, bodies and Earth as separate and as separable. Such separability might encourage physical experimentation, by separating individual components from the prior whole. It is debateable whether this tendency toward dualising and separating is inbuilt in our species or has been imposed through education and culture.

2.3 Nonduality and spiritual techniques

The term nonduality in this application to the human mind indicates a prior undivided state of consciousness. In a biblical sense, this is an original state of mind and of being, and in religious teaching, it is a state to which humans might be able to approach, if we work with the idea of metanoia, which is defined as a turning around of the mind to a completely new way of being; it means repenting and going beyond the usual state of mind to a higher or deeper understanding of reality. Maurice Nicoll suggests that metanoia is the way for humankind to reach a truly authentic understanding of the nature of being, and a state of self-realisation.[4] To move away from our dualising habits, we need to practise refraining from dualising, and to practise this repetitively, if we are to change our mind-set toward a more illuminated state of being and, perhaps eventually, reach a nondual state. Mystical theologians note that we cannot cause a unitive state of awareness to arise just by practising spiritual techniques, for a mystical experience appears to happen spontaneously. Yet the mystically inclined repeatedly practise such inner askesis[5] techniques as contemplation, prayer, silence, meditation and self-examination, while more extroverted worshippers will practise outer askesis such as praying aloud, singing praises, psalms and hymns, and engaging in worship in group settings. Although looking at the two approaches in this way may seem to be a dualising exercise, in reality most religious people have either an inner or an outer orientation, often termed 'introverted' or 'extraverted', which seems to be aligned with their personality. Those with an inner orientation may be mystically inclined toward the ineffable, while those with an outer orientation may be disposed to rational explanations and working in groups which teach

---

[4] Maurice Nicoll, *Living Time and the Integration of the Life* (Boulder and London: Shambhala, 1984), 4.

[5] Askesis is a term from ancient Greek which means 'exercise' and refers to spiritual and philosophical exercises included in the practice of Greek philosophy, which continued into the Roman and Christian world. These practices have been carried on within the early Church and in the Eastern and Orthodox Church, and have been recorded by such as Gregory of Nyssa, Pseudo-Dionysius, the anonymous author of the Cloud of Unknowing, Meister Eckhart, Henry Suso and Nicholas of Cusa. They have included specific types of contemplation, meditation, prayer and reading sacred texts. Askesis also involves working with attention, awareness and states of consciousness. The research that underpins this paper is from Julie A. Hawkins, *Nondual Consciousness and its Significance for Eco-philosophy and Eco-theology: Toward a Deepening Aesthetic Consciousness and Ethic*, PhD thesis (Armidale: University of New England, 2022); the thesis is available on request.

through more definable and concrete explanations. The first orientation appears to be experiential, while the second appears to be intellectual. These are not to be regarded as opposites, however, but as styles and approaches that are complementary, and if one is predisposed toward mysticism, this does not preclude one from engaging in intellectual study, nor the intellectual from exploring mysticism. It may be that, over time, we modern humans have lost the skill of developing our intuitive and intellectual faculties in unison. Interestingly, to practise spiritual askesis in both inner and outer traditions may bring the mind toward a more unified state by developing and deepening our skills in both approaches.

2.4 Nonduality and mysticism

In recent years, there has been an encouraging blossoming of nonduality teachings in the Western traditions. These nondual teachings tend to focus on the interconnectedness of all things and the profoundly deep states of consciousness that mystics have discovered through contemplative askesis, and described in their writings. These are states within which the sense of belonging and participation in a whole-world style of existence seems tangible and a most profoundly deep reality.[6] There is in religious practice a path of ascension, which consists of two interconnected directions, to suit the two aforementioned dispositions, whose approaches match their understanding of reality. The first approach is one of ascending from 'lower' to 'higher' consciousness (in an ascension model), and the second is one of deepening one's consciousness from a surface-orientation to a deep inner Core, associated with the heart.[7] The first *kataphatic* approach has a structured (upward and outward) emphasis that aspires toward the sublime transcendent, while the second has an *apophatic* (inward) emphasis that aspires toward relinquishing dualism and practising self-emptying of oneself (kenosis)

---

6 This use of the word 'deep' owes much to the works of William Ralph Inge DD, whose writings on Christian Mysticism study the 'deep experience, insight, understanding, religious feeling and orientation, and mysteries', many of which are also alluded to by Thomas Berry. In C.S. Lewis' fiction, the works of God's Creation are described as 'deep' in the sense of 'profound'. Paul Collins, Thomas Merton, Thomas Berry and other religious scholars refer to the deep things of God in the sense of their profundity. The term is also prominent in Deep Ecology and Integral Spirituality.

7 If a planet-based model of consciousness is used, the surface (at the planet's crust) represents our surface-orientation for our daily lifestyle, while as we engage in meditation or contemplations, our awareness settles and deepens toward the heart (the core) and a sense of profound peace and belonging can occur.

in favour of the Divine. Traditional practices are used to achieve both spiritual elevation and spiritual deepening, for these are inseparable, intertwined experiences in the scriptures and theological works. The deepening within oneself can ground the aspirant so that the experience becomes profoundly en-heartening, for the path to the Divine is found within, not outside of oneself. Thus, the apophatic technique involves going within to the deepest extent of the heart. By going 'deeper' within, the world that has usually been seen through a conceptually dualising filter is revealed as 'shallow', so that the intuition of a 'Real' world is approached more directly without the intervention of concepts and dogma; hence the world may be seen anew as a creation of Divine light. This would be regarded as a mystical illuminative experience.

Saint Augustine (354CE-430CE) recorded an experience of Illumination he once shared with his mother at their house in Rome. As they stood together at a window looking out over the Tiber, they were, he writes, 'in the presence of Truth', which:

> brought us to the point that any pleasure whatsoever of the bodily senses, in any brightness whatsoever or corporeal light, seemed to us not worthy of comparison with the pleasure of that eternal light, not worthy even of mention.[8]

In contrast to this, Saint Gregory of Nyssa (335CE-395CE) had written of the 'dazzling darkness' in an experience based on (and describing) Moses' journey up the mountain and into the Cloud in which God spoke to him; this idea is further elaborated by the unknown, possibly Syrian, monk who went by the name of Dionysius, when he wrote *The Divine Names* and *The Mystical Theology*, in the 5th century CE. *The Divine Names* set out the kataphatic (*via positiva*) path to God, while *The Mystical Theology* set out the apophatic (*via negativa*) path to God.

Introducing his translation of the works of Dionysius, Clifton Wolters writes:

> In *The Mystical Theology*, the controlling idea is the possibility of the soul's union with God, with the consequent deification of man. This is achieved by the soul's putting aside all knowledge obtained through reason and the use of the senses and by its entry into a 'cloud of unknowing'. Gradually it will be illuminated by a 'ray of divine darkness' and brought to a knowledge of God which transcends all that can be thought or said.[9]

---

8 St Augustine, *Confessions*, IX. X, Trans. F.J. Sheed (Stuttgart: Sheed & Ward), 23-5.
9 From Clifton Wolters' Introduction to his translation of Dionysius' *Mystica Theologia* under the title 'Dionise Hid Divinite' in *The Cloud of Unknowing and Other Works* (London: Penguin, 1978), 202.

These descriptions of a mystical shift in consciousness are examples of metanoia, in which Saint Augustine has described a kataphatic illuminative experience, and Dionysius an apophatic experience of the Divine darkness. These occur in Christian writings including Gregory of Nyssa's 'Life of Moses'. Here one must go beyond all that is visible, as Moses went into the dark cloud 'where God was'.

This darkness of God is also expressed in Psalm 18:11: 'He made darkness his covering around him, his canopy thick clouds dark with water', a verse which supports St Gregory's interpretation of the 'Divine darkness' in 'The Life of Moses'.

Thus, in the experience of Dionysius, the apophatic path is most significant. He writes:

> For it is through this passing beyond yourself and every other thing (and thereby cleansing yourself from all worldly, physical and natural love, and from everything that can be known by the normal processes of mind) that you will be caught up in love beyond the range of intellect to the super-essential ray of divine darkness. Everything else will have gone.[10]

Theologian Seely Beggiani writes that the God of Dionysius 'is by nature beyond being', since God is 'at a total remove from every condition, movement, life, imagination, conjecture, name, discourse, thought, conception, being, rest, dwelling, unity, limit, infinity, the totality of existence'.[11] Therefore, as Wolters suggests, 'Mystical experience, by which the soul has knowledge of him [God], can only come after a progressive shedding of all forms of human knowledge until the Absolute alone remains'.[12] This shedding famously constitutes, for Dionysius, 'the cloud of unknowing' we must enter to encounter God, to encounter the Real that 'transcends all that can be thought or said'.[13]

The Mystical Way of Dionysius is, as summarised by Wolters, 'the longing for union with God, the great effort demanded, the threefold way, the *via negativa*, the cloud of unknowing, and the indescribable realisation of it all on God's terms'.[14] Rejecting the idea that God or

---

10 Dionysius, *Mystica Theologia*, translated by Clifton Wolters as 'Dionise hid Divinite' in *The Cloud of Unknowing and Other Works* (London: Penguin, 1978), 209.
11 Seely Beggiani, 'Theology at the Service of Mysticism: Method in Pseudo-Dionysius', *Theological Studies*, 57, (1996): 205.
12 Clifton Wolters, 'Introduction to Dionysius' Mystical Teaching' in *The Cloud of Unknowing and Other Works*, (1978), 201.
13 Wolters, 'Introduction to Dionysius' Mystical Teaching', 202.
14 Wolters, 'Introduction to Dionysius' Mystical Teaching', 203.

Ultimate Being might be captured through human sensory experience and intellectual judgment that operates on the dualistic logic—semantic and practical—of the subject/object binary, it follows for Dionysius that 'Theology in all its aspects must deal constantly with the reality of God who remains incomprehensible, nameless and hidden'.[15] God, the Divine, is beyond all pairs of opposites, and so is nondual and may only be experienced in and through a consciousness that has ceased to dualise.[16] One who arrives at such a state of consciousness may have used some askesis practices as part of the spiritual journey.

3. Askesis and the Essenes

The theological tradition of spiritual askesis practised in monastic religious establishments is as old as the monastic lifestyle itself, as Philo has shown in his record of the practices of the Essenes from c. 200BCE to c. 200CE. Askesis had been practised by the ancient Greeks as part of their philosophy, and it became a noticeable part of Stoic philosophy. It was also practised in the Jewish Essene community.

Philo referred to the Essenes as *Therapeutae* and recorded their practices, describing their contemplative lifestyle in quiet, monastic communities. During the day's devotions, they meditate on and practice virtue, reading the scriptures allegorically, since 'they look upon their literal expressions as symbols of some secret meaning of nature, intended to be conveyed in those figurative expressions'. They also study their sect's ancient writings, which are regarded as 'memorials of the allegorical system of writing and explanation'. Following these as models, they spend the days contemplating and composing 'psalms and hymns to God in every kind of metre and melody imaginable', which they arrange 'in more dignified rhythm'.[17]

According to Philo, the Essenes' contemplative life was rich in scripture-based practices, conducive to spiritual growth and isolated from the ordinary cultural practices of their fellow Jews. This was their askesis for coming to know God, themselves, and the 'secret meaning of nature'. And it contains the common elements—contemplation, renunciation, self-discipline—of much metanoia- directed askesis.[18]

---

15 Beggiani, 'Theology at the Service of Mysticism', 201.
16 Wolters, 'Introduction to Dionysius' Mystical Teaching', 202.
17 Philo, *On the Contemplative Life*, or *Suppliants*, 5. The texts is found online at: http://www.earlychristianwritings.com/yonge/book34.html
18 Philo, *On the Contemplative Life*, 5.

The practices of the Essenes recall aspects of Jesus' life in the Gospels, of which contemplation and prayer in natural settings was a feature, and point toward further askesis in St Paul's Epistles.

Since the twentieth century, interest in the Essenes' use of ancient askesis has increased.[19]

3.1 Askesis in the teaching of Jesus, in St Paul's Epistles and in Evagrius' Praktikos

A reflection on Jesus' teachings, and the askesis recommended in St Paul's Epistles, will familiarise readers with the value of training in practices for enduring trials and temptations.[20] Engaging with askesis in the present time may help our culture approach transformative change via a more profound understanding and insight into the purpose and meaning of life.

A brief consideration of some of Jesus' teachings will clarify the type of behaviour he recommends to his followers. First, when Jesus says: 'Follow me', he means for his listeners to follow his way of living;[21] he also advises his listeners, 'If any wish to come after me, let them deny themselves and take up their cross and follow me'.[22] Jesus says in, Luke 6:27-28, 'Love your enemies, do good to those who hate you, bless those who curse you, pray for those who mistreat you' and, in Luke 6:31, he adds 'Do to others as you would have them do to you'. The behaviour Jesus encourages requires a shift in viewpoint, a metanoia, in his followers. In Luke 6:35-36, Jesus offers 'Instead, love your enemies, do good, and lend, expecting nothing in return ... Be merciful, just as your Father is merciful'. This advice suggests that acting from kindness, generosity, empathy and mercy will evoke these qualities in one's life, for these qualities in God are infinite, and practising them helps them to grow stronger.[23]

The injunction 'Do not judge, and you will not be judged; do not condemn, and you will not be condemned. Forgive, and you will be forgiven' is given in Luke 6:37. When one 'judges' and 'condemns', it is often due to particular points of view, because one may tend to think about people through a kind of 'polarising prism', which is another type of habit pattern that continues to separate one person from another; it is,

---

19 The discovery of the Dead Sea Scrolls near Qumran between 1947 and 1956 inspired interest in the Essenes.
20 Askesis should done under advice from a spiritual adviser.
21 Matthew 4:19; 8:22; 9:9, and Mark 2:14.
22 Mark 8:34.
23 These teachings, when acted on, may unlock profound values of empathy and compassion.

however, a habit which can be relinquished. When Jesus observes of the kingdom 'nor will they say, "Look, here it is!" or "There it is!" For, in fact, the kingdom of God is among you",'[24] the implication is that his disciples have not yet seen the Kingdom, nor are they aware of its presence. It seems clear that Jesus himself is aware of the Kingdom, and that it is within and amongst his disciples, where he is, with them.

In this connection, David Loy has stated, 'Reality is staring us in the face all the time, but somehow we misperceive it'.[25] This, he suggests, is because we look with an awareness that divides, at a world that is actually a unity, an interweaving of diversity and wonder. Our general cultural understanding of the world comes as a dualising framework through which we have learned to identify, label, categorise and judge the world we inhabit, turning it from a once wondrous unity into an apparent collection of objects; this is how the conventional, conditioned understanding of the world arises. In daily life we often remain near the surface of awareness in order to accomplish our daily tasks, although a deeper, more ultimate Reality may also be sensed. However, it cannot be perceived through a style of awareness that is still subject-objectifying rather than allowing the world to be as it is, that is, dividing and interpreting rather than simply perceiving and experiencing the world directly. Thus, in order to cease misperceiving Reality, as Loy suggests, one may practise refraining from thoughts that dualise. Thus, through contemplative practice, one might rest into a deeper state of understanding. A worthy goal then, would be for humans to understand Earth better, and to perceive its natural cycles and processes as well as its sacred, life-bearing qualities, both facets of a unified world.

St Paul, in the time of the early Churches, wrote a series of Epistles that addressed problems faced by Christian communities. One of these problems was that negative behaviour patterns had continued in believers, which he now asked the Churches to put aside, suggesting they put in place new, more Christ-oriented conduct.[26] These teachings are remarkable for their grasp of the dualistic habits which the new Christians would want to relinquish in order to be more like Jesus.

---

24 The footnote for this reference offers the alternative reading 'or within you'.
25 David Loy. *Nonduality: A Study in Comparative Philosophy* (New York: Humanity Books, 1988), 39.
26 The selections from which these quotations have been taken are found in Colossians 3:1-17 and Ephesians 4:14-32 and 5:1-4. Similar and related selections are located in Galatians 5:13-26; 1 Corinthians 1:13; and Philippians 3:12-17 and 4:4-9.

St Paul advises the Colossians to 'Put to death ... impurity, passion, evil desire, and greed (which is idolatry)', as these ways will attract 'the wrath of God'. He tells them to 'get rid of' all such things: 'anger, wrath, malice, slander, and abusive language', to give up lying and practices of the old nature, as they have now 'clothed' themselves with 'the new self, which is being renewed in knowledge according to the image of its creator'.[27] Although there seems to be a sense of dualism here in terms of the evil/good binary, it is when the 'new self' has gone beyond the 'old' that dualities vanish 'In that renewal'. For here 'there is no longer Greek and Jew, circumcised and uncircumcised, barbarian, Scythian, enslaved and free, but Christ is all and in all!'[28] It is in duality that oppositions are evident. Paul directs the people, as 'God's chosen ones', to 'put on' the qualities of the Divine as 'the new man'.[29] In this metanoia, oppositions will, ideally, have been transcended and unitive self will remain.

It might be possible that a fresh rendering of these Scriptures in an eco-theological context could be offered to the wider community, including information that addresses known causes of the climate crisis. These practices are all underscored by the Golden Rule, of which an ecological variant might be 'treat all life, and Earth, as you would like to be treated'. Such a rendering would honour both life and Earth.

The *Praktikos* of Father Evagrius Ponticus (345 CE-399CE) provided a set of contemplative methods and antidotes drawn from these sources: 'Christianity is the teaching of our Saviour Christ consisting of ... ascetical practice, the [contemplation of] nature, and theology'.[30]

Here, Father Evagrius describes 'Eight Patterns of Evil Thought': gluttony, sexual immorality, love of money, sadness, anger, acedia (listlessness), vainglory, and pride, and prescribes antidotes for each.[31] Examples of antidotes are given under 'Tactics for the Eight [Tempting] Thoughts', where the 'wandering *nous*' (distracted mind) is made stable by reading, vigils and prayer. Burning *epithumia* (desire) is quenched by hunger, toil, and solitude. Churning *thumos* (indignation) is calmed by the singing of psalms, patient endurance and mercy.[32] The use of antidotes is of great significance, as they enable a faster 'letting go' to occur.

---

27 Colossians 3:2-10.
28 Colossians 3:11.
29 Colossians 3:10, 3:12-15.
30 Evagrius Ponticus, *Praktikos*. The translation by Luke Dysinger is available at http://www.ldysinger.com/Evagrius/01_Prak/00a_start.htm
31 *Praktikos*: Sections 6-33.
32 Nous (Νοῦν) mind, epithumia (ἐπιθυμίαν) desire, and thumos (θυμὸν) Indignation.

Aside from askesis being a means to change outward behaviour, it provides encouragement and hope for an inner spiritual aspiration toward a better world. Although Father Evagrius' Desert practices are unlikely to suit the wider community, many people would benefit greatly from his contemplative approach.

Such practical training in spiritual askesis is capable of supporting whole communities in letting go of negative patterns of thinking and behaving, and moving toward more harmonious and insightful choices. By re-learning the significance of the internally connected aspects of the Human, the Natural, and the Divine, we may begin to address the societal need for spiritual guidance, by applying sensible practices in support of our children's future world. One crucial aspect would be to offer training for developing higher qualities of consciousness, while deepening the awareness of how to disengage from divisive behaviour, and how to discover deeper levels of inner peace.

We will now consider aspects of how human beings perceive (or misperceive) Earth, in the way innate sensory and aesthetic faculties are used.

4. Aesthetics and how we experience and relate to the world

As humans, we relate to Earth as Home, through our senses and aesthetic understanding and perceptions. We are familiar with traditional aesthetics being a set of principles concerned with the nature and appreciation of beauty, but perhaps less so with the Aesthetic branch of philosophy that deals with questions of beauty and artistic taste. According to Andrew Bowie, a scholar of Aesthetics, the term derives from the Greek term aisthanesthai, to 'perceive sensuously', while 'the new subject of "aesthetics" now focuses on the significance of natural beauty and of art'. Aesthetics, Bowie suggests, is now connected to 'the emergence of subjectivity as the central issue in modern philosophy', which is where 'the relevance of this topic to contemporary concerns becomes apparent'. As reflecting on aesthetics also involves 'a revival of Plato's thoughts about beauty as the symbol of the Good', Bowie suggests that aesthetics as a branch of philosophy deals with human subjective, sensory engagement with the world, with art, and with the beautiful—which includes Nature as the first Beautiful, later to be supplemented (occasionally supplanted) by a focus on visual artworks.

Such engagement involves, or is informed and shaped by, matters of proportion, colour, line, texture, and the balance of positive and negative space. On a more conceptual and subtle level, it involves allusions to other works of art and to cultures whose properties are considered valuable but intangible, although there seem to be tangible qualities detectable through one's inner senses such as intuition and the awareness of interconnectedness. These works of art may well evoke experiential elements and communicate profound content beyond the level of concepts and words. This aesthetic tangibility may be 'felt' and 'sensed' as almost physical. These elements take aesthetics beyond the functional and serviceable to what feels like a more deeply existential level of perceiving and being. Insofar as we humans see, know and perceive the world as other than functional and serviceable, we do so, in the broadest sense, aesthetically. Aesthetics can also be defined in connection with Ideas, and Tony Lynch has written in this context that 'the idea of beauty as the supreme aesthetic value is thought itself to be internally connected to the values of Justice or the Good, and to that of Truth'. Lynch adds, 'the idea is that aesthetic attention (awareness of internal connections, contrasts and unities, variations and idiosyncrasies, etc.) is itself essential of properly sensitive ethical vison, and to a discriminating non-dogmatic sense of the truths of the world.'[33]

In a sense, as human beings, we are grounded in the world through deepened aesthetic experience, which can be thought of as a holistic awareness of the whole-Earth. Beth Carruthers has suggested that 'a deeper aesthetic engagement with the world might help us arrive at a deep and necessary shift in our understanding of human, culture and world,' as 'a way of seeing anew'.[34]

Although our usual conceptualised division of the world into a succession of objects causes us to miss the Divine vision of a whole Nature—since this common world-view separates us from both Nature and the Divine—Thomas Merton discusses a deepened aesthetic sense of contemplation which differs from the deep Divine perception

> We meditate with our mind, which is 'part of' our being. But we contemplate with our whole being and not just with one of its parts. This means that the contemplative intuition of reality is a perception of value: a perception which is not intellectual or speculative, but practical and experiential. It is not just a matter

---

33 Lynch, 'On Aesthetics', *A Student Resource on Aesthetics in Philosophy* (Armidale: UNE, 2021).
34 Beth Carruthers, 'Call and Response: Deep Aesthetics and the Heart of the World', *Aesth/Ethics in Environmental Change* (Biological Station of Hiddensee and University of Greifwald, 2010), 131-141.

of observation, but of realisation. It is not something abstract and general, but concrete and particular. It is a personal grasp of the existential meaning and value of reality.[35]

Merton adds that 'such personal intuitions may be highly paradoxical and even, sometimes, disturbing'. In essence, 'one "knows" without knowing how he knows.'[36]

Thomas Berry also discusses deepened awareness, writing that 'the universe is so bound into the aesthetic experience, into poetry, music, art, and dance, that we cannot entirely avoid the implicit dimensions of the natural world'. He speaks of 'the wonder communicated most directly by the meadow or the mountains, by the sea or by the stars in the night'.[37]

Paul Collins deals with religious and spiritual faculties, and speaks of how real religious development teaches us 'that we know little or nothing of the *mysterium tremendum* that we call "God"'. All the most spiritually advanced can say is that 'they can perceive traces of the infinite in their experience'. He adds that 'these traces of transcendent mystery are often actuated by an encounter with nature', and notes that he is not speaking of 'peak experiences' (nor of 'Flow'), but 'profound metaphysical realisations', which 'point the recipient beyond the self. They open up a window into a broader context of meaning.'

> This type of experience is not so much a form of self-possession as an opening-out toward possession by a presence that is greater and deeper than the individual. Such experiences dwell more in the spiritual and transcendent realm than in the psychological.

Collins adds that his argument is that 'we find the divine in the midst of the world, and even ... in the midst of the secular'.[38] Thus we can understand this whole world as God's Earth, a 'kingdom' already here, which, with a shift in consciousness, can be perceived and experienced with authentic clarity.

We are used to operating through our senses and intellect, gathering input, processing it, then acting on it, an habitual approach with which we objectify from a relatively surface level of our awareness. However, adding intuition brings an additional depth to our experience, and

---

35 Thomas Merton, *The Inner Experience: Notes on Contemplation* (New York: Harper One, 2003), 59-60.
36 Merton, *The Inner Experience*, 60.
37 Berry, *The Great Work*, 17.
38 Paul Collins, *God's Earth: Religion as if matter really mattered* (Blackburn, Victoria: HarperCollins, 1995), 208-09.

positions us more 'within' the world than 'on' it, in the 'we live on Earth' sense; for we actually live within Earth's whole ecosphere, beneath an atmospheric layer that is around 10,000 kilometres deep. Rather than this being a dualistic point, we may consider that this information simply gives us a greater depth of aesthetic understanding of our planet, Earth. Using an awareness of our planetary surroundings, along with our active intellect and our activated intuition, there seems to be an extra dimension through which we perceive ourselves living in the world in a completely holistic way—a deep aesthetic sensibility. A further profound experience may be encountered during contemplation or meditation when the breath settles into a rhythmic pattern and quietens the mind, so that the awareness can rest more profoundly within oneself. When this occurs in an alignment of one's perceptions, bodily sensing, and intuition, a sense of an immersion of oneself within the world may be experienced.[39] To simplify, people in the modern West have become accustomed to using the mind in ways that enable a divided mental functioning for carrying out work-oriented tasks, often attempting to do several at once, with a faculty that thinks and divides; yet the intuitive and aesthetic faculties, as Merton, Berry and Collins have each expressed in their own way, are already aware of the wholeness of things. The re-joining of the two functions—intellect and intuition—brings a further, deep dimension to one's life.

5. Solutions in eco-theology: an educational way forward

Paul Collins advocates training the inner religious faculty in his book *God's Earth*.[40] Thomas Berry 'resituates' the human spirit 'within a sacred reality'.[41] Thomas Merton notes that his own spiritual upliftment transforms the world around him 'with the glory of God', suggesting that the way nature is perceived, experienced and treated is grounded in one's spiritual condition and world view.[42] If spiritual depth is able to improve one's ability to perceive and understand Earth through a non-dividing or non-dualising awareness, as 'God's Earth', then a subject that develops one's intuitive /creative faculty would be worthwhile content to add to

---

39 Mihaly Csikszentmihalyi's *Flow: the Psychology of Optimal Experience* New York: Springer, 1990), explores this concept in Chapter 4, 'The Conditions of Flow', 71-93.
40 Collins, *God's Earth*, 227.
41 Berry, *The Great Work*. Berry discusses such ideas in Chapter 14, 'Reinventing the Human', 159-165.
42 James Finley, *Merton's Palace of Nowhere: A Search for God through Awareness of the True Self* (Notre Dame, Indiana: Ave Maria Press, 1992), 144.

educational curricula. A deeper way of engaging with the world through intuitive and religious faculties might be beneficial for students to learn. If students can be given exercises to assist them in further engagement with the natural world, and even to work in the nascent industries of ecosystem restoration and renewal, then it is advisable for those skills to be taught at all levels of education. An educational focus on skills that help students engage with knowledge about natural processes will prepare people to live with an awareness of and engagement with the planetary ecosphere. Since we humans share this planet with all other known species of life,[43] it is sensible to prepare students to live in an awareness of how to interact appropriately with our fellow species.

We must contribute reasons for the coming generations to have hope. A grassroots shift in educational focus is possible if we make community adult education more easily available within our localities. Therefore, increasing educational opportunities connected with environmentally-based activities at local, regional, national, (and planetary) levels is one strong approach. Another would be to train people to share ecological literacy within the community, to help mediate and educate populations toward re-engagement with Nature and restoration of eco-systems in local areas. We need to have new ideas if we are to begin to resolve this desperate need for a transformation in the way people are aware of, and inter-relate with, our planet Earth.

6. Including an inter-faith approach

To implement contemplative training would assist community groups which have a spiritual focus, to learn ways to develop and focus the awareness. Exploring aesthetically- inspired activities will engage community members in a range of creative approaches to widening the general awareness of nature, and ecological matters might be woven into such pursuits. These could be achieved through a variety of faith-based contexts, in a companionable spirit. A focus on aesthetic appreciation of artworks and natural environments, coupled with sessions of creative and contemplative activities, might draw participants with a range of faith-based approaches toward a productive engagement with the natural world, in ways that are consistent with the faiths of participants.

Three eco-philosophical concepts are important in this context: a) humans sharing the planet with other species, b) humans participating in Earth's ecosphere, and c) humans engaging in a diverse range of experimental nature-based activities to approach a more integrated

---

43 Thomas Berry has much to say on this matter in *The Great Work*.

understanding of living respectfully with (and within) Nature. These three approaches would provide useful foci for creative activities concerning visual and performing arts in community settings. One goal would be to work toward a wider understanding of the world's non-human species as 'companion species' rather than as 'lesser creatures', perhaps while engaging in community discussions. A further goal might be to use community activities to encourage a fresh understanding of Earth as a whole-world, rather than as a collection of countries, isolated on continents and islands. A final goal could be to view Earth as an ecosphere in which all inter-connected facets of the whole-Earth operate as a unity. J. Stan Rowe has written that 'this clearer perspective as to who we are, where we are and what we evolved from, will eventually revolutionize how we know ourselves and our environments', because it represents a different reality than that constructed by partial knowledge in isolation. Rowe suggests that, 'in the profounder ecological sense, the world is now known as a unity. The various spheres--atmo, hydro, litho, and bio--are intertwined and related, both in the historical and cultural sense'.[44]

This understanding of Earth as a unity has long been known by Indigenous people all over the world. They understand quite readily that the 'othering' of Nature has been due to a dissonance between modern industrialised civilisation and the natural, and that Nature's suffering has not been recognised—by the industrial mode of thinking—as being of consequence. Therefore, an inter-cultural inter-faith dialogue will enrich the way cultures relate to nature, and share a range of approaches, including indigenous nations' understandings of the land and the relations they experience with non-human species and their environments. Another point is that Indigenous communities can help their societies deal with climatic changes, particularly since they have lived in closer intimacy within natural environments, and can advise and oversee ways of working with the elements during bushfire and flood seasons. Indigenous cultures all over the world have maintained their innate knowledge of interrelations between species, which has enabled them to live in authentic interconnectedness with their environment and fellow creatures. They have an advanced understanding of the need to maintain natural ecosystems as homes for non-human species. The tendency in western society to consider nature as 'other', may have been encouraged to more easily allow exploitation of animals as well as minerals and other material resources, treating all of these at once as 'resources'

---

44 J. Stan Rowe, 'Ecosphere Thinking' (March, 1987), from http://environment-ecology.com/holistic-view/129-ecosphere-thinking.html

made for human use. However, there has been little consideration that all creatures suffer when their lives are shortened as a result of exploitation. This is not good stewardship.

If the solution to our various issues concerning the Ecosphere is to transform our consciousness by means of metanoia, then this may be partly achieved through encouraging a mixture of wider educational opportunities across all religious and cultural boundaries, sharing in experiential events that involve Nature, a more diverse and accessible spiritual education, and the sharing of techniques from the ancient traditions of askesis, and of living within Nature, in the direction of moving communities and populations toward an elevation of planetary consciousness.

7. Mediating re-engagement between humans and nature

Importantly, ecosphere thinking can bring about a shift in culture, away from viewing the world as ripe for exploitation, and toward understanding the need for planetary balance.

J. Stan Rowe's approach was to increase literacy about the biosphere and ecosphere, and encourage people to engage more with their natural surroundings. A range of approaches to sharing experience in Nature might be useful in this endeavour, including guided contemplative exercises with a focus on aesthetic and creative experience in partnership with the natural world.[45]

Berry suggests an inspirational range of approaches to reinventing the human experience of Nature,[46] which will repay further examination.

We might consider how our mind relates to the world as we contemplate it. Do we feel separate, or do we begin to experience ourselves as 'participants in Earth'? 'How does this occur?' 'What are the barriers to this experience?' 'What might it involve?' Such reflective questioning helps us to feel how our presence in the world is experienced in an intellectual sense, a bodily sense, and an intuitive sense.

Even during the work-based aspects of our lives, where we are employed to work and live in built-up areas within cities and towns, we can contemplate and experience Nature directly (rather than through

---

45 Joanna Macy has written on 'The Work That Reconnects', a program designed to help humans reconnect with the natural world, including Interfaith and Intercultural content. Joanna Macy and Molly Brown, *Coming Back to Life* (Gabriola Island, BC: New Society Publishers, 2014).
46 Berry, *The Great Work*, Chapters 14 and 15.

indirect technological media); for the sky is always above, and trees are in the streets, plants can be grown at the roadside and indoors, and companion animals can live or visit with humans in these environments. We can begin to re-plan our cities to include natural mini-eco-systems.

Developing our inner faculties through study and skills-training, particularly including contemplative skills, will open us naturally into new perspectives of being. From this, nondual values, ethics, virtue-ethics, and aesthetics may be understood as spiritual experiences of nature and life. Exploring the nature of Reality is a life-long task. Because we humans are all interconnected within the biosphere and all Earth processes are interdependent, our hearts and minds are able to open deeply (during contemplation and meditation) into an expansive awareness that widens to experience the wonder of our interwoven presence with all life, within the world.

8. An experiential approach to human-nature re-engagement through mediation and education

Mediating involves reintroducing people to Nature, helping those who wish to spend more time in human-nature interactions. Here we set out a list of potential approaches which have been derived in part from the type of practices commonly used in Daoism, Zen and Yoga, and in many further Indigenous contexts which focus on direct experience. There are also additional western sources for many of these types of exercises. Other venues for nature-orientation activities include such spiritual activities as drumming and healing workshops, which use incense, music, dancing, and exercising as ways for approaching the Sacred, including environmental groups which seek an immersive re-engagement with Nature. In the list of experimental activities that follows, some activities have a sensory and aesthetic orientation, while others involve experiencing differing ways of approaching Nature, including experimenting with subjective encounters.

The following types of experimental activities involve simple meditations in natural areas, reading nature poetry and seeking deeper understanding of reflective experiences.

- Practise contemplation and a sense of interconnectedness with life. Feel interconnectedness, through guided experiential practices.
- Experience the wholeness of Earth, and presence with the life of the world.

- Sometimes encounter nature through a window, a photo, or an idea; sometimes go outside and experience Nature directly, with a peaceful mind.
- Re-engage with Nature, being aware of sky above, ground below and life all around. In the sacred natural energy, feel the Divine as Present.
- Enjoy vitality and beauty in the land. Life is everywhere, and everywhere is life.
- After experiencing a noisy environment, enter the peace of the trees; relax into that peace, participate in it, feel it spread out in all directions.
- Discovering how Nature is sometimes objectified, step back from the dualising impulse. Regain a sense of friendliness toward Nature and receive it from trees, birds, flowers, and the breeze.
- Relax when standing, sitting and being in Nature, inseparable from your surroundings. Enjoy Beauty, the aesthetic of life, flowers and trees.
- Deepening your perceptions, experience the World directly as God's Earth.

9. Afterword

Can modern western culture find fresh ways forward for this present time? As we see, there are many approaches which remain true to ancient theological values and ethics while implementing the most suitable practices of traditional contemplatives, meditators, and even renunciates. Learning to reduce approaches to life that dualise and objectify, and habits that seem to be quite deeply ingrained, can modern westerners follow the most appropriate of these practices that were once only followed within religious communities? And since these are already taught within some secular schools and community education contexts, can this type of education become more available in all local communities? This would seem to be an important way forward for our post-modern culture. In conclusion, I recommend that spiritual and nature-orienting askesis be taught with ecological literacy in communities, and reconnecting with natural ecosystems through mediation.

Chapter Eight

The *habitus*, reflexivity and an Ignatian spirituality that does justice

Sandie Cornish

Introduction

This paper is concerned with the interplay between structure and agency. It examines the relevance of the *habitus* and reflexivity to an Ignatian approach to social justice. The findings of a case study exploring the interaction of Catholic Social Teaching (CST) and Ignatian spirituality within the praxis of the Jesuit Conference Asia Pacific (JCAP) Social Apostolate Network in relation to vulnerable migrants in Asia in the period 2008 – 2011 point to a link between reflexivity and the capacity to integrate, synthesise and move between these sources of praxis.[1] This secondary analysis places the data in dialogue with Mouzelis' restructuring of Bourdieu's theory of practice.[2]

For Bourdieu, the *habitus* is a set of dispositions or generative schemata that is the major link between social structures and practices. However, Mouzelis points out that a reflexive disposition can be acquired via socialisation, giving the example of religious communities that stress the importance of the inner life and thus socialise members into a reflexive *habitus*.[3] Reflexivity may be understood as casting one's gaze back on oneself as an actor. Mouzelis' work makes space for both the pre-reflexive action characteristic of the *habitus* and also for the routine exercise of reflexive accounting, conscious strategising, and rational calculation.

This paper demonstrates that both the *habitus* and personal reflexivity are useful in understanding the experience of members of the Network. It argues that the shared praxis of the Network can be described as a reflexive

---

1 Sandra Jayne Cornish, 'How Catholic Social Teaching and Ignatian Spirituality Interact within the Praxis of the Jesuit Conference Asia Pacific Social Apostolate Network in Relation to Vulnerable Migrants in and from Asia' (Doctoral thesis, North Sydney, Australian Catholic University, 2016), https://doi.org/10.4226/66/5a9db4213360d.
2 Nicos Mouzelis, 'Habitus and Reflexivity: Restructuring Bourdieu's Theory of Practice', *Sociological Research Online* 12, no. 6 (2007): 9, https://doi.org/doi:10.5153/sro.1449.
3 Mouzelis, 'Habitus and Reflexivity', 3.

habitus and shows how particular Ignatian practices embody apophatic and cataphatic reflexivity. Thus, a reflexive Ignatian *habitus* may both mediate CST in a distinctive way, and contribute to its development.

The interplay of structure and personal agency is a long-standing question in sociology, and it underpins diverse thinking within the Catholic social justice tradition concerning structures of sin. This paper argues that spiritualities that socialise followers into a reflexive *habitus* can be an important resource in addressing structures of sin. The exploration of these questions is timely in the light of the priority that Francis, the first Jesuit Pope, gives in his teaching to social, economic, and ecological justice and the role of spirituality within this teaching.

The JCAP case study

The JCAP Social Apostolate Network and its engagement with vulnerable migrants from Asia in the period 2008–2011 was chosen as a case study because migration is a major ethical challenge and a significant proportion of the world's migrants were from Asia during the period studied.[4] Further, with over one hundred years of Papal CST on migration,[5] and teachings from the Federation of Asian Bishops' Conferences (FABC) on migration since 1970,[6] the relative influence of, and potential interplay between, the international and local teachings within praxis could be examined. A focus on Ignatian spirituality was warranted because of its influence as the spirituality of the largest order of religious men in the world, and of several other religious institutes and movements. Finally, because I have observed, networked with, and journeyed alongside people and groups inspired by Ignatian spirituality,[7] it was possible to adopt a community engagement approach, consciously engaging

---

4 International Organisation for Migration, 'World Migration Report 2011: Communicating Effectively About Migration', 2011, http://publications.iom.int/system/files/pdf/wmr2011_english.pdf, 68.

5 Fabio Baggio and Maurizio Pettena, eds., *Caring for Migrants: A Collection of Church Documents on the Pastoral Care of Migrants* (Strathfield, NSW: St Paul Publications, 2009).

6 Jonathan Y Tan, 'Inculturation in Asia: The Asian Approach of the Federation of Asian Bishops Conferences', ed. Vimal Tirimanna, *Reaping a Harvest from the Asian Soil: Towards an Asian Theology* (Bangalore: Asian Trading Corporation, 2011).

7 These engagements have included periods working for the Jesuit Refugee Service International Office in the early 1990s, employment by the Australian Province of the Jesuits in the fields of formation and social ministry from 2005 to 2010, involvement in JCAP research tasks from 2008 to 2011, and the provision of specialist input on the Jesuit justice tradition and CST to the international tertianship program based in

synergies between the methodology of contemporary CST, the dynamics of Ignatian spirituality, and a praxis approach to practical theology, in order to generate emergent knowledge.

A community engagement approach informed the case study.[8] Data was gathered through semi-structured in-depth interviews and content analysis was conducted using the tools of grounded theory.[9] Contact with potential research participants who were, or had been, involved in JCAP's work with vulnerable migrants was facilitated by JCAP leaders. Information letters and consent forms, approved by the Australian Catholic University Research Ethics Committee, were provided to each potential research participant and written consent was secured before interview. The thirteen research participants included eight Jesuits, two of whom were still in training for ordination to the priesthood, two female religious and three lay women. The interview participants came from Australia, Indonesia, Malaysia, the Philippines, Singapore, South Korea, Spain, Taiwan and Vietnam. They had been involved in work with vulnerable migrants in Cambodia, Indonesia, Malaysia, Singapore, Taiwan, Thailand, Vietnam and in pan-regional settings. The 'J' and 'R' codes associated with interview participants indicate that they are Jesuits or other religious – there are no references to any of the lay participants in this paper. Together with a number, they provide a unique identifier for each of the research participants. Internal validation of the data, and the theorising that emerged inductively from it, was achieved by providing feedback on the key insights that were emerging from the initial analysis of interview data to interview participants and key leaders in JCAP and its Social Apostolate Network. External validation of the coding and analysis of the data was achieved by engaging the services of an independent researcher.

Sydney from 2004 to 2011. The author was a member of the JCAP Migration Task Force and worked together with other Task Force members to support the JCAP Social Apostolate Coordinator to animate, promote and coordinate JCAP's work on migration from 2009 to 2011.

8 Jude Butcher, Luke A. Egan, and Ken Ralph, 'Community Engagement Research: A Question of Partnership' (Australian Catholic University, March 14, 2008), https://www.researchgate.net/publication/228435738_Community_engagement_research_A_question_of_partnership

9 Steinar Kvale and Svend Brinkmann, 'Interviews: Learning the Craft of Qualitative Research Interviewing' (Thousand Oaks, California: Sage, 2009), 202.; Kathy Charmaz, 'Constructing Grounded Theory: A Practical Guide Through Qualitative Analysis' (London: Sage Publications, 2006), 2-4.

Some questions raised by the case study

The interview data confirmed that Ignatian spirituality and CST were both sources of the praxis of the research participants and that these sources interacted primarily in the participants' approach to action. The consistency of research participants' accounts of their own praxis, and their observations of the praxis of Jesuit organisations and of other members of the Network, indicated that there was a shared Network praxis. This shared praxis was experienced by research participants as an Ignatian 'way of proceeding'. Indeed, Ignatian spirituality often mediated CST for the research participants; they were not conscious of the source in CST of many concepts that they were using and which they experienced as Ignatian.[10] For example, here one Jesuit identifies the option for the poor as an element of Ignatian spirituality rather than originating in CST:

> The Jesuits that work for the migrant ... we have many encouragements from the spirituality of the Jesuits. The first thing that preferential option for the poor, for me that's the first motivation because I see the migrant, with my personal experience the migrant is the poor, the poorest among the poor ... and when the spirituality is the preference, option for the poor, the Jesuit is encouraged to think about them and work for them. (J8)

Another Jesuit uses CST principles to assess action even while claiming not to be acting in a manner informed by CST:

> In my case, I don't go to the Catholic Social Teaching to do what the Catholic Social Teaching says ... But for me the criteria comes, and the first one is, the most important thing is, the dignity of the person. (J1)

Even among those research participants who showed evidence of reflecting critically on their motivations, action and thinking, and on the dynamic interconnection of these elements of praxis, several Ignatian practices, such as discernment, were often taken for granted, rather than critically examined. Together with the lack of consciousness of the sources of concepts being used, this raises the question of the role of the *habitus* in the praxis of the Network.

Although the case study did not set out to examine the personal or team reflexivity of the members of the Network, the focus of research participants' reflexivity emerged as the central phenomenon from the content analysis of the interview data. Different focuses of reflexivity that were demonstrated by research participants were associated with

---

10 For further details of this research, see Cornish, 'How Catholic Social Teaching and Ignatian Spirituality Interact'.

different patterns in the way in which they drew on CST and/or Ignatian spirituality. Some participants cast their gaze back on themselves as actors in a one-dimensional manner by reflecting only on their action. Others reflected also on their thinking about issues and situations but did so separately from reflection on action; their focus of reflexivity was two-dimensional. A third cluster of participants reflected critically on their action, thinking, and on the interaction between them. Only members of this third cluster, who demonstrated a holistic focus of reflexivity, were able to integrate, synthesise and move easily between sources of praxis including CST and Ignatian spirituality. In this example, a Jesuit research participant moves easily between Ignatian spirituality, primal religions, and traditional cultures in his reflection:

> In indigenous religiosity we talk about everyday sacredness. It is not just in the place of worship... it's an experiential sacredness that we talk about. So the spirit world is not just out there ... one can access it any time. But actually it articulates very well with Ignatian spirituality, seeing God in all things would be, you know, the Ignatian way of saying God is everywhere therefore God is in our sacred space ... he is everywhere ... The other thing I realised in doing the retreat with the students at the university level is, to me you realise that God is at work in your cultures. Not their Christian cultures, but their ... traditional cultures. And then to push the boundary a bit to say that God is at work in your traditional beliefs, so we said the religiosity of the people, including traditional religions is also where God is at work ... It's not just in humans but also around them, in nature, in cultures, in traditional or primal religions now we call it ... They may not call it Ignatian spirituality. (J3)

This finding raises the question of how personal and/or team reflexivity may inform the praxis of people and organisations inspired by Ignatian spirituality. Hence this paper is concerned with the interplay of structure and agency within the Network, and with the relevance of the *habitus* and reflexivity more specifically.

Drawing on the interviews conducted for the case study, this paper places the experience of the Network in dialogue with Mouzelis' restructuring of Bourdieu's theory of action.[11] It argues that the Network's shared praxis can be understood as a reflexive *habitus* and demonstrates how particular Ignatian practices embody apophatic or cataphatic reflexivity.[12]

---

11 Mouzelis, 'Habitus and Reflexivity'.
12 Nicos Mouzelis, 'Self and Self-Other Reflexivity: The Apophatic Dimension', *European Journal of Social Theory* 13, no. 2 (2010): 271–84.

The *habitus* and reflexivity

The concept of reflexivity dates back to the beginnings of sociology and has been understood in a variety of ways. While Mead saw reflexivity as 'the turning back of the experience of the individual upon [her- or himself]',[13] Archer's influential contemporary work defines it as 'the regular exercise of the mental ability, shared by all normal people, to consider themselves in relation to their (social) contexts and vice versa'.[14] One of Archer's insights is that people may exercise reflexivity differently—their internal conversations differ. She sees this as being linked with the relations that they establish with their social contexts, especially their socialisation in family of origin, and their main concerns. Through her empirical work, Archer identifies four modes of reflexivity—communicative reflexivity, autonomous reflexivity, meta-reflexivity and fractured reflexivity—which stem from different kinds of internal conversations.[15] Research participants in the case study also exercised reflexivity in different ways; however, the differences that emerged from the data were not in relation to a mode of reflexivity but, rather, the focus of their reflexivity—they focused their reflection on themselves as actors on different things.

Archer emphatically rejects Bourdieu's theory of action, and especially his concept of the *habitus*, as over- emphasising structure and neglecting agency.[16] Other theorists have tried to reconcile, combine or hybridise the two approaches,[17] an effort rejected by Archer.[18]

As we have noted, for Bourdieu, the *habitus* is a set of dispositions or generative schemata that is the major link between social structures and practices. As Mouzelis explains, 'social structures, via various socialisation

---

[13] Mead, 1934, 134 quoted in Charalambos Tsekeris, 'Reflections on Reflexivity: Sociological Issues and Perspectives', *Contemporary Issues* 3, no. 1 (2010): 28–36. 28.
[14] Margaret Archer, *Making Our Way Through the World: Human Reflexivity and Social Mobility* (Cambridge, UK: Cambridge University Press, 2007), 4.
[15] Margaret Archer, *Structure, Agency and the Internal Conversation* (Cambridge, UK: Cambridge University Press, 2003).
[16] Margaret Archer, 'Routine, Reflexivity and Realism', *Sociological Theory* 28, no. 3 (2010): 272–303.
[17] Gisli Volger, 'Power between Habitus and Reflexivity—Introducing Margaret Archer to the Power Debate', *Journal of Political Power* 9, no. 1 (2016): 65–82, http://dx.doi.org/10.1080/2158379X.2016.1149309; Ana Caetano, 'Defining Personal Reflexivity: A Critical Reading of Archer's Approach', *European Journal of Social Theory* 18, no. 1 (2015): 60–75; Ana Caetano, 'Coping with Life: A Typology of Personal Reflexivity', *The Sociological Quarterly* 58, no. 1 (2017): 32–50.
[18] Archer, 'Routine, Reflexivity and Realism'.

processes, are internalised and become dispositions, and dispositions lead to practices which, in turn, reproduce social structures'.[19] The dispositions of the *habitus* are not usually consciously present to their carriers, but nonetheless give them a 'feel for the game' when they enter a 'field' characterised by a system of positions. Mouzelis challenges Bourdieu's view that reflexivity only emerges when a crisis arises because the *habitus* and the system of positions of a 'field' are incongruent.

Mouzelis' restructuring of Bourdieu's theory of action makes space both for the pre-reflexive action characteristic of the *habitus*, and the routine exercise of reflexive accounting, conscious strategising, and rational calculation. He says the *habitus* doesn't strictly determine the practices but rather operates as a limiting framework within which a great number of practices may be produced. Bourdieu argues that when the *habitus* carrier enters a 'field', its 'positions', will shape practice, Mouzelis, however, adds that the interaction with actual players (who may or may not reproduce the practices expected of their role or position) also shapes action. To dispositional and positional structures, he adds figurative or interactive structures. Mouzelis holds that a player needs to combine the taken-for-granted practical logic of dispositions with the reflexive-calculative logic resulting from interaction in actual situations. Thus, reflexivity emerges when there are incongruities between dispositional, positional, and figurative structures, or *intra-habitus* contradictions. Rational and/or reflexive calculation also appears when people are reflexive, irrespective of how congruent or incongruent dispositions are vis-a-vis positions or figurations.[20]

Mouzelis points out that a reflexive disposition can be acquired via socialisation. He gives the example of religious communities that stress the importance of the inner life and thus socialise members into a reflexive *habitus*. He emphasises apophatic reflexivity as a counterpoint to what he perceives to be an overemphasis on cataphatic reflexivity. Apophatic reflexivity turns inwards to remove obstacles, such as thinking and decision-making processes, which prevent the spontaneous emergence of personal goals[21] or open ended self-self and self-other relationships.[22] Cataphatic reflexivity, meanwhile, is activistic and cognitive; the self, in a purposive manner, chooses a goal and the best means of achieving it.[23]

---

19 Mouzelis, 'Habitus and Reflexivity', 1.
20 Mouzelis, 'Habitus and Reflexivity', 2.
21 Mouzelis, 'Habitus and Reflexivity', 3.
22 Mouzelis, 'Self and Self-Other Reflexivity', 272.
23 Mouzelis, 'Self and Self-Other Reflexivity', 272.

These are ideal types and elements of both modes may be found in a person's reflexive processes.

I will demonstrate that both the *habitus* and personal reflexivity are useful in understanding the experience of the Network. Moreover, I suggest that Mouzelis' concept of a reflexive *habitus* is a good fit for the shared Network praxis uncovered by the case study. His concepts of apophatic and cataphatic reflexivity help to throw light on the reflexivity of particular Ignatian practices. Limitations of the interview data preclude the systematic exploration of team reflexivity, hence further empirical work would be needed to explore the task reflexivity and social reflexivity dimensions of team reflexivity within the Network.[24]

An Ignatian *habitus*

As we have seen, the *habitus* refers to a set of dispositions or generative schemata that link social structures and practices. Meanwhile, a spirituality may be seen as a way of understanding God, the world, and one's place in it, expressed in values, attitudes, motivations or dispositions, commitments and practices.[25] In fact, one strand in the literature on Ignatian spirituality sees it as a living tradition with a particular way of proceeding that continues to take shape through expression by people and communities in concrete contexts.[26]

The expression 'our way of proceeding' has a long history and particular resonance for the Jesuits. It was a favourite phrase of Ignatius' and appears many times in the Constitutions of the Society of Jesus.[27] Jones explains it as an 'Ignatian mindset or approach which distinguishes an Ignatian culture or ethos from others'.[28] General Congregation 34 (a major international meeting of the Jesuits held in 1995) described it

---

24 Marie Adela and Didier Truchot, 'Emotional Dissonance and Burnout: The Moderating Role of Team Reflexivity and Re-Evaluation', Stress and Health 33 (2017): 179–89.
25 Michael Mason, Andrew Singleton, and Ruth Webber, *The Spirituality of Generation Y: Young People's Spirituality in a Changing Australia* (Mulgrave: John Garratt Publishing, 2007), 39–41.
26 David L. Fleming, *What Is Ignatian Spirituality?* (Chicago: Loyola Press, 2008); William A. Barry and Robert G. Doherty, *Contemplatives in Action: The Jesuit Way* (Manila: Jesuit Communications Foundation, 2002).
27 Charles Healey, *The Ignatian Way: Key Aspects of Jesuit Spirituality* (New York: Paulist, 2009), 101.
28 Ross Jones, 'Jesuit Speak: A Glossary of Jesuit Terms, People and Phrases', ed. Martin Scroope and Sandie Cornish, *Ignatian Spirituality for Today: Key Readings for Busy People* (Sydney: The Loyola Institute, 2008), 254.

as 'certain attitudes, values, and patterns of behaviour' and went on to articulate eight characteristics of the Jesuit way of proceeding which were deemed most significant for contemporary times.[29] These eight characteristics or dispositions are: 1) a deep personal love of Christ, 2) being a contemplative in action, 3) being an apostolic body within the church, 4) being in solidarity with those most in need, 5) being in partnership with others, 6) being called to learned ministry, 7) being people sent, always available for new missions, and 8) being ever ready to seek the *magis* (that is, the ever greater glory of God, the ever fuller service of our neighbour, the more universal good, the more effective apostolic means).[30]

Thus, Ignatian spirituality can be seen as a set of internalised, embodied dispositions towards the meaning of the social world, which are promoted through initial formation which socialises people into an Ignatian *habitus* in which these dispositions are expressed in Ignatian practices. Here J4 reflects on the role of initial formation in his involvement in humanitarian action:

> I think the Jesuits initiated me into this concern. It was heavy on helping those around the margins of society, those who are marginalised when I joined the Society [of Jesus]. So, I guess it was, it was the Society [of Jesus], that inculcated this concern in the first place. I guess it was, it was the Jesuit formation, you know.

Caetano's empirical work shows that the way each person reflects upon themselves in the world can change over the course of life. Changes in circumstances, contexts, particular life experiences, and on-going socialisation processes can influence this.[31] Ongoing formation in the Ignatian 'way of proceeding' includes the promotion of dispositions, practices and priorities which in turn reproduce Ignatian structures in the various contexts within which followers find themselves. It is an ongoing socialisation process that includes the development of reflexivity through socialisation into dispositions and practices which I will demonstrate in the next section to be reflexive. The three different ways in which the research participants in the case study focused their reflexivity may be

---

29 Society of Jesus, 'General Congregation 34, Decree 26: Characteristics of Our Way of Proceeding' (Rome: Curia of the Superior General, 1995), n 1.
30 General Congregation 34, 'Decree 26'.
31 Ana Caetano, 'Reflexivity and Social Change: A Critical Discussion of Reflexive Modernization and Individualization Theses', *Portuguese Journal of Social Science* 13, no. 1 (2014): 69.

typical of stages on a journey, or they may be end points for particular individuals.

The characterisation of Ignatian spirituality as a *habitus* makes sense of the lack of consciousness of the sources of concepts being used, and of the uncritical reproduction of Ignatian practices, by some research participants. Such concepts and practices have become internalised and are pre-reflexive. J4 expressed a somewhat ambiguous view on this possibility. Here he rejects the need for conscious cognitive deliberation before any action, but also resists the idea of internalised dispositions resulting in spontaneous practice:

> I'm afraid to say that it's instinct, it's common sense that takes hold when you see or when you find yourself in a situation and then you have to make decisions, you have to do something about it. Catholic social teaching doesn't come as easily, no, although some might say 'well it's been ingrained in you, it has become spontaneous' ... I never follow in that way though. Honestly, it's about in front of you you've got people dying, are you going to just stand there and watch? Of course not! I need to do something, and I don't know if that's just common sense, or you know over the years we've been in formation and somehow values got into our mind, but ... I don't know it's just a human thing to do.

Those research participants who reflected only on their action took for granted the Ignatian practices which they and/or their organisations had adopted, describing but not critiquing them. For example, here J7 describes his work with migrant workers in terms that echo the characteristics of the Jesuit way of proceeding previously introduced:

> In the work I think as Ignatian spirituality I am required to reflect, we also rally other people come together, come together to work as a team and sort of strengthen our resource by pulling more people and on more skill come to deal with the matter. And at the same time ... there is another sort of level we need to deal with like sort of educate workers of their rights, make them, empower them, make them feel strong that they need to sort of unionise themselves or stand together, to defend their rights and so to make them aware of their human rights, their worker rights and of their rights as a normal worker.

Those research participants who reflected in a two-dimensional way on action and thinking, but not on the interconnectedness of the two, described but did not critique sources of thinking in addition to describing their action. For example, J5 simply declares 'my faith determines how I decide things—I'm a Christian, I know that respect for people, charity, love is our core values'.

As Caetano notes, there is in fact repetition and structure in social dynamics and people cannot always be on the alert and consciously think through every decision and action.[32] Bourdieu's 'practical sense' makes sense; through an acquired 'feel for the game' or formation in 'our way of proceeding', an actor may know how to act in a context without thinking about it. Again, J4 explains:

> Our first instinct when we see any situation like that is to ask ourselves what can I do? It's not that I should convene first, I should have a meeting first, no what can I do and then afterwards, let's have a meeting to talk about what we have done, not the other way around.

But the *habitus* is not only a structured structure, it is also a structuring structure—it generates practices that re/create social structure. Ignatian spirituality takes shape through placing the resources of the tradition in dialogue with context to continually reinterpret these sources and generate action. For example, the General Congregations (GCs) of the Jesuits have the task of authoritatively interpreting the Constitutions of the Society of Jesus through time and of setting international priorities for mission.[33] In addition to such instances of communal apostolic discernment (discerning together for mission), the exercise of reflexivity by individual *habitus*-carriers, such as the research participants, can also generate new practices and contribute to the creation of new structures.

Those research participants who reflected critically on their action, thinking and the interconnectedness of the two, and who drew on both CST and Ignatian spirituality in multidimensional ways, were able to contribute to the ongoing development of Ignatian spirituality and of CST as sources of praxis. The interaction of the two sources of praxis was demonstrated to be mutual and generative for most of these research participants. For example, R1 spoke of her involvement in the development of the influential JRS philosophy of 'accompany, serve, and advocate' saying 'even when I joined the JRS they didn't have this thing "to accompany, to serve, to advocate"—that grew out of things that we all did together'. She also described her creation of enculturated

---

32 Caetano, 'Coping with Life', 34.
33 *The Constitutions of the Society of Jesus and Their Complementary Norms* (Saint Louis: The Institute of Jesuit Sources, 1996), n. 17.

physical symbols of key themes from CST as a result of an Ignatian process of accompaniment and conversation with the local community. It seems then that the exercise of reflexivity may be a mechanism through which different sources can be integrated or synthesised and new practices generated.

Reflexive Ignatian practices

Vogler believes that reflexivity can turn the *habitus* discursively – actors can distance themselves from their *habitus* by making it discursive. Thus, *habitus* and reflexivity are polarities rather than mutually exclusive explanations; one or the other may be more explanatory in a particular case.[34] Meanwhile, Caetano's empirical work yielded five reflexive profiles, three of which have a structural nature. She concludes that disposition and reflexivity are simply different notions that account for distinct components of action—the unconscious and conscious mechanisms behind practices.[35] Mouzelis, however, points out that reflexivity can be acquired via socialisation, in other words, that a *habitus* can be reflexive, producing reflexive practices.[36] I will now demonstrate how two core Ignatian practices are inherently reflexive.

The Spiritual Exercises

St Ignatius of Loyola's Spiritual Exercises are a key source of Ignatian spirituality and are widely considered to be his major contribution to western spirituality.[37] The Exercises are a handbook for those helping others to search for God in which Ignatius recorded the insights that he gained from his own search for God. The Exercises consist of four stages, or 'weeks', which may vary in length and contain a structured set of spiritual activities or methods. They are a foundational experience that connects all Jesuits, and many others who share in the Ignatian charism. Undertaking the Spiritual Exercises is part of the preparation to become a Jesuit priest or brother, and the Exercises are undertaken again

---

34 Volger, 'Power between Habitus and Reflexivity – Introducing Margaret Archer to the Power Debate', 75.
35 Caetano, 'Coping with Life: A Typology of Personal Reflexivity', 49.
36 Mouzelis, 'Habitus and Reflexivity'.
37 Dean Brackley, 'The Call to Discernment in Troubled Times' (New York: The Crossroad Publishing Company, 2004); Javier Melloni, 'The Exercises of St Ignatius of Loyola in the Western Tradition', Inigo Texts Series (Leominster: Gracewing, 2000).

during the final stage of Jesuit formation. They can be seen as a key tool of socialisation into the Ignatian *habitus*. Several Ignatian dispositions and practices grounded in the Exercises are reflexive in nature. Due to limitations of space, I will focus on the examen and discernment.

Indifference

A statement of worldview known as the Principle and Foundation stands at the heart of the First Week of the Exercises.[38] In it, Ignatius asserts that human beings are created to praise, reverence, and serve God, and that all created things should be used, or not used, to the extent that they serve this goal. The First Week is a purgative way, a process of letting go, of emptying, or of purification. It is about becoming free from all inordinate attachments and biases in order to make choices that lead to this end for which human beings have been created. Ignatius calls this 'indifference'. Indifference is a prerequisite for sound discernment and is cultivated, among other ways, through the regular practice of the examen.

In a similar way, Mouzelis, referencing Eastern Orthodox spirituality, speaks of an apophatic reflexivity that adopts a *via negativa* in which barriers to direct encounter with the divine are stripped away, allowing the spontaneous emergence of genuine personal goals or open-ended self-self and self-other relationships.[39] The direct encounter with the divine of which Mouzelis speaks is consistent with Ignatius' insistence that God deals directly with people through their deepest desires. The Ignatian concept of deepest desires is also similar to Archer's belief that subjects deliberate through internal conversations on their 'ultimate concerns', that is, their values and commitments that make up a meaningful existence.

The examen

The First Week of the Exercises introduces the examen, also known as the examination of consciousness, as a regular practice to help people become more aware of God's action in their lives.[40] It follows these steps:

---

38 St Ignatius of Loyola, 'The Spiritual Exercises', *The Spiritual Exercises of St Ignatius: A New Translation Based on Studies in the Language of the Autograph* (Makati City, Philippines: St Pauls, 1987), n. 23.
39 Mouzelis, 'Self and Self-Other Reflexivity'.
40 St Ignatius of Loyola, 'The Spiritual Exercises', n. 43.

1. give thanks to God for favours received,
2. ask for the grace to know one's sins and to rid oneself of them,
3. a systematic review of one's thoughts, feelings, words, and deeds over a period of time,
4. ask for forgiveness of faults,
5. the resolution to amend one's way, looking to the future and planning action.

The examen is intended to be a daily practice continued beyond the spiritual retreat in which one undertakes the Exercises. The third step of the examen is clearly an invitation to the daily exercise of personal reflexivity. In the Ignatian spirituality literature, it is described as an invitation to notice God's action in oneself and in the world, and to develop the capacity for contemplation.[41] It also involves the on-going effort to notice and let go of inordinate attachments as noted above. Ignatian spirituality, however, is not simply contemplative but also active, as we saw in the identification of being contemplatives in action as a key characteristic of the Ignatian way of proceeding. The fifth step of the examen links reflexivity with the further development of practice. The examen is also about purposively choosing the path of action that best responds to God's call. Hence the examen engages the exercise of both apophatic and cataphatic reflexivity.

The examen can be employed collectively as well as personally, for example international documents of the Jesuits, such as the Decrees of their GCs, often follow the format of the examen quite explicitly. Further empirical work could explore the use of a collective examen in the team reflexivity of Ignatian organisations.

Whether personal or communal, the examen prepares the ground for discernment—a practice by which people and groups read their interior spiritual movements in order to make choices that respond to God's call.

Discernment

The Second Week of the Exercises is centered on making an 'election' or well-ordered choice about one's life through the process of discernment. This is consistent with Archer's assertion that through reflexive internal conversations people deliberate on the best way to establish a life

---

41 Timothy Gallagher, *The Examen Prayer: Ignatian Wisdom for Our Lives Today* (New York: Crossroad, 2006), 118–21.

project or *modus vivendi* consonant with their ultimate concerns. The subject's 'ultimate concerns' provide a 'sounding board' for these internal conversations.[42] For Ignatius, the ultimate concern is responding to God's unique call to each person or group to love and serve God. For example, GC 36 Decree 1 says that 'rather than ask what we should do' the Jesuits 'seek to understand how God invites us ... to share in' the 'ministry of reconciliation God has begun in Christ'.[43] As we have seen, the Exercises position apophatic reflexivity as a necessary preparation for the exercise of the cataphatic reflexivity required to choose the course of action that best responds to this call.

Discernment is introduced in an appendix to the Exercises that includes two sets of rules for discernment in different circumstances.[44] Ignatius speaks of the movements produced in our souls by good and bad spirits, and associates these either with the Spirit of God, and the angels, or with Satan, or the 'enemy of our human nature'.[45] Lonsdale believes that one does not need to accept this pre-Freudian theoretical framework in order to practise discernment. He stresses the direction in which a person's feelings are leading—towards love, growth, and relationship or towards destructive forms of behaviour that undermine solidarity and destroy love and community—rather than their origin.[46] The bad spirit can be seen as leading people to become less fully human and to disordered relationships. The good spirit can be seen as leading people towards becoming more fully human, towards integral human development, and right relationships.

Turning attention back on the self to notice the interior movements of spiritual consolation and desolation is critical to Ignatius's treatment of discernment. Consolation is characterised by an increase in faith, hope, and love, whereas desolation is its opposite.[47] The rules for discernment in the First Week suggest that when people are caught up on the wrong path, false consolation can block change.[48] Conversely, when a person is

---

42 David Farrugia and Dan Woodman, 'Ultimate Concerns in Late Modernity: Archer, Bourdieu and Reflexivity', *The British Journal of Sociology* 66, no. 4 (2015): 628.
43 General Congregation 36, 'Decree 1: Companions in a Mission of Reconciliation and Justice', *Documents of General Congregation 36 of the Society of Jesus* (Rome: Society of Jesus, 2017), https://jesuits.eu/images/docs/GC_36_Documents.pdf. n 3.
44 St Ignatius of Loyola, 'The Spiritual Exercises'. n 131-136.
45 St Ignatius of Loyola, n. 329-336.
46 David Lonsdale, 'Discernment of Spirits', ed. George W Traub, *An Ignatian Spirituality Reader* (Chicago: Loyola Press, 2008), 178-81.
47 St Ignatius of Loyola, 'The Spiritual Exercises'. n 316- 317.
48 St Ignatius of Loyola, n. 314.

on the right path, they may be blocked by desolation.[49] Ignatius suggests that we need to be patient and not reverse well-made decisions at the first sign of opposition or trouble.[50] These interior movements are not merely cognitive, they are also affective.

Mouzelis points out that Eastern Orthodox spirituality considers thinking, decision making and even imagination as obstacles which are to be peripheralised or subdued in order to experience the divine energy directly.[51] Ignatius, on the other hand, engages the imagination, uses thought experiments, and proposes one technique (amongst others) of discernment that is entirely rational and cognitive—simply listing and considering pros and cons. However, Ignatian spirituality is not simply a way of thinking; it is a way of the heart and engages all of the senses. Ignatius proposes meditation exercises in which one ponders the words of Scripture, as well as contemplative exercises in which one places oneself imaginatively within the action, attending to the sights, sounds, smells and feelings that arise. For Ignatius, thinking and imagination are spaces in which the person can have a direct experience of the divine. Indeed, Ignatian spirituality is deeply incarnational; God is to be found in all things. The disposition of indifference may lead different people to let go of different things in order to have the inner freedom to find and follow the will of God.

While religious communities may commonly focus on the inner life and socialise members into a reflexive *habitus*, different spiritualities may give greater emphasis to either apophatic or cataphatic reflexivity, and they may combine them in distinctive ways. The dynamics of the Spiritual Exercises and the practices of the examen and discernment each hold apophatic and cataphatic forms of reflexivity in creative balance. This distinctive feature of the reflexive Ignatian *habitus* of the Network can be summed up in the phrase 'contemplatives in action'.

A question for Catholic Social Teaching

Like Ignatian spirituality, CST is a living tradition that continues to take shape through expression by people and communities as they place its sources and resources in dialogue with reality in concrete contexts. It, too,

---

49 St Ignatius of Loyola, n. 315.
50 St Ignatius of Loyola, n. 318-319.
51 Mouzelis, 'Self and Self-Other Reflexivity'.

can develop by turning its gaze back on itself, refining its understanding of social processes.

The interplay of structure and agency come into focus in CST in the concept of structures of sin. During the 1960s, Latin American liberation theology and German political theology were critical of a focus on the private rather than social dimension of sin.[52] The concept of social sin or structures of sin suggests that social structures, processes and institutions can reflect and embody sin and constrain human action, entrenching and encouraging sin and making it harder for people to act justly. In other words, structure can constrain agency. Kristin Heyer explains that understandings of social sin vary from 'limiting it to the effects or embodiment of personal sin, to an expansive sense of all sin as primarily social, with personal sins as mere manifestations of social sin'.[53]

In his teachings, John Paul II affirmed the concept, clarifying CST's stance on the significance of structures of sin and their relationship with personal freedom and responsibility. In *Reconciliatio et Paenitentia*, he explains social sin as the result of the personal sins:

> of those who cause or support evil or who exploit it; of those who are in a position to avoid, eliminate or at least limit certain social evils but who fail to do so out of laziness, fear or the conspiracy of silence, through secret complicity or indifference; of those who take refuge in the supposed impossibility of changing the world, and also of those who sidestep the effort and sacrifice required, producing specious reasons of a higher order.[54]

For John Paul II, situations, institutions, structures, and societies are not the subject of moral acts—real responsibility for social sin lies with individuals. In *Sollicitudo Rei Socialis*, he identifies the 'all-consuming desire for profit' and 'the thirst for power' as typical structures of sin.[55] Structures of sin create obstacles for people and institutions that are difficult to overcome. They are rooted in personal sin, consolidating it, helping it to 'grow stronger, spread, and become the source of other sins'.[56]

---

52 Kristin Heyer, *Kinship Across Borders: A Christian Ethic of Immigration* (Washington DC: Georgetown University Press, 2012), 37–39.
53 Heyer, 37.
54 John Paul II, *Reconciliatio et Paenitentia*, 1984, n. 16. https://www.vatican.va/content/john-paul-ii/en/apost_exhortations/documents/hf_jp-ii_exh_02121984_reconciliatio-et-paenitentia.html
55 Pope John Paul II, *Sollicitudo Rei Socialis* (SRS), 1987. n 37. https://www.vatican.va/content/john-paul-ii/en/encyclicals/documents/hf_jp-ii_enc_30121987_sollicitudo-rei-socialis.html
56 SRS, n. 36.

Daniel Finn favours a critical realist approach to sociology and sees social structures as systems of human relations among social positions. They have causal impact in people's lives through 'the restrictions, enablements, and incentives which structures present to individuals who operate within them'.[57] Such causal impact may be either positive or negative. People retain free will, but some choices are more costly than others.[58] Finn charges that CST:

> should go beyond simple statements that social structures exist and have an impact, to analyse what they are, how they arise, how they are reproduced over time, how they can be changed, and most importantly how they have powerful causal impact through human freedom.[59]

I suggest that sinful structures can be internalised in a *habitus* that reproduces them, for example, through the taken for granted 'supposed impossibility of changing the world' that Pope John Paul II points out. This case study points to the possibility of a reflexive *habitus*—a *habitus* that actively socialises members into reflexive practices that can generate new dispositions and practices rather than simply reproducing existing structures. The concept of a reflexive *habitus* can simultaneously explain the unconscious or nonvoluntary aspect of social sin while affirming the freedom and responsibility to critique unjust structures and generate new practices and structures—structures of grace. Demonstrating how Ignatian spirituality can be understood as a reflexive *habitus* suggests the importance of spirituality as a way of changing structures of sin. The emphasis that Pope Francis gives to spirituality in the final chapters of both *Laudato Si'* and *Fratelli Tutti* points in the same direction.

Pope Francis as an Ignatian *habitus*-carrier

At the heart of the Jesuits' contemporary understanding of their mission is 'the call to share God's work of reconciliation in our broken world'.[60] It is expressed in a three-fold commitment to reconciliation with God, with one another, and with the whole of creation, which addresses both

---

57 Daniel K Finn, 'What Is a Sinful Social Structure?', *Theological Studies* 77, no. 1 (2016): 151.
58 Finn, 'What Is a Sinful Social Structure?', 152.
59 Finn, 'What Is a Sinful Social Structure?', 163.
60 General Congregation 36, 'Decree 1: Companions in a Mission of Reconciliation and Justice'. n 21.

personal sin and sinful structures.[61] It is hardly surprising then that these are key themes in the teaching of the first Jesuit Pope, especially in his two social encyclicals to date.

While Pope Francis sets out five general 'lines of approach and action' in chapter five of *Laudato Si'*, the final chapter culminates in a call to ecological spirituality as the key to change. Francis says that a commitment as lofty as 'passionate concern for the protection of our world' requires 'a spirituality capable of inspiring us' rather than doctrine alone.[62] He sets out elements of an ecological spirituality and calls for a personal and communal 'ecological conversion' in order to achieve 'reconciliation with creation'.[63]

According to Francis, Christian spirituality proposes a different way of understanding 'quality of life' from that of the technocratic and consumeristic paradigm that dominates our world.[64] It encourages a prophetic and contemplative lifestyle marked by moderation, simplicity, gratitude, detachment from possessions, the avoidance of the dynamic of domination and the recovery of a 'healthy humility' and a 'happy sobriety'.[65] Francis points out that 'inner peace is closely related to care for ecology and for the common good' and that 'an integral ecology includes taking time to recover a serene harmony with creation, reflecting on our lifestyle and our ideals, and contemplating the Creator who lives among us and surrounds us'.[66] Such a spirituality is not merely personal but also 'civic and political' affecting not only inter-personal relationships 'but also macro-relationships, social, economic and political ones'.[67] An ecological spirituality entails a sense of kinship with all people and all of creation, expressed in both inter-personal and structural action in favour of care for the most disadvantaged or vulnerable members of the 'splendid universal communion' of God's creatures.[68] These understandings of the world,

---

61 General Congregation 36, 'Decree 1: Companions in a Mission of Reconciliation and Justice'. n. 21-30; see also *General Congregation 35, Decree 3: Challenges to Our Mission Today: Sent to the Frontiers* (Oxford: The Society of Jesus in Association with Way Books, 2008), n 12-36.
62 Pope Francis, *Laudato Si'*(LS), 2015. n 216. https://www.vatican.va/content/francesco/en/encyclicals/documents/papa-francesco_20150524_enciclica-laudato-si.html
63 LS, n. 218-219.
64 LS, n. 222.
65 LS, n. 222, 224.
66 LS, n. 218-219.
67 LS, n. 231.
68 LS, n. 220.

values, dispositions and practices can also be seen as elements of a reflexive Ignatian *habitus*.

In *Fratelli Tutti*, Francis focuses on reconciliation among people and communities. Here he elaborates on his frequent call for a culture of encounter, dialogue, and accompaniment, and stresses the contribution that religions can make to social harmony.

In a world marked by the 'parallel monologues' of social media,[69] Francis calls for real dialogue in which we approach, speak, listen, look at, come to know and to understand one another, and find common ground.[70] He says that a culture of encounter means that we 'should be passionate about meeting others, seeking points of contact, building bridges, planning a project that includes everyone' and that this should become 'an aspiration and a style of life'.[71] He urges us to 'hear the true stories' of victims of violence and people pushed to the edges, to 'look at reality through their eyes' and to 'listen with an open heart to the stories that they tell'.[72] Francis says that 'no one can possess the whole truth or satisfy his or her every desire' and so we need a 'dialogic realism' in which we remain faithful to our own principles while recognising that others also have the right to do the same.[73]

Similarly, in his encouragement of a more synodal way of being Church, Francis promotes the practice of spiritual conversation as part of the preparation for the Synod on Communion, Participation and Mission at the diocesan, Bishops Conference and Continental levels. GC 36 presents spiritual conversation as 'an essential tool that can animate apostolic communal discernment' that involves 'an exchange marked by active and receptive listening and a desire to speak of that which touches us most deeply ... with the objective of choosing the path of consolation that fortifies our faith, hope and love'.[74] Its use within the Society of Jesus was initiated by Ignatius himself.[75]

---

69 Pope Francis, *Fratelli Tutti* (FT), 2020, n 200. https://www.vatican.va/content/francesco/en/encyclicals/documents/papa-francesco_20201003_enciclica-fratelli-tutti.html
70 FT, n. 198.
71 FT, n. 216.
72 FT, n. 261.
73 FT, n. 221.
74 General Congregation 36, 'Decree 1: Companions in a Mission of Reconciliation and Justice'. n 12.
75 Laurence Loubières provides an introduction to spiritual conversation within the Society of Jesus: 'Spiritual conversation: a heart-to-heart dialogue'. https://jesuits.ca/stories/spiritual-conversation-a-heart-to-heart-dialogue/.

Francis ends *Fratelli Tutti* by pointing to religious belief as the ultimate foundation of a sense of being one human family.[76] He says that without openness to God as 'Father of all' there can be 'no solid and stable reasons for an appeal to fraternity' and that the 'effort to seek God' helps believers of different religions to recognise one another as 'truly brothers and sisters'.[77] Meanwhile, a 'desensitised human conscience ... and the prevailing individualism accompanied by materialistic philosophies that deify the human person' have replaced transcendent principles with material values. Hence the mission of the Church must engage the political sphere to 'reawaken the spiritual energy' that can animate the common good.[78]

The dispositions and practices promoted by Francis' social teaching encourage us to reflect on our own positioning and perspectives, to be open to critical reflection on them in the light of the experiences and perspectives of others, and to embrace 'indifference' and responsiveness to God's will. They can be seen as practices of reflexivity with potential to generate new practices and structures and they are strongly linked to Ignatian spirituality and its 'way of proceeding'.[79] Francis may be seen as a carrier of a reflexive Ignatian *habitus*.

Conclusion

Neither Bourdieu's *habitus* nor personal reflexivity alone adequately explain the results of the case study. There was evidence of pre-reflexive action, and the exercise of reflexivity that was evident was not adequately explained by the presence of a crisis. The characterisation of Ignatian spirituality as a *habitus* makes sense of the lack of consciousness of the sources of concepts being used, and of the uncritical reproduction of Ignatian practices, by some research participants.

Discernment is a distinctively Ignatian characteristic of the shared Network praxis identified by the case study. And, as we have demonstrated, this core practice of Ignatian spirituality is inherently reflexive. Formation in Ignatian spirituality and socialisation into the Ignatian 'way of proceeding' encourage the development of reflexivity through practices such as the examen and discernment.

---

76 FT, n. 272.
77 FT, n. 272, 274.
78 FT, n. 276.
79 General Congregation 36, 'Decree 1: Companions in a Mission of Reconciliation and Justice'. n 11.

The experience of the Network reflects Mouzelis' insights that reflexivity can be acquired by socialisation and that the *habitus* of religious communities may be reflexive. For example, GC36 Decree 1, reflecting on a key tool of socialisation into the *habitus* of the Society of Jesus, says 'the question that confronts the Society today is why the Exercises do not change us as deeply as we would hope. What elements in our lives, works, or lifestyles hinder our ability to let God's gracious mercy transform us?'[80]

Unlike Eastern Orthodox spirituality in which apophatic reflexivity is dominant, Ignatian spirituality holds apophatic and cataphatic forms of reflexivity in creative balance through the dynamics of the Spiritual Exercises and their on-going expression in practices such as the examen and discernment. While a reflexive *habitus* may be common among faith-based social and ecological justice organisations, the nature of the spirituality that inspires different organisations could result in quite different forms of reflexivity and hence distinctively different expressions of praxis.

The possibility of spiritualities forming people in reflexive practices points to the potential power of spirituality in addressing structures of sin. Pope Francis' social teaching reflects this position, giving significantly more attention to the role of spirituality in social, economic and ecological transformation than his predecessors.

---

80 General Congregation 36, 'Decree 1: Companions in a Mission of Reconciliation and Justice', n. 18.

Chapter Nine

What is spiritual health?

Peter Carblis

Introduction

Practical theology is essentially operational. Healing is at the core of its mission. The task of the practical theologian is to think through the implications of the *Missio Dei*, to understand their application in the myriad fields of human endeavour and provide contextualised guidance for practice and living. The *Missio Dei* has both salvific and eschatological elements. The salvific elements have healing at their core. The eschatological elements describe the end state or outcomes that the work of the salvific elements will bring about. The eschatological elements envisage and declare the restoration and fulfilment of humanity's and creation's goodness as purposed by their Creator.

To fulfil their mission, then, practical theologians need theologically sound operational definitions of healing and health. In particular, they need to pay attention to the conceptualisation and application of spiritual health that allows for authentic practice in pluralistic settings. This paper proposes a New Testament understanding of spiritual health grounded in the statement of the New Covenant.

The paper proceeds in two main sections. In the first section, it provides a critical review of current attempts to engage with the meaning of spiritual health and explores the current consensus around its definition. The second section expands and centres this consensus on a New Covenant understanding.

The first section begins by examining the relationship between the concepts of health, healing, and holiness. It argues that reductionist tendencies of the modern age have failed to eliminate consideration of the spiritual aspect of health and healing in their definitions. Echoes of the spiritual dimension of health remain loud, however, in the etymologies of these words and in current popular intuitions about health and healing. It considers the approach of the World Health Organisation (WHO) to health and its recognition of the dimensions of physical, mental, social, and spiritual well-being. It considers conceptions of health and healing in modern medicine and the approach to mental health taken in recent years in the emergence of positive psychology. While noting that all aspects of this dimension are relevant to the practical theologian, it draws particular attention to the concept of spiritual health and considers recent attempts to define spiritual health and healing.

The second section begins by criticising the approaches developed so far as insufficient because of their generality. This section includes a more specific consideration of the place of healing and the attributes of the spiritual health implied within the Biblical narrative that culminates in the statement of New Covenant, a promise of interior renovation and transformation.[1] It will not at this point consider other passages that could be related to spiritual health, such as the fruit of the Spirit and the beatitudes. The focus on the statement of the New Covenant is because of the priority of this passage as the culmination of the Biblical narrative of covenant and its structure as a statement of intent. The paper concludes by briefly noting the breadth of Christian services whose mission contributes to the development and promotion of spiritual health thus defined.

Defining health and healing
A failed reduction

Current attempts to define health suffer from the recent separation and demotion of religion and spirituality from medicine so often encountered in developed economies. In less developed economies, there is often little or no separation.[2] This demotion reduces the meaning of health to the empirical constraints of modern medicine and denies or ignores health's essential spiritual components. It has been said that Western medicine 'shorn of every vestige of mystery, faith, or moral portent, is an aberration in the world scene'.[3]

---

[1] Hebrews 8:10–12.
[2] Harold George Koenig, 'Religion, Spirituality, and Health: The Research and Clinical Implications', *ISRN Psychiatry* 2012 (16 December 2012): 1, https://doi.org/10.5402/2012/278730; Harold George Koenig, Michael E. McCullough, and David B. Larson, *Handbook of Religion and Health* (Oxford University Press, 2001), 24–49.
[3] Thomas G. Plante, ed., *Religion, Spirituality, and Positive Psychology: Understanding the Psychological Fruits of Faith* (Santa Barbara, Calif: Praeger, 2012), xvi.

This denial has resulted in medicine becoming unable to offer a clear operational definition of healing.[4] Health has too often been reduced to the absence of disease, injury, or impairment with a focus on curing rather than healing.[5] This tendency has often resulted in the dehumanising reduction of patients to little more than organ systems and diseases. The one who should be the healer becomes little more than an impersonal and disinterested biomechanical technician. It is not surprising, then, that modern attempts to arrive at a clear and comprehensive definition of health that do not adequately incorporate its spiritual dimensions have proven to be incomplete. Such attempts are essentially reductive. They are effectively trying to define something in terms of less than that which it is. Such efforts will always prove frustrating and inadequate.

There is, however, increasing resistance to the demotion of spirituality and religion. A sustained emphasis in the literature on the development of continuous healing relationships between medical practitioners and their patients is evidence of this resistance. Studies relating to nurse-patient relationships and the significance of spirituality and spiritual care in nursing are prominent in the nursing literature.[6] Sulmasy argues for the extension of the biopsychosocial model of care to include the spiritual concerns of patients.[7] Vieten et al. proposed sixteen spiritual and religious competencies for psychologists categorised as attitudes, knowledge and skills.[8] Proposed as baseline competencies, their scope is limited and avoid engaging with the particularities essential to spiritual and religious beliefs (p. 10). Moreia-Almeida et al. reported on the approval by World Psychiatric Association (WPA) of seven spiritual and religious considerations that, regardless of the precise definitions and particularities of spiritualities and religions, should be central to the clinical, academic and ethical aspects

---

4 Thomas R. Egnew, 'The Meaning of Healing: Transcending Suffering', *Annals of Family Medicine* 3, no. 3 (May 2005): 256, https://doi.org/10.1370/afm.313.
5 Charles J. Corcoran, 'The Catholic Physician, Health and Holiness', 1980, 211; Egnew, 'The Meaning Of Healing', 255; Christina M. Puchalski, 'The Role of Spirituality in Health Care', *Proceedings (Baylor University. Medical Center)* 14, no. 4 (October 2001): 352.
6 Puchalski, Christina M., Robert Vitillo, Sharon K. Hull, and Nancy Reller. 2014. 'Improving the Spiritual Dimension of Whole Person Care: Reaching National and International Consensus'. *Journal of Palliative Medicine* 17 (6): 642–56; Fiona Timmins and Sílvia Caldeira, 'Understanding Spirituality and Spiritual Care in Nursing' 31, no. 22 (18 October 2015): 50–57.
7 A Biopsychosocial-Spiritual Model for the Care of Patients at the End of Life', *The Gerontologist* 42, no. suppl_3 (1 October 2002): 24–33.
8 Cassandra Vieten et al., 'Spiritual and Religious Competencies for Psychologists', *Psychology of Religion and Spirituality*, 2013, 7, 10.

of psychiatry.⁹ Despite these positive trends, there remains an attitudinal malaise in the medical world that is hostile to spirituality in any form.¹⁰

Other attempts to escape the rigidity of empirical norms have defined health as the ability to cope with the demands of daily life, transcending suffering, or a state of balance or equilibrium established between a person's self and their social and physical environment.¹¹ These attempts are also inadequate. Failing to adequately recognise the spiritual aspect of health, they despairingly demand that those who suffer intractable ill-health 'recover' by simply redefining health as the ability to endure that which should not be.

The *Oxford English Dictionary* evidences the reductiveness of current usage by limiting health to the soundness of the body and the due and efficient discharge of bodily functions. The same entry marks the association of health with spiritual, moral or mental soundness and even salvation as archaic. Health, thus defined, obscures the broader more holistic intuitions and understandings embedded in the meaning of the word and its cognates. This reduction is damaging. By obscuring the spiritual aspect of health, it denies the element of hope embedded in a full concept of health and prevents development of the conceptualisation and integration of the spiritual dimension.

The spiritual dimension is and always has been an inseparable component of *health, heal, healing* and *holiness*. The etymologies of these words reveal the inextricably wovenness of themes in these words that relate to and integrate physical, psychological and spiritual wholeness. Similar intricacies exist within the health and healing related words in both testaments.¹²

The English words, *health, heal,* and *healing* have emerged from Old English roots shared with Old High German and other Germanic and Norse languages. Together these words referred to a category of overlapping concepts that included wholeness, soundness of body,

---

9   'WPA Position Statement on Spirituality and Religion in Psychiatry', *World Psychiatry* 15, no. 1 (February 2016): 87–88, https://doi.org/10.1002/wps.20304.
10 Michael Balboni and Tracy J. Balboni, *Hostility to Hospitality - Google Books* (New York: Oxford University Press, 2018); Lester Liao, 'Spiritual Care in Medicine', *JAMA* 318, no. 24 (26 December 2017): 2495.
11 Harald Brüssow, 'What Is Health?', *Microbial Biotechnology* 6, no. 4 (July 2013): 341; Norman Sartorius, 'The Meanings of Health and Its Promotion', *Croatian Medical Journal* 47, no. 4 (August 2006): 662; John Glenn Scott et al., 'Healing Journey: A Qualitative Analysis of the Healing Experiences of Americans Suffering from Trauma and Illness', *BMJ Open* 7, no. 8 (1 August 2017): 1.
12 W. Foester, 'σῴζω, σωτηρία, σωτήρ, σωτήριος', in *Theological Dictionary of the New Testament Σ*, ed. Gerhard Kittel and Gerhard Friedrich, vol. 7 (Grand Rapids: William B. Eerdmans Publishing Company, 1971), 965; Frederick J. Gaiser, *Healing in the Bible: Theological Insight for Christian Ministry* (Baker Academic, 2010).

freedom from sickness, the process of healing, remedies, well-being, safety, prosperity, spiritual health, moral soundness, and salvation. The word *holy* derives from the Old English *hál* which referred to being uninjured or whole. This root is still reflected in the saying 'hale and hearty.' The pre-Christian usage of *hálig/heilag* is likely to have referred to something inviolate that must be preserved whole and cannot be damaged with impunity.[13]

Despite the operational naturalism of the many if not most of the educated elite and practitioners of medicine and their abandonment of anything spiritual, evidence for the continuation of these associations is prolific in popular culture. Too often this has handed attention to the spiritual dimension of healing to dangerous quacks, charlatans, and well-intentioned but ill-informed naïveties. Problems that arise from this are beautifully illustrated in the opening verse from Cher's still popular song *Gypsies, Tramps, and Thieves*:

> I was born in the wagon of a travelin' show
> My mama used to dance for the money they'd throw
> Papa would do whatever he could
> Preach a little gospel, sell a couple bottles of Doctor Good[14]

Four dimensions of health

Perhaps the most influential definition of health in the current era is that written into the preamble of the World Health Organization. Approved in 1948, the same year that the United Nations adopted and proclaimed the Universal Declaration of Human Rights,[15] the WHO constitution defined health as 'a state of complete physical, mental and social well-being and not merely the absence of disease or infirmity'.[16]

Although the constitutional statement of this definition has remained unaltered since its first declaration, the World Health Assembly acknowledged the spiritual dimension in resolution WHA37.13 at the thirty-seventh World Health Assembly in 1984.[17] of health as being a state of physical, mental, social, and spiritual well-being. Attempts, including a resolution

---

13 Egnew, 'The Meaning Of Healing', 250; Scott et al., 'Healing Journey', 1.
14 Bob Stone, *Gypsies, Tramps and Thieves*, Recorded by Cher (Universal Music Group, 1971), https://www.imdb.com/title/tt9475990/.
15 Frank P. Grad, 'The Preamble of the Constitution of the World Health Organization', *Bulletin of the World Health Organization*, 2002, 4.
16 WHO, 'Basic Documents', World Health Organization Governance, 2020, 1, https://apps.who.int/gb/bd/.
17 Alexander Manuila, ed., *EMRO: Partner in Health in the Eastern Mediterranean* (Alexandria: World Health Organization in the Eastern Mediterranean, 1991), chap. 4. This gave rise to the current understanding

of the executive board of the WHO, to have the World Health Assembly revise the definition in the constitution in accord with this decision, have so far not been implemented. The failure of the World Health Assembly to fully incorporate this dimension into its constitution may not be because there is a failure to recognise the significance and importance of the spiritual dimension of health. It is more likely to be because of the complexities involved in understanding it in a way that encompasses the competing worldviews of the philosophies, religions, and secularities that dominate the world stage.[18]

Despite this diversity, the attendant complexities, contests and the occasional polemic, there is now an extensive and growing literature that demonstrates the benefits of attending to the spiritual dimension in health practices. Attention to the spiritual dimension can no longer be left in the 'too hard basket'. Important benefits of attention to the spiritual dimension are too evident to ignore. Evidence is mounting that indicates that spiritual beliefs and practices enhance both the physical and mental dimensions of health. Several studies and reviews have shown how attention to the spiritual dimension improves a wide range of physical and mental conditions. Physical benefits include reductions in blood pressure, cerebrovascular disease, cardiac conditions, immune disorders and cancer, and increased longevity. Mental benefits include how people understand health, and cope with and become resilient in the face of ill-health, pain, and disability.[19]

The psychological dimension

Medicine is not the only area in which a resistance to the reductive tendencies of modern health practices has emerged. Just as in medicine there is a developing resistance to the reduction of its task to the curing of conditions and diseases, the positive psychology movement has turned from its focus on disorders to identifying what constitutes and promotes psychological health and well-being. Foci of the positive psychology movement have been identifying and conceptualising character strengths and virtues, understanding the cognitive, emotional and relational

---

18 Francesco Chirico, 'Spiritual Well-Being in the 21st Century: It's Time to Review the Current WHO's Health Definition', *Journal of Health and Social Sciences* 1 (15 March 2016): 13.
19 Peter C. Hill and Kenneth I. Pargament, 'Advances in the Conceptualization and Measurement of Religion and Spirituality: Implications for Physical and Mental Health Research.', *American Psychologist* 58, no. 1 (2003): 64–74.

elements of well-being, examining subjectivities related to psychological health, seeking insights into its biological underpinnings, applying it to develop coping strategies and contextualising it within special populations and settings.[20]

A constant theme within this literature has been the recognition of the strong contribution of religion and spirituality to psychological health. Compton and Hoffman arranged their book *Positive Psychology: The Science of Happiness and Flourishing* around the themes for the fruit of the Spirit from Galatians 5. 22–23.[21] Peterson and Seligman, writing what they intended to be a positive version of the *Diagnostic and Statistical Manual of Mental Disorders* (DSM) (pp. 7-10),[22] developed a six-category system made up of wisdom and knowledge, courage, humanity, justice, temperance, and transcendence. They included *Spirituality (Religiousness, Faith, Purpose)* as an element of the strength of transcendence.[23]

The spiritual dimension

Several attempts have been made to address the spiritual dimension in ways that encompass its diversity. Among these are *The Four Domains Model* proposed by Fisher,[24] a joint publication of five spiritual care associations in North America that produced *The Impact of Spiritual Care*,[25] and a concept analysis of spiritual health carried out by Jaberi et al.[26] What follows briefly outlines these in turn.

---

20 William C. Compton and Edward Hoffman, *Positive Psychology: The Science of Happiness and Flourishing*, Third edition (Thousand Oaks, California: SAGE Publications, 2019).
21 Compton and Hoffman.
22 Christopher Peterson and Martin Seligman, *Character Strengths and Virtues: A Handbook and Classification* (Washington DC: American Psychological Association / Oxford University Press, 2004).
23 Peterson and Seligman, 599–624.
24 John W. Fisher, 'The Four Domains Model: Connecting Spirituality, Health and Well-Being', *Religions* 2, no. 1 (2011): 17–28.
25 NASCA, 'The Impact of Professional Spiritual Care' (North American Spiritual Care Associations: A joint publication of ACPE: The Standard for Spiritual Care & Education, Association of Professional Chaplains, Canadian Association for Spiritual Care, National Association of Catholic Chaplains, Neshama: Association of Jewish Chaplains, 2018), https://indd.adobe.com/view/2d555e8f-5d1a-47bf-ad94-760092053d0b.
26 Jaberi, Azita, Marzieh Momennasab, Shahrzad Yektatalab, Abbas Ebadi, and Mohammad Ali Cheraghi. 2017. 'Spiritual Health: A Concept Analysis'. *Journal of Religion and Health* 58 (5): 1537–60.

The Four Domains model

Fisher argues that spiritual health is a dynamic, innate and emotive dimension of overall health that permeates and integrates the other dimensions of health.[27] He presents it as being comprised of the four overlapping dimensions of the personal, the communal, the environmental and the transcendental. These are illustrated and laid out in Figure 1 and Table 1 below.

In his view, Fisher[28] concurs with earlier writers such as Eberst,[29] who wrote of the spiritual dimension as being deeper than a 'surface manifestation' and the avenue through which the other dimensions of health interact; Banks et al.,[30] who wrote of it as a unifier of the other dimensions of health; and Greenberg[31] and Ram,[32] who wrote of the inseparable unity of body, mind and spirit.

Figure 1. Fisher's Four Domains Model*

Personal	Communal	Environmental	Global
Meaning, Purpose and Values	Morality, Culture and Religion	Care, Nurture and Stewardship	Transcendent Other
Self Awareness	In-depth personal relations	Connectedness with Nature	Cosmic Force
Joy	Forgiveness	Awe and wonder	Ultimate Concern
Peace	Justice		God
Identity	Love		Faith
Self-esteem	Hope and faith		Adoration
			Worship

* John W Fisher, 'Spiritual Health: Its Nature and Place in the School Curriculum', PhD thesis, April 1998, 192, http://minerva-access.unimelb.edu.au/handle/11343/39206.

27 Fisher, 'The Four Domains Model', 17.
28 Fisher, 'The Four Domains Model'.
29 Richard M. Eberst, 'Defining Health: A Multidimensional Model', *Journal of School Health* 54, no. 3 (1984): 101.
30 Rebecca L. Banks, David L. Poehler, and Robert D. Russell, 'Spirit and Human-Spiritual Interaction as a Factor in Health and in Health Education', *Health Education* 15, no. 5 (1 September 1984): 16–19.
31 Jerrold S. Greenberg, 'Health and Wellness: A Conceptual Differentiation', *Journal of School Health* 55, no. 10 (1985): 403–6.
32 Eric R. Ram, 'Spiritual Leadership in Health', *World Health*, 1988, 3.

Table 1. Domains of Spiritual Health and Well-being*

	Personal	Communal	Environmental	Transcendental
Knowledge Aspect Filtered by worldview	Meaning, purpose, and values	Morality, culture (and religion)	Care, nurture, and stewardship of the physical eco-political and social environment	Transcendental Other Ultimate concern (Tillich)
Inspirational aspect Essence and motivation Filtered by beliefs	Human spirit creates awareness Self-consciousness	In-depth personal relations Reaching for the heart of humanity	Connectedness with Nature or Creation	Cosmic force – for New Age God – for theists Faith
Expressed as	joy, fulfillment peace, patience freedom humility identity integrity creativity intuition self-worth	love forgiveness justice hope and faith in humanity trust	sense of awe and wonder valuing nature or creation	adoration and worship being: at one with Creator of the essence of the universe in tune with God
Assessed by	attitude and demeanour individual behaviour participation contentment body language	behaviour toward others tolerance service respect contribution to commonweal	extent of identification and unity with the environment	quality of relationship with the transcendent other
Developed through	encouragement self-talk teacher model personal development	relating to others devotions religious values	communion with nature awareness and awe peak experiences	commitment nurture meditation/prayer worship

* Fisher, 'The Four Domains Model', 23.

North American Spiritual Care Associations

Arguing that human beings experience spirit just as they experience their minds and bodies, and distinguishing between religion and spirituality, the North American joint publication provided a generic definition of spirituality as follows:

> Spirituality is a dynamic and intrinsic aspect of humanity through which persons seek ultimate meaning, purpose, and transcendence, and experience relationship to self, family, others, community, society, nature, and the significant or sacred. Spirituality is expressed through beliefs, values, traditions, and practices.[33]

In contrast, they referred to religion as:

> an organised system of beliefs, practices, rituals and symbols designed (a) to facilitate closeness to the sacred or transcendent (God, higher power or ultimate truth/reality) and (b) foster an understanding of one's relationship and responsibility to others in living together in a community.[34]

The authors of this publication argued compellingly for the importance of certified and trained spiritual care professionals or chaplains and for their ability to serve across a wide range of spiritual conceptions. They make, however, no mention of spiritual health. This omission may not be inappropriate because the multicultural and multi-spirituality nature of the environments in which such practitioners serve precludes anything but the most general of interactions. In such settings, the spiritual care professionals act more as spiritual companions than as therapists. Their role is to accompany rather than to heal (even though healing may take place because of their involvement).

Concept analysis of spiritual health

Jaberi et al. conducted an extensive concept analysis of the attributes, antecedents and outcomes of spiritual health.[35] They searched major databases to find over 400 papers that investigated this concept. The definition they propose is:

> spiritual health is a dynamic, developmental, conscious, multidimensional, and universal process that activates through spiritual awareness, personal capacity, and potentials for transcendence.[36]

In their findings, they summarised the critical attributes of spiritual health under headings of transcendence, meaningfulness and purposefulness, faithfulness, harmonious interconnectedness, multidimensional and holistic

---

33 NASCA, 'The Impact of Professional Spiritual Care', 5.
34 NASCA, 5; Koenig, McCullough, and Larson, *Handbook of Religion and Health*, 18.
35 Jaberi et al., 'Spiritual Health', 1540.
36 Jaberi et al., 'Spiritual Health', 1551.

being, and integrating power/energy (pp. 1541-1545). They summarised the antecedents of spiritual health under the headings of capacity and potentiality for transcendence, and spiritual awareness (pp. 1547-1549) and its outcomes under the headings of well-being and moral development (pp. 1549-1550). They diagrammed their findings in Figure 2.

Figure 2: Antecedents, Attributes and Outcomes of Spiritual Health*

Antecedents	Attributes	Outcomes
Spiritual awareness Capacity and potentiality for transcendence	Transcendence Becoming meaningful and purposeful Faith Harmonious interconnection Integrative energy Multidimensional and holistic being	Well-being Moral development

* Jaberi et al., 'Spiritual Health', 1550.

What is particularly helpful in this approach is its identification of outcomes. Their model suggests that the community represented by their samples expects that spiritual health results in both moral development and well-being. Spiritual ill-health might, therefore, be recognised in the absence of these same attributes.

Limitations

Definitions of spirituality and spiritual health, such as those proposed by Fisher, the North American Chaplains, and Jaberi et al., are the distillation of decades of discussion and research and are of great value. They provide validated constructs that are acceptable to most if not all the differing and competing conceptions that reside within the cultures, philosophies, and religions they represent or seek to encompass. They are, however, limited by their high levels of abstraction and generalisation. They cannot challenge or address the core issues of the various universal claims of the cultures, philosophies, and religions that they attempt to encompass. They do, nevertheless, lay the ground for a healthy pluralism in which each system of belief can operate in recognition of and dialogue with the other without having to surrender core tenets.

At the particular level, these belief systems differ profoundly. More needs to be done to identify the ground level particularities and opportunities for dialogue and cooperation that reside within them. Such further work is only possible within each system. Despite the fashion of 'inclusivism' common to this age, it is important to realise that all belief systems are by their nature exclusivist. This is so even if they claim to be inclusivist. Inclusivism, by its very nature, excludes what is not seen to be inclusive. All global religions are both exclusive and inclusive. They are exclusive in that they hold to one set of tenets to the exclusion of others. They are inclusive in that they invite all to adopt their tenets. The same is true of the global humanisms that invite all to join their soft relativisms that reduce religions to 'energising spiritualities rather than substantive articulations' of truth and the good life.[37] Religions can only embrace such relativisms at the cost of becoming diluted and syncretised.

Biblical perspective

What follows is a discussion about spiritual health within the particularities of a Biblical perspective. At its core, a Biblical perspective is a conception of reality that is grounded, first in the sovereign, creative and redemptive action of the triune One who is the uncreated source of all that exists, materially, spiritually and otherwise (all things seen and unseen), second in the incarnation, ministry, passion, resurrection and ascension of the One through whom all things exist,[38] third in the history of salvation embedded in the Biblical narrative, and fourth in the active work today of the uncreated Spirit, the giver of life who hovered over the face of the deep in the creation narrative. This faith perspective unapologetically rejoices in the ongoing concerted work of the uncreated, transcendent, and immanent One, the Creator, who continues to draw all humanity toward its created purpose in the state of well-being and wholeness for which it was created. This state of well-being and wholeness is spiritual health. Having both protological and eschatological import, this state is and must be the ultimate telos of all healing.

A Biblical conception of spiritual health that expresses this state and aligns readily with contemporary general conceptualisations, without being restricted to them, is readily found in the Hebrew concept of *shalom*. *Shalom* is a ubiquitous word in the Old Testament. Its

---

37 Cf. Miroslav Volf, *Flourishing: Why We Need Religion in a Globalized World*, Kindle edition (New Haven: Yale University Press, 2015), 101.
38 Cf. John 1:1-16.

core meaning relates to the divine order of the world characterised by prosperity, happiness and well-being at the personal, communal, environmental and global levels. It refers at the same time to the order of the world understood as a beneficial whole and to conduct that accords with that order.[39] Plantinga writes:

> The webbing together of God, humans, and all creation in justice, fulfillment, and delight is what the Hebrew prophets call shalom. We call it peace, but it means far more than mere peace of mind or a cease-fire between enemies. In the Bible, shalom means universal flourishing, wholeness, and delight—a rich state of affairs in which natural needs are satisfied and natural gifts fruitfully employed, a state of affairs that inspires joyful wonder as its Creator and Saviour opens doors and welcomes the creatures in whom he delights.[40]

Shalom satisfies at all four of Fisher's levels.[41] It is personal, communal, environmental and global at the same time. It also accords with the definition of spirituality proposed by NASCA,[42] and the conceptualisation of spiritual health arrived at by Jaberi et al.[43]

Shalom describes the outcome of redemption; this is nowhere clearer than in Isaiah 53:5-6:[44]

> 5 But he was wounded for our transgressions;
> he was crushed for our iniquities;
> upon him was the chastisement that brought us peace,
> and with his stripes we are healed.
> 6 All we like sheep have gone astray;
> we have turned—everyone—to his own way;
> and the Lord has laid on him
> the iniquity of us all.

The word translated 'peace' and associated with healing in verse five is shalom. The Septuagint translated it with *eirene*. This is also the word that underlies 'peacemakers' in the Beatitudes[45] and 'peace' in the fruit of the Spirit.[46]

---

39 F.J. Stendebach, שלום, in Theological Dictionary of the Old Testament, ed. G. Johannes Botterweck, Helmer Ringgren, and Heinz-Josef Fabry (Grand Rapids: William B Eerdmans Publishing, 2006).
40 Cornelius Plantinga, *Not the Way It Should Be: A Breviary of Sin* (Grand Rapids: William B Eerdmans Publishing Co., 1995), 10.
41 Fisher, 'The Four Domains Model'.
42 NASCA, 'The Impact of Professional Spiritual Care'.
43 Jaberi et al., 'Spiritual Health'.
44 Isaiah 53:5-6, English Standard Version.
45 Matthew 5:9.
46 Galatians 5:22.

Spiritual health and the New Covenant

The statement of New Covenant in Hebrews 8:10-12 is one of three New Testament passages that align with the nature and outcomes of spiritual health and spirituality as identified by Fisher, NASCA, and Jaberi et al. The others are the Beatitudes (Matthew 5:3-12) and the Fruit of the Spirit (Galatians 5:22-23). The Beatitudes address issues of moral development in the context of well-being. The word variously translated 'blessed', or 'happy' is makarios, which signifies an inner state of being that 'refers overwhelmingly to the distinctive religious joy which accrues to man from his share in the salvation of the kingdom of God'.[47] The fruit of the spirit refers to nine personal or communal attributes related to well-being and morality that are outcomes of living in harmony with the Holy Spirit. What is new in the New Covenant (Ezekiel 36:25-26; Jeremiah 31:33b; Hebrews 8:10-12) is centred on the promise of the internalisation of God's law through the work of the Holy Spirit. The operative stichs are Jeremiah 31:33b, Hebrews 8:10b, and Ezekiel 36:27. Hebrews 8:10b is:

> I will put my laws in their minds,
> and write them on their hearts.

In this stich, 'minds and hearts' is a hendiadic expression that refers comprehensively to human interiority[48] and 'law' refers primarily to the Decalogue understood as a statement of the natural law of the Creator, the primary ground of morality, the ground and goal of all virtue, and a guide for moral formation.[49]

In these three passages, the New Covenant is tied to the Abrahamic thread of the covenantal focus of the narrative of redemption. This thread begins with the condition of blamelessness in the covenant with Abraham,[50] is expanded in the condition of compliance with the Mosaic laws,[51] and renewed and reset in the New Covenant, a promise that God himself will bring about the blamelessness required of Abraham and his descendants by God's direct intervention in the minds and hearts of those subject to the covenant.

---

47 F. Hauck and G. Bertram, 'μακάριος, μακαρίζω, μακαρισμός', in *Theological Dictionary of the New Testament: Λ-N*, ed. Gerhard Kittel, Geoffrey William Bromiley and Gerhard Friedrich (Grand Rapids: William B. Eerdmans Publishing, 1967), 367.
48 Carblis, 188-98; Barry C. Joslin, *Hebrews, Christ, and the Law: The Theology of the Mosaic Law in Hebrews 7:1-10:18* (Milton Keynes: Paternoster, 2015).
49 Carblis, 188-98; Barry C. Joslin, *Hebrews, Christ, and the Law: The Theology of the Mosaic Law in Hebrews 7:1-10:18* (Milton Keynes: Paternoster, 2015).
50 Genesis 17:1-2.
51 Exodus 19:5-6 and thereafter.

The centrality of the New Covenant is emphasised in the words spoken by Jesus when he took the cup at the last supper. Consider Luke 22:20:

> And he did the same with the cup after supper, saying, "This cup that is poured out for you is the new covenant in my blood".

The association of redemption with healing and covenant in the New Testament is explicit and emphatic in the Benedictus.[52] In this passage, Zechariah, at the birth of his son, John the Baptist, prophesied that the Lord God of Israel, remembering his holy covenant sworn to Abraham, had 'raised up a horn of salvation (*keras soterias*)', who would give 'knowledge of salvation (*soterias*)', the result of which would be the ability of God's people to serve God without fear 'in holiness and righteousness'. The 'horn of salvation', alluding to Psalm 18:2, in which YHWH is identified as David's saviour, is the Messiah, Jesus.[53] In this prophecy, John's role was to go before and prepare the way.

Throughout the New Testament, the word, *soteria*, and its verbal cognate, *sozo*, carry the sense of making alive and making healthy.[54] They also occur extensively in ancient Greek literature. Their meanings include saving from peril, keeping alive, pardoning, being cured or preserved in good health, and the preservation of the inner being or nature of men or things.[55] The New Covenant is therefore a covenant of spiritual healing through the work of God. Its outcomes are therefore expressions of spiritual health. The effect of this covenant is a transformation of the inner life of those subject to it and which gives rise, in Willard's words, to:

> the kind of person from whom the deeds of the law naturally flow. The apple tree naturally and easily produces apples because of its inner nature.[56]

This is a person whose life is naturally aligned with and complies with the deontic, principle-based, and virtue- dimensions of God's law. The question then arises 'What are the attributes of this kind of person?' These may be derived by asking 'What are the personal attributes of a person who would naturally live according to the values that underlie the precepts of the Decalogue?' Table 2 suggests what these attributes might

---

52 Luke 1:67-79.
53 Mikeal C. Parsons, *Luke*, Kindle edition (Grand Rapids, Michigan: Baker Academic, 2015), loc. 1706.
54 Foester, 'σῴζω, σωτηρία, σωτήρ, σωτήριος', 990.
55 Foester, 966-68.
56 Dallas Willard, *The Divine Conspiracy: Rediscovering Our Hidden Life in God* (San Francisco: Harper, 1998), 142.

be, as well as to suggest the kind of a society to which that kind of person might contribute. The division of the precepts combines various Ancient, Jewish, Catholic, Orthodox and Protestant traditions.

Table 2. Inner Personal and Societal Attributes and the Decalogue

Precept of the Decalogue	Personal	Societal
I am the Lord your God who brought you out of Egypt, the house of slavery. Exod. 20:2, Deut. 5:6	Covenant Faithfulness Recognition and honouring of the God of creation as the God of the Bible. It also includes recognition of the covenant initiated through Abraham and continued in the Biblical Narrative through the New Covenant to the present day.	A society which recognises all human beings as made in the image and likeness of the Creator and, therefore, worthy of deep respect and care.
You shall have no other gods before me. Exod. 20:3, Deut. 5:7	Reverence for God and His image in each person.	Humble societal acknowledgement of the superiority to God over humankind and anything seen or unseen.
You shall not make for yourself an idol. Exod. 20:4-6, Deut. 5:8-10	Exclusive commitment to God as revealed in the Bible.	A society which accepts reality as defined by God and is free from false images and ideologies.
You shall not make wrongful use of the name of your God. Exod. 20:7, Deut. 5:11	Respect for the holiness of God's name.	A society free from magic, superstition, presumption, and blasphemous disrespect.
Remember the Sabbath and keep it holy. Exod. 20:8-11, Deut. 5:12-15	Mindful commitment to sacred time.	A society ordered toward healthy rhythms of worship, rest, and prayerful reflection.
Honour your mother and father. Exod. 20:12, Deut. 5:16	Embracing of family values and responsibilities.	A society which values, respects, is committed to and cares for children and the aged.

Precept of the Decalogue	Personal	Societal
You shall not kill/murder. Exod. 20:13, Deut. 5:17	Respect and reverence for life and relationships.	A society that lovingly approaches relationships, and life and death related ethical issues from the understanding that life, as found in individuals and relationships, is sacred.
You shall not commit adultery. Exod. 20:14, Deut. 5:18	Commitment and purity in relationships.	A society ordered toward supporting the family as the institution ordered to create the environment in which human beings can be born and raised in stable families and which disavows and discourages approaches to sexuality that see others as a means of gratification or objects of lust.
You shall not steal. Exod. 20:15, Deut. 5:19	Productivity and generosity	A society ordered economically toward equity that encourages the kind of personal productivity and generosity that enables all who earn to live responsibly and generously.
You shall not bear false witness. Exod. 20:16, Deut. 5:20	Integrity	A society which values truthfulness and accuracy in communication, especially when it might affect the reputation or well-being of another.
You shall not covet neighbour's house, wife, servants, or property. Exod. 20:17, Deut. 5:21	Appreciative and thankful	A society which encourages an appreciative approach to life and the well-being of its members and discourages envious competition.

Christian service and spiritual health

Jaberi et al.'s definition of spiritual health (see above) may therefore be expanded as follows:

> Spiritual health is a dynamic, developmental, conscious, multi-dimensional, and universal process that activates through spiritual awareness, personal capacity, and potentials for transcendence, *and progresses toward well-being and morality as covenantally expressed by the internalisation of God's values, as expressed in his law, through the work of the Holy Spirit.* [passage in italics added by the author.]

The definitions of spirituality of Fisher and NASCA that were discussed earlier might similarly be combined and amended by the author to read:

> Christian services and ministries that contribute to spiritual health, thus defined, include all that fall within professions related to pastoral care, education, mental health, and medicine. Processes in these areas may take the shape of spiritual direction, therapy, or pedagogy broadly defined. All such practices must first involve discernment of how the Holy Spirit might be leading a person toward covenant outcomes. The goal of these practices is to help the recipients of these services gain insight into and cooperate with the leading of the Holy Spirit in their lives.

Conclusion and summary

Health has an unavoidable spiritual dimension. This is attested across cultures and ages in the language and history of health and healing. Recent attempts in medicine as practised in developed economies to arrive at definitions of health that omit the spiritual dimension of health have proved inconclusive and reductionistic. A consequence of this flawed approach has been to see the disproportionate prominence of attention given to the spiritual dimension of health by quacks, charlatans, and the naïvely uninformed. Counter to these trends has been a parallel attentiveness to the spiritual dimension of health in the nursing and other literatures as well as the inclusion of the spiritual dimension as an aspect of health by the WHO. Decades of research and commentary have arrived at a clear consensus about a general concept of spiritual health that adequately frames the articulation of a Biblically-based approach to spiritual health, spirituality and healing grounded in the terms of the

New Covenant. This approach allows for authentic practice in pluralistic settings involving pastoral care, education, mental health, and medicine without threat of syncretism or dilution. As we have seen, recent work by Fisher, North American spiritual care associations and Jaberi et al. have attested to this consensus.

Chapter Ten

In the beginning was the Word: the place of AI technology in the integral approach

Beatrice Green

Introduction

'In the Beginning was the Word.' This proclamation that opens the Gospel of John indicates the sheer outpouring of divine grace that has brought creation to birth, given us humanity and life, and sustains all within an eternal merciful embrace, while we, as a whole creation, become, over time, what our loving God wills us to be.

'Word', in the context of the Gospel of John as a whole, must be interpreted as Trinitarian and Eucharistic in the widest sense. The theologian and philosopher, Raimon Panikkar, a great exponent of interfaith dialogue, has expressed this creatively, guided by Hindu spiritual insight: '(The) total living word (reveals that) God, humanity and the universe ... are constitutively connected ... (in a) *cosmotheandric* communion'.[1] Likewise, the Benedictine monk and Christian *sannyasi*, Bede Griffiths, understood John 17:21, 'that they may all be one, even as you, Father, are in me and I am in you, may they also be in us' as being the most profound expression of the kind of intimate relationship God offers us—together with all created life.[2]

We honour mystical experience of such interconnectedness within Christian tradition. For example, the medieval mystics, the German Dominican, Meister Eckhart, the Flemish Augustinian, John van Ruysbroeck, and the English Anchorite, Julian of Norwich, from their different

---

[1] Raymond Panikkar, *The Vedic Experience Mantramañjarī: An Anthology of the Vedas for Modern Man and Contemporary Celebration*, Fourth Edition (Pondicherry: Narendra Prakash Jain, 1983), 89-92.
[2] Bede Griffiths, 'East and West: The Mystical Connection with Father Bede Griffiths', in an interview by Michael Toms (Ukia, CA: New Dimensions Media, 20 Sep 1983). The Gospel quotation is from the NRSV Bible.

contexts, describe how it was revealed to them that the whole of creation is loved, known and held by God eternally.

Yet it is only human to feel perplexed by apparently contradictory impulses, destructive natural forces, genetic malformations, human error and evil intent. Herself questioning such negative pressure, Dame Julian writes how Jesus responded to her in a vision, telling her that, despite sin in the world, 'all shall be well, and all shall be well, and all manner of thing shall be well'.[3] Today, modern science and space exploration provide evidence that there is from the beginning the drive for life that manifests in constantly greater complexity. Such currents have been well demonstrated by scholars such as the palaeontologist, Père Teilhard de Chardin, and in the present time physicist David Bohm. Over the past 50 years, we have seen a veritable explosion of information available through constantly developing technologies that have, along the drive for life tangent, provided extraordinary help, for example in health and communications. With these developments comes a gearing up of what we call 'AI'. This so-called 'artificial intelligence' taunts human imagination with the threat of 'going rogue'. It is on this particular area that I wish to focus in an exploratory approach to help inform a more positive attitude in place of fear or apprehension.

Integral thinking, the AQAL diagram, and AI

There are two common themes in the writing of Bede Griffiths, David Bohm, transpersonal psychologist and integral thinker, Ken Wilber, and exponent of Integral Philosophy, Steve McIntosh. These represent the expectation of a new consciousness to which humanity is being called by the Spirit, and the understanding that the whole cosmos is a complex web of interdependent dynamic relationships.

Inseparable from these themes, for all four persons, is the emphasis on the vital importance of the practice of contemplation.[4] The 2019 tome, *Smart Spacetime: How Information Challenges Our Ideas about Space, Time and Process*[5], indicates to me that its author, scientist/technologist

---

3 Julian of Norwich, *The Revelations of Divine Love of Julian of Norwich*, trans. ed. James Walsh SJ (London: Burn and Oates, 1961), 171.

4 See Beatrice Green, 'The Different Guises of Christ: Towards an Integral Consciousness' in *Weaving Theology in Oceania: Culture, Context and Practice*, eds. Beatrice Green and Keiti Ann Kanongata'a (Newcastle upon Tyne: Cambridge Scholars Publishing, 2020), 72, 73.

5 Mark Burgess, *Smart Spacetime: How Information Challenges Our Ideas about Space, Time and Process* (Oslo: XtAxis Press, 2019). Glenn O'Donnell, leading IT practitioner, innovator and visionary since 1980, in his endorsement of Burgess' earlier work, *In Search of Certainty*, recommends Burgess as 'one of the best minds'.

Mark Burgess, also belongs in this group. He emphasises process and deep interrelatedness and, although he does not mention 'a new consciousness', it is implicit. Like Bohm (who believes in spirituality and regards himself as an agnostic),[6] Burgess does not overtly profess a personal religious faith, but both authors are visionary and emphasise the need for deep listening and acute awareness.[7]

I have commented previously on Steve McIntosh's critique of Ken Wilber's AQAL diagram that is pivotal to the thrust of his argument for integral consciousness.[8] Burgess' concepts assist us to assess and to comment on the significance of McIntosh's critique in order to appreciate where and how AI fits in. It will be best to briefly recollect the argument so far.

AQAL—All Quadrants, All Levels, All Lines, is modelled as a square divided into four quadrants. In each quadrant a diagonal line runs from the centre of the square to the corner. These lines (or 'streams') represent the directional flow of evolutionary change within each quadrant. The levels or stages are specifically designated along each diagonal line in each quadrant. The two quadrants on the left of the square are the subjective domain; the two on the right, the objective domain. The Upper Left (UL) quadrant delineates the evolutionary levels of the interior human reality, self-actualising, the 'I', (first person singular); the Lower Left (LL) the plural of this (first person plural), that is, the human interactive reality and culture, the 'we'; the Upper Right (UR) represents the 'individual exterior', biological and behavioural, (third person singular, 'it'); the Lower Right (LR) is the 'exterior-collective', the social systems. Each of these stages describes a new level of consciousness that is acquired through transcendence and inclusion. This indicates that each prior fundamental stage, or level, is the birth-place of the next 'significant' stage. That is, each stage is vital for and intrinsic to the next process of transcendence. Furthermore, while correspondences can be diagrammatically demonstrated, from quadrant to quadrant, the

---

6 See, David Bohm, 'Science, Spirituality, and the Present World Crisis', https://www.davidbohmsociety.org/david-bohm/audio-and-video/#science-spirituality-and-the-present-world-crisis
7 Burgess says, 'We are not here to punish ourselves, fulfil others' expectations, or work exclusively for pay without gratification. We only get one chance, so we should strive to be happy.' 'Happiness' (2009), http://markburgess.org/blog.html.
8 For Wilber's and McIntosh's diagrams, see Green, 'The Different Guises of Christ', 74-78. These images are also accessible online. For Ken Wilber: https://integrallife.com/four-quadrants/. For Steve McIntosh: https://www.stevemcintosh.com/books/integral-consciousness/chapter-two-the-internal-universe/.

evolutionary flow and change do not necessarily actually proceed at the same pace, quadrant to quadrant.

Burgess' exposition on the significance of AI leads me to take another look at Steve McIntosh's declaration that Wilber's fourth quadrant is unnecessarily separated from the 'it' above, that the whole of the right side of the square should all really be the one objective domain. McIntosh considers that some of the systems in the lower right quadrant are 'artefacts' that have no 'inside' or organic centre, and as human constructs they do not properly correspond with the organic changes in other quadrants. McIntosh prefers a tri-partite diagram—the good, the beautiful and the true—which he shows diagrammatically as a 'nested sequence of evolutionary emergences', concentric circles with a ragged outer circle differentiating the 'artefacts' from the organic life.[9]

Spacetime, AI, limitations and the infinite

Studying *Smart Spacetime* leads me to better appreciate the significance of the intimacy of the human/artefact relationship that must include AI, and also the all-important difference between the two. Following Burgess' line of thought, I recognise that, with any industrial, technological and informational system along Wilber's evolutionary stream in the LR or 'its' quadrant, the organic connection must remain inferred. The artificial part is *entirely* dependent on the human part in the relationship where the human part must always be held to be responsible.

Time and space are not separate objectifiable notions, but intrinsic/integral to our known reality. Each is entwined inseparably with the other, meaningless on its own, hence 'spacetime.' Spacetime, which defines our perception of the universe as a whole and the multi-verses we inhabit, such as citiverse, econoverse and technoverse, demonstrates process that further links 'give and take'. This is a principle that is grounded in the proposition that there is no 'sender' without a 'receiver', expressed, as early as 1948, as 'Shannon's Law', and described by Burgess as 'promise theory ... a simple reference model for spacetime'.[10]

Evidence for these principles originates in the gaseous origins of the universe from the 'Big Bang,' 13.8 billion years ago, to the clumping

---

9 Steve McIntosh, *Integral Consciousness and the Future of Evolution: How the Integral Worldview Is Transforming Politics, Culture and Spirituality* (St Paul, Minnesota: Paragon House, 2007), in Green, 'The Different Guises of Christ', 76.
10 Burgess, *Smart Spacetime*, 116.

of primal elements, formation of stars and planets, the origins of biological life, and the emergence of human life. There is 'promise' in the 'condensed singularity' described by David Bohm, whereby all that will be is implicated in an enfoldment, as it were, that is explicated in an original expansion of the basic ingredients for life—though not deterministically, because novelty and creative inter-play are integral ingredients. We can perceive a 'receiver' along the tangent of such an expansion. However, in the first instance, is the receiver the emptiness that 'calls' to life? We can imagine how an empty blackboard 'begs' to be written on. Does emptiness have a beckoning power? When 'all' is in God, and God is 'all' can the emptiness prior to the Big Bang have meaning outside of God? Justin Martyr's *logoi spermatikoi* are one side of the equation, the other is the womb of empty waiting holding a sigh of longing to be. According to the Christian mystics and integral thinkers, nothing truly exists outside the web of deep, dynamic interconnectedness.

Burgess shows how the same principles of 'promise theory' are basic to processes that build, govern, and develop 'artificial intelligence' that is bound up with the interior spacetime of computer technology. 'Spacetime processes become 'smart' when they promise outcomes that anticipate the needs of a particular context.'[11] Spacetime processes exist at different scales. And, as in nature where the microcosm and macrocosm, though interdependent, are governed by different laws, scale matters.

The term, 'Artificial Intelligence', as Panikkar pointed out and Burgess would agree, is nonsensical; 'artificial' is fine as describing something not natural or spontaneous; 'intelligence', however, is problematic and contentious.

Burgess points out that there may be a basic capacity for 'selection and elimination of junk' in the algorithmic artificial reasoning of the huge cloud data-bases with their great stores of memory and fast retrieval of the same in service of human pursuits. Massive amounts of data are 'netted up' for use by the modern search engines.

However, the human mind only is capable of discerning depth of truth and verifiable evidence from the purely speculative, the purposefully erroneous, biased or bigoted, or propagandist. Burgess finds intelligence in the human capacity for 'recursive' reasoning, something a machine cannot do. For, example, 'If she had not taken that job last week, she would still be alive today'. Human intelligence has developed through story-lines deeply etched in the human memory in a complex web of

---

11 Burgess, *Smart Spacetime*, 490.

scaled truth, gravity and performance made by the interactions of rational and complex, emotional, imaginative, body, creative intelligence. If AI could ever compare, it would be 'millions of years' off in the future. 'Talk of AI and robots displacing humans is just lazy thinking.'[12]

Similarly, Bede Griffiths, distinguishing 'intuition ... the feminine power of the mind' with the power of self-reflection, as being distinct from 'reason,' describes it as a source of knowledge not accessible by an empirical method. This particular self-awareness, expressed by Jacques Maritain as 'beneath the sunlit surface of the mind', where dreams and images take shape, Griffiths compares with the traditional Chinese wu wei, or action in inaction. This 'intuition', which is the self-reflection of the passive intellect, is an integrative bodily, psychological and mental awareness through which arise 'image, symbols...dance and song, and beyond this ritual sacrifice...prayer and ecstasy'.[13]

Interpreting AI in the AQAL diagram

So, then, in light of Burgess' decades of research and work with IT and AI, how may we interpret the 'bulge'—the 'explosion' of information and technology, and AI along the diagonal line in Wilber's fourth quadrant? Are these systems, described as 'artefacts' by McIntosh, confusedly out of place? As has been noted above, the four areas of evolutionary change do not have to proceed at the same comparable rate. At this point in time, the movement of change in the LR (Lower Right) quadrant is speeding along very fast, as regards information technology and 'AI'. The result of this has been beneficial for a great many people, for example, educationally and in medical science, such as the development of prosthetic limbs and computer assisted micro-surgery. It also assists efforts to find sources of alternative energy in order to curb climate change, and the detection of threatened species for the sake of their preservation. And, admitting also that there are obvious risks involved in the human handling and direction of such powerful tools, how do these 'artefacts' as McIntosh names them fit in with the rest of Wilber's diagram?

Perhaps the answer is that changes in the other three quadrants will take place. For example, the *Journal of Anatomy* has recently published a

---

12 Burgess, *Smart Spacetime*, 492.
13 See Bede Griffiths, *The Marriage of East and West: A Sequel to the Golden String* 2nd Ed (London: Fount Paperbacks, 1983), 150-171 in Beatrice Green, *A Christological Interpretation of the Golden String of Bede Griffiths Spiritual Journey*. The Degree of Doctor of Philosophy (Brisbane, QLD: Australian Catholic University, 2011).

study of 'microevolution of modern humans' that describes more babies being born without wisdom teeth, with extra bones in legs and feet, and the median artery in the forearm that used to disappear after birth now remaining in more and more people in what is expected to become the norm within 80 years.[14] In Wilber's AQAL diagram, these changes would be significant in the UR (Upper Right) quadrant.

Furthermore, while McIntosh argues that 'artefacts' have no 'inside', the fact is they are operated by human intelligence according to particular human motives, for good or ill. As AI is increasingly developed in the service of medical science, entertainment, security and defence, alternative energy production and space exploration, we humans must keep right control of decision-making, and be acutely awake to the risks. 'Heaven forbid the weaponisation of AI (for high-speed warfare or cyber warfare)'.[15] Furthermore, for the sake of justice and human equality, we will need new laws for a machine-enhanced world. Greater complexity will mean more points of interaction within greater human specialisation through 'the proxies and intermediaries of machinery'. We will need to keep our heads in order to 'adapt (and maintain) a human sense of purpose'.[16] Unless we do so, we cannot hope to properly exercise our privileged role as co-creators with Christ.[17]

Pope Francis, in *Laudato Si'*, commenting on the speed of technological development without regard for deep human values that include respect for the natural environment, urges us 'to slow down ... to recover the values and the great goals swept away by our unrestrained delusions of grandeur' (n. 114). On the one hand, he quotes St John Paul II, 'who stressed the benefits of scientific and technological progress as evidence of "the nobility of the human vocation to participate responsibly in God's creative action"'. On the other hand, he notes that creative human activity is a 'form of power involving considerable risks' (n. 131) and that the resulting issues 'require constant attention and a concern for their ethical implications' (n. 135).[18]

---

14 Teghan Lucas, Jallya Kumaratilake and Maciej Henneberg, 'Recently Increased Prevalence of the Human Median Artery of the Forearm: A Microevolutionary Change' *Journal of Anatomy*, 237 (2020), 623–631. https://doi.org/10.1111/joa.13224
15 Burgess, *Smart Spacetime*, 492.
16 Burgess, *Smart Spacetime*, 493.
17 For 'co-creation' see Philip Hefner, 'Evolution of the Created Co-Creator' in *Cosmos as Creation: Theology and Science in Consonance*, ed. Ted Peters (Nashville: Abingdon, 1989), 226-228.
18 Pope Francis, *Laudato Si': On Care for Our Common Home* (2015). https://w2.vatican.va/content/francesco/en/encyclicals/documents/papa-francesco_20150524_enciclica-laudato-si.html

In order to keep ahead, and also maintain a world that is human-friendly, it will mean investment in education both towards science and technology and human wholeness (holiness). Individual differences cannot just be ironed out or, worse, obliterated. Furthermore, the relationship between the human and their artificial creation is likely, in many cases, to become increasingly more intimate. This could very well prompt organic change, neurologically, physically, culturally and spiritually. Considering all of this, the practice or habit of regular silent meditation and/or contemplative prayer, as the integral thinkers I introduced at the start, Griffiths, Bohm, Wilber and McIntosh insist, is vital.

Conclusion

Wilber's and McIntosh's diagrams may be used separately and together to discern, describe and better understand the whole or different aspects of the human journey in the evolutionary process of change. The aim is movement into integral thinking, a new level of consciousness which would, no doubt, at least help us to handle AI.

Finally, let us return to the words from the Gospel of John that Bede Griffiths held so central, and complete the sentence: '... that they may all be one; even as you, Father, are in me and I am in you, may they also be in us so that the world may believe that you have sent me'. As Jesus' friends, we are exhorted to show the world that the source of Christ's words and works is God, Abba, who unites us in a profound familial bond of love. As St Paul points out in his letter to the Romans, this love for one another and our natural world is proof and seal of our unity with God, the goal for the whole human family and all of creation. Our loving God has sent us forth into the universe on an extraordinary journey. We can expect that AI technology will be an important aspect of it that we, as co-creators, must strive to develop, share and use wisely.

Part Three

Creating Healing Communities

Chapter Eleven

Embracing voices of dissent: Women, spiritual authority and the Church[1]

Catherine Lambert

Introduction

'Rachel', a participant in my recent doctorate research, described her decision to leave a particular church community. She lamented, 'They couldn't cope with me. And I couldn't cope with them'. What 'Rachel' described was her beginning to speak of her own ideas and experiences and her subsequent movement away from the external authority of the faith community. Her new ideas about faith and God became an unwanted voice of dissent in the community and her easiest option was to leave.

This essay shares some findings from my research with women at the edge of the church.[2] To begin, I highlight the key themes of education and self-knowledge which arose from initial interviews with my sample group concerning their experiences of the journey to the edge of the church. The second part of the paper examines the significant theme of spiritual authority with particular emphasis on the women's discovery of their inner authority. The significant place of experience for women learning to trust their own authority is emphasised, along with the resulting difficulties in authentication by the community. I then bring anecdotal evidence from the experiences of my sample group into conversation with

---

[1] This essay arises from research towards my PhD thesis through the University of Divinity, Melbourne. I acknowledge the contribution to this research from Pilgrim Theological College and the Uniting Church Synod of Victoria and Tasmania through the Robert James Brown Postgraduate Scholarship, the Uniting Church of Western Australia through the Roland Geise Memorial Fund and the Ian Marshall Memorial Fund and the Janette Gray RSM Fund through the Janette Gray PhD Scholarship.

[2] My research methods were approved by the University of Divinity HREC procedures. My research involved interviewing 13 women from across Australia. The women were diverse in age and denominational background. All participants identified as being on the edge of the church. The identities of the women are protected by the use of pseudo-names.

the work of Karl Rahner to explore the clash that can occur between inner authority and the external authority of the institutional church. To conclude, I present resulting reflections regarding conformity and dissent and propose a movement beyond traditional views of faith education, development and formation towards an emphasis on faith validation. My hope is that churches will not just cope with women's voices of dissent, but embrace them for the betterment of the church.

Women's journeys to the edge of the church: education and self-knowledge

All of the women interviewed as part of my research grew up in a church environment. Their stories varied according to their denomination, the extent of their family's involvement and their continued commitment to their faith community into adulthood. The point of connection, however, was their description of the journey of realisation that found them on the edge of the church. I encountered very little animosity towards the church in the women's stories, only a deep grief that they no longer felt spiritually nourished by these communities. Largely, the response of women was that their church upbringing had been a foundational and grounding influence in their early formation. A key aspect of this for many of the participants was faith education and the subsequent development of self-knowledge.

The interviewees all included anecdotes referring to their adult religious or theological education. Some of the narratives recalled formal education, including the completion or desire to pursue research at a post-graduate level. The form of education, however, did not change the weight of influence this played in the women's lives. One participant, 'Helen', described her reaction to attending a workshop hosted by her local church in which the speaker presented a theological perspective that challenged traditional doctrine and interpretation of scripture. 'Helen' remembered:

> [He] kind of turned a whole heap of things upside down. And he challenged me on a whole heap of fronts that had never been challenged before. It was one of the moments in your life where you go, 'Oh my gosh, I can't unhear what I've heard. And I can't pretend like that hasn't meant anything to me.' And it just kind of blew my world apart and at that point I said, 'I can't keep doing this. Where am I going to go from here?'

Her new knowledge contributed significantly to the deconstruction of childhood images of God and understandings of faith. The foundational understandings that 'Helen' had once held dear needed to be challenged before a new door could be opened presenting new language and perspectives.

Theological or faith education, in its various forms, contributes to the dismantling of well-established faith structures that have provided safety and support in early formation. Rebecca Chopp and Mark Taylor define the process of reconstructing theology as both 'reworking theology's symbols and doctrines in various ways and also a continual re-engaging of the diverse communities that Christians address and with whom they must work today for an emancipative restoration of personal and social flourishing'.[3] In relation specifically to women, Mary Belenky and her colleagues describe 'constructed knowledge' as beginning with an effort to 'reclaim the self by attempting to integrate knowledge that they intuitively felt was personally important with knowledge they had learned from others'.[4] Chopp brings the more general constructivist theological concerns together with a specific feminist approach as she describes freedom for women as 'more than interrupting current discourses and practices', but also involving finding ways to 'name the possibilities and dreams of freedom as emancipation and transformation'.[5] This process involves deconstruction and reconstruction. Peter Bentley, in his model of spiritual formation, identifies surrendering or letting go of our attachment to old patterns and habits as an important phase that opens the way for transformation.[6]

The exposure to differing interpretations of Scripture, doctrine and theological understandings invites the learner to look beyond their own patterning and begin to critique and question. Although this may cause considerable discomfort and angst, education also has a liberating role on the journey to the edge of the church. For the women in my sample group, theological education began an awakening. The revelation of new

---

3 Rebecca S Chopp and Mark L Taylor, eds., *Reconstructing Christian theology* (Minneapolis: Fortress Press, 1994), 20-21.
4 Mary Field Belenky, Blythe McVicker Clinchy, Nancy Rule Goldberger and Jill Mattuck Tarule, *Women's Ways of Knowing: The Development of Self, Voice, and Mind*, (New York: Basic Books, 1986), 134.
5 Rebecca S. Chopp, *The Power to Speak: Feminism, Language, God* (New York: Crossroad, 1989), 11.
6 Peter Bentley, 'Bridging the Old and the New in Spiritual Direction,' in *Companioning at the Edges: Exploring New Dimensions of Spiritual Direction in Australia*, eds. Peter Bentley and Ann Lock (Ashburton, VIC: Wellspring Centre, 2021), 15-16.

understandings, interpretations and experiences allowed the women to begin to deconstruct old patterns that had not been life-giving and explore a broader terrain of new traditions, fresh interpretations, and alternative language.

The education received by the women was in a direct and dynamic relationship with their own development of self-knowledge. The nature of the programs and workshops the women engaged in often resulted in an examination of the self. 'Michelle', referring to her involvement in adjunct programs of her church, explained that:

> Even though [the programs] were still within the traditional bounds of the church, they were movements that actually called you to look at yourself. So, it wasn't head stuff. It was just, you know, more than that. And that, I think, changes your own internal dynamics.

Although the development of self-knowledge occurred in a myriad of forms for the women, discovery of the Enneagram held particular significance for at least half of the women interviewed. These women had been introduced to the Enneagram in the form of a workshop run independently or as part of a spiritual formation program.[7] Most continued their exploration with subsequent reading. For some, their sharing was merely a brief revelation of their Enneagram number. In other cases, the women shared more deeply of the impact encountering the Enneagram had upon their life. 'Rachel' recalled her feelings in attending an Enneagram workshop:

> It was the first time in my life when I felt like I wasn't a broken toy. Like, I'd been on a massive journey already and my theology was in pieces and all of that stuff, but inside I still felt broken. Who I was, was not who I was supposed to be.

Learning about the Enneagram and its relevance in personal life does not only impact psychologically, but also spiritually. Studies have demonstrated that knowledge of the Enneagram can 'connect a deep part of [her] personality with a deep part of God's personality in order to

---

7 The Enneagram is a system which presents human personality as nine interconnected types. There are nine basic types and sub-types determined by the wings (or adjacent types). Knowing your Enneagram type can assist in identifying patterns in times of strength and stress.

strengthen [her] intimacy with God'.⁸ The women interviewed shared how their use of the Enneagram as a tool allowed them to find healing and acceptance within themselves, be more open and gracious to the difference in others, and discover a unique giftedness that led to new modes of service and expression within their communities.

Australian Cistercian monk, Michael Casey, argues that the gaining of self-knowledge is a vital spiritual discipline for 'all who aspire to live a spiritual life'.⁹ Coming face-to-face with themselves and embarking on a journey of self-discovery became a precursor for the women in discovering and trusting their own inner spiritual authority. Viewing oneself not as flawed or dysfunctional, but with understanding and forgiveness in times of compulsion, led to a place of self-love where trust and strength were built. The gaining of self-knowledge is often not a comfortable process as darker, hidden parts of life are exposed. Unearthing self-knowledge may leave the individual vulnerable as they open themselves to experience and explore the pain in their lives.¹⁰

Women's discovery of inner spiritual authority

A key theme among the women engaged in my research was the discovery of their own inner spiritual authority. Although this is considered a natural element of faith development, this process was not always easy for the women. A helpful entry to investigating individual spiritual authority is James Fowler's work regarding personal faith development. Fowler, a theologian and developmental psychologist, published a six-stage theory for faith development based upon Piaget's theory of cognitive development and Kohlberg's theory of moral development.¹¹ His renowned work explores the concept of authority in terms of its location as internal or external to the individual. The locus of authority is defined as 'to whom or to what did she [or he] look for decisive guidance as regards to decisions about actions or beliefs'.¹² Fowler argued that, as faith develops in the individual, the locus of authority transitions from external to internal. In

---

8 Christopher Kam, 'Integrating Divine Attachment Theory and the Enneagram to Help Clients of Abuse Heal in Their Images of Self, Others, and God' *Pastoral Psychology*. 67, no. 4 (2018): 351. See also Adele Ahlberg Calhoun, *Spiritual Rhythms for the Enneagram: A Handbook for Harmony and Transformation* (Downers Grove, IL: IVP Books, 2019).
9 Michael Casey, *Grace: On the Journey to God* (Brewster, Massachusetts: Paraclete Press, 2018), 91.
10 For a more thorough exploration of the place of self-knowledge in the spiritual journey see Casey, *Grace*, 91-107.
11 James W. Fowler, *Stages of Faith: The Psychology of Human Development and the Quest for Meaning*, 1st ed. (San Francisco: Harper & Row, 1981).
12 Fowler, *Stages of Faith*, 241.

early life, the individual refers to a valued group or community as their source of authority. The consensus of the group becomes the held belief of the individual. The relocation of authority within the self occurs between the Synthetic-Conventional Faith (third) and Individuative-Reflective Faith (fourth) stages. A readiness for transition from stage three occurs when clashes or contradictions between valued authority sources become evident.[13]

This movement in the locus of authority is not simply switched from an external source to the individual's inner source. The judgment of others remains important in the Individuative-Reflective individual; however, their expectations and counsel are submitted to an 'internal panel of experts' who reserve the right to select the course of action and take responsibility for their choices.[14] Other external factors still have influence on the individual and their strength will vary according to the manner in which the faith community has evolved a pattern of authority around the individual. As Fowler describes it, the public church which has procedures and leadership skills that allow for conflict and struggle, include diverse voices in discussion and are serious about reconciliation, is more likely to assist the individual whose locus of authority has moved inward.[15] Unfortunately, this is not always the case and external leadership often presumes spiritual seniority and authority, viewing themselves as the sole source of religious truth.[16]

Writing as a feminist and a practical theologian, Nicola Slee (2004) has successfully brought together Fowler's Faith Development Theory with the importance of the inter-relational in her research concerning women's faith development.[17] From her interviews with women, Slee identified distinctive 'faithing' strategies or processes used by women to create meaning in their life experiences and patterns for how faith development occurred. Although Slee's sample group was limited in size and diversity, her research is considered important for those in ministry with women.[18]

---

[13] Fowler, *Stages of Faith*, 173.
[14] Fowler, *Stages of Faith*, 179.
[15] James Fowler, *Weaving the New Creation: Stages of Faith and the Public Church*, 1st ed. (San Francisco: HarperSanFrancisco, 1991), 159.
[16] Fowler, *Weaving*, 160.
[17] Nicola Slee, *Women's Faith Development: Patterns and Processes* (Aldershot, UK: Ashgate, 2004).
[18] Karen E. Smith, Review of 'Women's Faith Development: Patterns and Processes', by Nicola Slee, *Journal of Contemporary Religion* 21, no. 2 (2006): 270-271; Christie Cozad Neuger, Review of 'Women's Faith Development: Patterns and Processes,' by Nicola Slee, *International Journal of Practical Theology* 9, no. 2 (2005): 333-335.

Of the six strategies identified by Slee, three contain a communal aspect. The importance of 'conversational faithing' in providing women with a place of potential epiphany is described as the presence of an attentive other in the woman's life.[19] The sharing of one's spiritual life in dialogue with another brings the individual's inner authority into conversation with an external voice in a mutual manner. 'Narrative faithing' involves storytelling for meaning-making. Slee argues that telling one's story is primary and fundamental to identity formation.[20] Although it is possible to record one's story purely for oneself, it is implied that a story has a reader or a listener who connects with the narrative in some way. 'Personalised faithing' refers to the way that faith is articulated with reference to spiritual exemplars. Parental figures, mentors, teachers and spiritual guides serve to offer a point of security and relatedness in a world that can seem meaningless and fragmented. These people serve as a concrete example of an incarnational ideal. They 'enshrine faith in a human other'.[21] Although Slee emphasises the importance of community in faith development of women, she maintains Fowler's focus on the necessary shift in the locus of authority from an external to internal source.

All of the women engaged in my research recalled stories which clearly illustrated this shift in authority in their spiritual lives. Although, for many, the judgment of others remained important, their choices now relied on their own inner authority to select the course of action and take responsibility for their choices. One participant, 'Marion', explained this using the language of her Catholic faith construct. She describes how she adopted 'primacy of conscience' as her method of making informed decisions, rather than simply accepting the edicts of the church. Essentially, 'Marion' was distinguishing between the external authority of the institution and her new-found trust in her own inner authority.

'Candice' describes this time as a stretching that challenged her traditional views and gave her a broader understanding of God. She recounts a conversation with a church leader about atonement that was pivotal in claiming her own inner spiritual authority:

> She said, 'I just don't understand what you're not getting. Don't you believe in God's wrath?' And I just went—it was like the shutters opened—and I just went, 'No! I don't think I do' and that was personal authority, for me, and it took a lot of courage to actually say it. In that split second after she asked that question, I toyed with saying, 'Oh, yeah. Of course, I do'. But I actually had

---
19 Slee, *Women's Faith*, 62-65.
20 Slee, *Women's Faith*, 68-70.
21 Slee, *Women's Faith*, 70-74.

this moment of reckoning where I just realised, 'No. I don't'. So, to say that out loud was actually liberating. It felt like a victory for me.

Although the movement from an external to an internal locus of authority takes time, there are some moments that the women recount as points of revelation. Often these moments include the woman hearing her own inner voice speak for the first time. The courage of 'Candice' to share her own beliefs allowed her voice to be heard not only by the leader she spoke with, but by herself. 'Candice' shared that, preceding such instances, the presence of a spiritual director or mentor provided a safe space to gain confidence in her inner spiritual authority. The women practised using their voice with people of safety before speaking their mind in spaces that were perceived as less protected.

Although the quest to discover inner spiritual authority is not unique to women, the challenge for women within the patriarchal structures of the institutional church is particularly burdensome.[22] Work specifically focused on women's experience must consider the unique challenges for women in discovering their inner spiritual authority. Slee's findings concerning faith development suggest that women move through the processes of alienation and awakening. During alienation, women experience a profound loss of self, faith, and authentic connection to others.[23] This process is often the call into the growth and development of the subsequent process of awakening, where women discover a new self and a new orientation.[24] The process of awakening involves finding language and metaphors that describe the new 'subjective knowledge' that has taken the place of the previously 'received knowledge'.[25] This process of awakening is equated in women with the finding of their own voice.[26] For contemporary women, the discovery of their inner spiritual authority also brings a new self-awareness and self-assurance. The voice the woman finds is the expression of this new self to the world. Finding ways to express this within the constraints of the institutional church can be challenging and disheartening.

---

22 Nicola Slee, *Fragments for Fractured Times: What Feminist Practical Theology Brings to the Table* (London: SCM Press, 2020), 16. Kochurani Abraham, *Persisting Patriarchy: Intersectionalities, Negotiations, Subversions* (Cham, Switzerland: Palgrave Macmillan, 2019), 19.
23 Slee, *Women's Faith*, 81.
24 Slee, *Women's Faith*, 110.
25 Slee, *Women's Faith*, 105.
26 Ursula King, *Women and Spirituality: Voices of Protest and Promise* (New York: New Amsterdam, 1989), 2.

Both Fowler and Slee's work in faith development are helpful in considering a movement to an internal locus of authority as a natural progression in the individual's faith journey. The extent to which there is freedom to develop in this way depends greatly on the community context in which the individual is situated. Faith traditions across history and from different cultures have developed their own methods of combating dissidence within their communities, sometimes with dire consequences. The authority held by the church, therefore, holds great power in terms of individual faith development.

Women's Personal Lived Experience of the Divine

Forty years ago, Dorothee Sölle, searching for liberating strands within the patriarchal church tradition for feminist Christians, identified mystical theology as a resource.[27] Her argument was based on the experiential nature of mysticism and an understanding of God that is not dominating or viewed as other. Sölle defines mysticism as 'the knowledge of God through and from experience'.[28] Drawing on their own experiences, women are deconstructing the patriarchal and inherited patterns of religious institutions into uncharted spaces that are life-giving.[29] Women's attraction to a more mystical way of life to honour their own lived experience is not a new phenomenon.[30]

The spiritual journey of the women interviewed was strongly experiential, a reality predicted and strongly endorsed by feminist theologians.[31] During the conversations, the women shared a variety of experiences ranging from intimate, spiritual encounters to significant relational and life events. The anecdotes recalled all bore significance for the woman in her spiritual life. Explicitly or implicitly, many of the women engaged in some form of theological reflection prior to or during

---

27 Dorothee Sölle, 'Mysticism, Liberation and the Names of God: A Feminist Reflection,' *Christianity and Crisis* 41, no. 11 (1981): 179.
28 Dorothee Sölle, *The Silent Cry: Mysticism and Resistance*, trans. Barbara and Martin Rumscheidt (Minneapolis: Fortress Press, 2001), 45.
29 See for example, Abraham, *Persisting Patriarchy*, 14-15. Sabrina Muller, *Lived Theology: Impulses for a Pastoral Theology of Empowerment*, (Eugene, OR: Cascade Books, 2021), 31. Muller refers to lived theology being grounded in experience.
30 The writings of women mystics throughout the centuries are illustrations of this, including Hildegaard of Bingen, Hadewijch of Brabant, Mechthild of Magdeburg, Marguerite Porete, Teresa of Avila and Julian of Norwich.
31 Slee, *Women's faith*, 170-73. Kathleen R. Fischer, *Women at the Well: Feminist Perspectives on Spiritual Direction* (London: SPCK, 1989), 12. Beverley J Lanzetta, *Radical Wisdom: A Feminist Mystical Theology* (Minneapolis: Fortress Press, 2005), 41.

our conversation. Their ability to integrate their experiences into the wider story of their lives displayed a trust in their own authority and an ability to notice the Divine at work in and through their experiences. Beverley Lanzetta, in proposing a new feminist mystical theology, 'affirms the revelatory and prophetic in women's experience'.[32]

The perceived need to authenticate an individual's religious experience is a contentious issue in the relationship between the individual's spiritual authority and that of the community's external authority. It is one thing for an individual to claim they have directly experienced God, but is there a need for the community to verify this in order to trust their authority? This brings into question the mysterious nature of the spiritual and religious. William James' *The Varieties of Religious Experiences* is considered a classic text in understanding the nature of spiritual occurrences.[33] Of particular interest to this study are James' conclusions about whether we can invoke religious experiences as authoritative. He answers this question in three parts. First, he concludes mystical states, when well-developed, are absolutely authoritative over the individual to whom they come.[34] He argues that the experience itself creates a knowing or a truth by which the person finds a force to live. Secondly, James suggests no authority emanates from religious experiences 'which should make it a duty for those who stand outside of them to accept their revelations uncritically'.[35] He describes the religious experiences of mysticism as privileged and isolated, however, these should not be considered superior in authority. Lastly, James concludes religious experiences break down the authority of the non-mystical, rationalistic consciousness that is based on the senses alone.[36] Although the individual experience carries no authority for others, it cannot be denied that there exist mystical states unable to be explained with rational thought.

In her convincing argument, Grace Jantzen, an historian of spirituality, describes James' understanding of mysticism and religious experience as 'misguided and inadequate'.[37] After examining James' contribution and his large influence on subsequent writing, Jantzen measures his

---

32 Lanzetta, *Radical Wisdom*, 13.
33 William James, *The Varieties of Religious Experience: A Study in Human Nature, Being the Gifford Lectures on Natural Religion Delivered at Edinburgh in 1901-1902* (New York: New American Library, 1958).
34 James, *The Varieties*, 323-324.
35 James, *The Varieties*, 324-325.
36 James, *The Varieties*, 32, 327.
37 Grace M. Jantzen, 'Mysticism and Experience,' *Religious Studies* 25, no. 3 (1989): 295, https://doi.org/10.1017/S0034412500019867.

understanding against the accounts of two mystics: Bernard of Clairvaux and Julian of Norwich. From her reading, she concludes that the concentration upon religious experience is unhelpful, as the goal of mysticism is, in fact, union with God.[38] She asserts union with God is experiential in a broad sense; however, it cannot be equated with intense experiences such as visions, voices or feelings of ecstasy. This argument supports the view that, although the individual's presenting experience may be a starting point, it is the relationship with God that is central.

Both Robert Oakes and John Hick struggle with the complexity of religious experience. Hick's examination of the validity of religious experience draws on the different levels of human experience and their interpretation. He argues it is this complexity that creates ambiguity.[39] Acknowledging that religious experiences are not always theistic, Hick then examines the idea of union with God. He concludes that a truly unitive experience cannot be expressed or reported as there would be no memory of an event where the individual's distinct consciousness ceased to exist.[40] Hick does not deny the possibility of such experiences as, 'for someone who sees the world religiously it is rational to experience life that way'.[41] Oakes, on the other hand, examines the problematic concept of a self-authenticating religious experience.[42] He admits that there is always the possibility that such an experience is deluded and, since the individual could be mistaken, the conclusion could be made there is no such thing as a self-authenticating experience. Oakes continues, however, to define a self-authenticating religious experience as 'a veridical experience of God which is sufficient to guarantee that the person having that veridical experience could never have any justification for questioning its veridicality'.[43] Oakes' view is similar to that of James. The experience has authority for the individual, but not necessarily for others.

Lawrence Cunningham offers some practical advice for discerning the authenticity of a religious experience.[44] He raises the question

---

38 Jantzen, 'Mysticism', 313.
39 John Hick, 'Religious Experience: Its Nature and Validity,' in *Disputed Questions in Theology and the Philosophy of Religion* (New Haven: Yale University Press, 1993), 17-20.
40 Hick, 'Religious Experience', 27.
41 Hick, 'Religious Experience', 31.
42 Robert A. Oakes, 'Religious Experience and Rational Certainty,' *Religious Studies* 12, no. 3 (1976): 311-318, https://doi.org/10.1017/S0034412500009409.
43 Oakes, 'Religious Experience', 314.
44 Lawrence S. Cunningham, 'Authority and Religious Experience,' *The Way*, no. 92 (1998): 9-19.

of the relationship of such experiences to the authority embedded in the believing community. Without simplifying the complexity of authentication, Cunningham suggests opening a dialogue where questions can be asked regarding how the experience brings insight and reality to the Word of God as it is preached in the tradition, how it helps one grow as a person and how it may lead the individual to further develop the fruits of the Spirit.[45] Using examples, Cunningham demonstrates the use of discernment and authority as more of an art than a science, stressing the need to find a balance between the freedom of the Christian and the unity of the community.[46] Cunningham concludes his examination, of what he describes as a complex issue, with a simplistic quote from Rabbi Gamaliel: 'If the experience is a human one it will fail but, if it is from God, it cannot be overthrown'.[47] Although this view may be adopted by many, it is a disappointing conclusion to what is otherwise a good discussion on the topic of authority and religious experience.

The varieties of approaches to individual religious experiences highlight the complexity of finding methods to validate their authenticity. The experiences themselves may be very ordinary or more extraordinary in nature and may challenge the authority of the community at different levels. The need for a safe space where open exploration of such experiences can occur is much needed to find a place of discernment and discovery which moves beyond right and wrong, orthodox or heretical, acceptable and not. This occurs in supportive relationships rather than situations where judgment is acceptable.

Conflicting authorities and women's push to the edge of the church

The central place of experience in the stories of these women was significant. How they processed these experiences, with whom they shared them and the reactions they received from those who listened all played an influential role in their spiritual journeys. This had either a positive or negative effect depending on the woman's own sense of spiritual authority and the severity of the reactions from external sources of authority. Unfortunately, for many women the institutional church has not provided the space to explore and discover their own inner spiritual authority. As demonstrated in my research, this can result in individuals feeling pushed to the fringes of the church or leaving the faith community.

Despite their favourable appreciation for the place of the church in their lives, each woman shared stories of tension, abrasion, and conflict

---

45 Cunningham, 'Authority', 13-14. For fruits of the Spirit see Galatians 5:22-23.
46 Cunningham, 'Authority', 17-19.
47 Cunningham, 'Authority', 18.

with the institutional church. The context of these situations varied, often involving issues of leadership, decisions of the church, use of language, conflicting theologies, or reactions to the woman's own sense of calling. The confines of this article allow me to share the experiences of only three women: 'Stephanie', 'Candice' and 'Kelly'. These anecdotes are but a sample of the many difficult and painful stories shared.

Many of the women felt trapped within prescribed roles that did not echo their own sense of calling. For some, this reflected the restricted role of women within their particular denomination. For others, this arose from stereotypes around gender roles. 'Stephanie' shared:

> I guess my whole life has been me throwing myself into religious activities that were predominantly children and families ministry because I was a girl and that was the only thing that was okay for you to do.

As a young mother, 'Stephanie' was nominated for a leadership role within her church community. She spoke with the minister about her sense of calling and was told, 'Your primary role is to be a mother, go home'. This dismissal of women's sense of calling was common amongst the women.

On experiencing their own alienation from the church community, many of the women subsequently became more aware of others who found themselves on the margins. This is illustrated clearly in 'Candice's' story of leaving a church community in which she had exercised leadership and been heavily involved. After refusing to sign a prescribed statement of faith, her membership was revoked, and she was no longer allowed to serve in leadership roles. As 'Candice' stood at the back of the church after an annual general meeting in which she was not able to participate, she spoke with a long-term attender of the church whom she knew to be gay. She said,

> 'Did you come to the AGM today?' And he said, 'Oh no, I never come'. And I said, 'But you've been involved in this church for ages. How come?' And he said, 'Well, I guess I've never qualified as a member in this church'. So, I think that was the final nail in the coffin for me and really gave me the courage and the conviction to say, 'Sorry, see you later. I'm outta here'.

Often the women would not make the decision to leave a church community based entirely on their own experience. It was their ability to identify with the treatment of others and see patterns of behaviour that extended beyond their own circumstances that had more influence.

The conflict created between the women and church leaders regarding theological views also affected the women's recoil from the use of traditional, patriarchal language. This arises in many forms of church life but is particularly evident in worship. Many of the women shared that they were not able to sing the old hymns or participate in the prayers anymore because of the patriarchal or outdated language. 'Kelly' passionately clarifies why her occasional visits to church are not a good experience for herself or the community:

> Simply because they're using this language...it's such a male language. It is so violent. Like, they're not even aware how violent it is. And then they get utterly offended when I point out that.

Her choice not to remain silent within the church community had not been received warmly and was a cause of conflict. In all three of these situations, the women's discovery of their own inner spiritual authority created tensions with the external authority of their church community.

Individual Spiritual Authority and the Faith Community

The clash of individual spiritual authority and the external authority of the ecclesiastical hierarchy is a recurring issue throughout the history of the church. Jesuit theologian, Karl Rahner, attempted to address the issue of how the church can encourage individuals to grow in personal faith while remaining in community.[48] He had a vision, in the mid-twentieth century, of a future church that could return to its roots and trust more in the authority of God. He offers an image of hope that embraces both individual, inner authority and the need for a community of faith.

Rahner emphasises the authority of the experience of God over the institutionalised authority of the church. As he describes it, the office of the church has a functional character, but does not necessarily represent the reality for the members. He argues that the church of the future must be a de-clericalised church where the officeholders, in humility, allow for the spirit to breathe where it will. This charismatic element of the church can never be regulated, and the authority of the officeholders must be an authority of freedom. The officeholders will only have as much effective authority as is given to them freely by the believers. In such a community, those in positions of authority will change in reaction to criticism, have the courage to reverse decisions and will cause no damage by admitting their uncertainties and doubts.[49]

---

48 Karl Rahner, *The Shape of the Church to Come* (London: S.P.C.K, 1974).
49 Rahner, *The Shape of the Church*, 57-59.

Supporting the argument for a de-clericalised church, Rahner also appeals to the church to remain true to being a community of real spirituality. He observes that there is too little talk about the mystery of God in the church and, therefore, it lacks vitality and has become defensive of its own teaching.[50] He argues that when the church speaks out in authority against heresy, it should not appeal to the teaching authority of the church's magisterium, but to the living Spirit of faith. He acknowledges the difficulty of more open church structures where it is not easy to define membership and assign the limits of orthodoxy upon the members.[51]

Karl Rahner's insights concerning ecclesiology have been applied much further afield than Europe. His assertion that the authority of the experience of God should be prioritised over institutionalised authority informs the situation of the Australian women interviewed. The dissenting voices of the women often led them to be viewed as trouble-makers. The question which arises from Rahner's vision for the church is whether the voices of women speaking from their own inner spiritual authority will be heard by leaders of the church.

Conformity and voices of dissent

In many of these stories shared by the women there is a common theme of no longer fitting within the church institution. 'Alice' described this saying, 'It was like the shoes were too tight'. 'Rachel' used the image of a root-bound plant that needed to find new soil to survive. For many years, some of these women attempted to conform to the practices and beliefs of their associated faith communities. The combination of theological education, increased self- knowledge and the resulting trust in their own inner spiritual authority led to their defining themselves as dwelling on the edge of the church. This raises questions about how the institution maintains conformity within its communities and how it manages voices of dissent.

Simon Oxley describes dissent as emerging from commitment and conviction rather than being viewed as complaining or fault finding.[52] He argues that dissent needs to be nurtured for the sake of a healthy community. Instead, as the contemporary women of my research illustrate,

---

50 Rahner, *The Shape of the Church*, 82-87.
51 Rahner, *The Shape of the Church*, 95-98.
52 Simon Oxley, 'Nurturing Conformity or Dissent. What is the Function of Christian Formation?', *Journal of European Baptist Studies* 14, no. 3 (2014):34-46.

our church institutions value conformity, often under the guise of formation. Formation fashions or moulds the individual into a predetermined outcome. This can occur consciously or subconsciously. The women interviewed in this research became aware of the limiting nature of the church which led them to state that 'the shoes are too tight'. The voices they had discovered arising from their inner spiritual authority were not welcomed within their church communities. Voices of dissent, however, hold a valid alternative and conformity does not encourage learning and growth.[53] The women in this study no longer felt a need to conform to meet their human need to be loved, valued, and accepted. Their decision to reside on the edge of the church, although in many cases filled with grief, opened doors to new ways of expressing their faith life and finding a community that was liberating and more spacious.

For the women interviewed, the church had provided a nurturing space to experience religious education, develop a sense of self and even discover their own inner spiritual authority. Their growth within the church could be described under the heading of faith education and development. Largely, these activities were encouraged by the faith communities until the woman found her voice and spoke from her own authority and experience. Now heard as an unorthodox voice of dissent, the women experienced being silenced, removed from leadership or simply being dismissed. Their experience could not be further from Oxley's view that voices of dissent should be valued as an opportunity for growth in the community.[54]

The challenge for the church from the Australian women interviewed, and from both Rahner and Oxley is to listen to the voices of dissent in their midst. The women longed for their personal experiences to be taken seriously and validated. This does not mean that every voice will contain authority that is relevant for the whole community. The women did not mention needing others in the community to agree with their viewpoint. They did, however, talk about the need to be heard and have their personal experience of faith validated by the community. Rather than reacting in fear to the voice of dissent to eradicate any possibility of unorthodox belief, the church community may find they benefit from the stretching and challenging that occur from engaging with difference.

---

53 Oxley, 'Nurturing', 39-44.
54 Oxley, 'Nurturing', 39-44.

Conclusion

The participants in my research described how 'the shoes [of the church] were too tight'. In this essay, I have issued a challenge to our churches to provide a broader space for those who embark on the journey of discovering inner spiritual authority. Our churches deliver programs promoting faith education and development which encourage people to examine their long-held faith constructs. Learning to trust their own personal experiences of God, women can struggle to find their own voice within the patriarchal tradition of the church. When their opinions and views seem at odds with the external authority of the faith community, women's voices of dissent may be viewed as troublesome. Rather than repeating patterns of fear and control where these differing views are silenced and ostracised from the community, we need to practise intentional listening. Embracing the voices of dissent within our midst and validating the lived experience of all people will only broaden and grow the possibilities for the community of faith into the future.

Chapter Twelve

Anxious behaviours at the interface between pastors and congregations

Kathy Matuschka

Introduction

Have you noticed how things are more likely to go wrong when people are anxious? When I was a physiotherapist working in a hospital, it sometimes seemed to me those clients who behaved anxiously were more likely to experience adverse events. When people are anxious, they may not listen well or think reflectively, often unaware of the effect they are having on others. In cases of severe, persistent anxiety, it can be difficult for the staff and family members caring for them to avoid becoming anxious. It was my impression that sometimes the presence of anxiety induced a feedback loop in which no one was behaving at their best!

The research project described below began with my personal experience as a lay leader within a congregation going through an anxious time. I noticed that some of our behaviours as leaders, though well-intended, seemed to make matters worse rather than better. For example, I made assumptions about others' motivations rather than asking clarifying questions, reacted quickly when offended, spoke too much and listened too little. In my desire to help heal my congregation's wound, I instead contributed to an anxious feedback loop.

Through my work in Ministry and Mission in my denomination's district office, I also observe signs of anxiety, particularly around the relationships between pastors and congregations. It is not uncommon to hear congregational members say, 'If we get just the right pastor, he[1] will solve our problems', as if everyone is going to forget current and historical differences and get on board behind this imagined 'right pastor'.

---

[1] The pronoun 'he' is used because the LCA ordains males exclusively at this time.

The highs and lows of interdependence

Christians understand congregations to be local manifestations of Christ's body, the church.[2] This organic metaphor assumes an interdependence between individuals. Since we understand ourselves to be simultaneously sinners and saints, it is not surprising that this interdependence can have both positive and negative expressions. Put another way, humans can be at our best as well as our worst within group settings. This research project offered insights into how we behave within congregations, and the possible effect of anxiety on group behaviour.

Does anxiety within congregations prompt behaviours that lead to emotional dynamics that may undermine our freedom to grow more like Christ? Rabbi Edwin Friedman's work validated my research interest:

> The emotional processes in a family always have the power to subvert or override its religious values. The emotional system of any family...can always 'jam' the spiritual messages it is receiving.[3]

Based on their respective disciplines of theology and psychology, Schults and Sandage concur with Friedman: 'relational systems contexts are "cultures of embeddedness" which can support spiritual formation and transformation but can also impede progress or even shape the pathology of spiritual malformation.[4]

My path into this area of research began with some publications by the Alban Institute.[5] Alban were specialist publishers of resources to help leaders facilitate healing and transformation within their congregations.[6] The Alban reading led to Friedman's book cited above: Friedman offers insight and wisdom into the 'blessed messes' that sometimes characterise faith communities.[7] In turn, Friedman pointed to Murray Bowen's Family Systems Theory.

---

2 1 Corinthians 12:27.
3 Edwin H. Friedman, *Generation to Generation: Family Process in Church and Synagogue* (New York: Guilford, 2011), 6-7.
4 Fount LeRon Shults and Steven J. Sandage, *Transforming Spirituality: Integrating Theology and Psychology* (Grand Rapids: Baker Academic, 2006), 172.
5 E.g., Peter L. Steinke, *Congregational Leadership in Anxious Times* (Hendon: Alban Institute, 2006.) or Beth Ann Gaede, ed., *When a Congregation is Betrayed: Responding to Clergy Misconduct* (Hendon: The Alban Institute, 2006).
6 For more about the Alban Institute, see https://alban.org/about-alban/history/.
7 When referring to Friedman's work, 'faith community' acknowledges his Jewish context. In this paper, 'Congregation' is used only in the context of Christian faith communities.

Research objective

My aim was to use Bowen's family systems concepts (which will be discussed shortly) to better understand our behaviour within congregations through a psychological lens, and then to investigate the potential usefulness of these concepts for inviting transformation. The qualitative research employed document analysis and semi-structured interviews to explore the following question: To what extent can theories of differentiation and/or co-dependency be of use for understanding the pastor-congregation relationship in Lutheran Church of Australia Queensland District (LCAQD) congregations?

Why restrict the research into congregational emotional dynamics to the relationship between pastors and congregations, rather than between members of congregations? First, issues between pastors and congregations are often reported or discussed, so I expected that my interview subjects would also have something to say on this topic. Secondly, my denomination has reference documentation that defines expectations of the relationship between pastors and congregations,[8] allowing me to compare expected and actual behaviours.

This research was motivated by my experience that while congregational conflict and anxiety are distressing, they also provide an opportunity to understand ourselves in new ways, and possibly become more authentic and accepting of ourselves and of one another. I was looking not only for clearer insights to the presenting problem but also for understandings that might inform my approach to congregations as systems.

It was the thought that emotional dynamics can work against what God's spirit would do within the soul of our community that underpinned this research. There were elements of a transformative philosophy at play in that 'the research contains an action agenda for reform that may change lives of the participants, the institutions ... and the researcher's life'.[9]

Significance of this research for our mission to heal

Healing begins when there is acknowledgment that something is wrong. All going well, the problem is then diagnosed, and an efficacious remedy

---

[8] The doctrinal statements and theological opinions of my church body are gathered here: https://www.lca.org.au/departments/commissions/cticr/

[9] J.W. Creswell and J.D. Creswell, *Research Design: Qualitative, Quantitative, and Mixed Methods Approaches* (Los Angeles: Sage publications, 2017), 9.

is both available and utilised. While as Christians we believe that the remedy for soul conditions is found in the gospel of Jesus Christ through the power or God's Spirit, we often lack awareness of what is wrong within ourselves or our communities. Those who would be healers within congregations sometimes notice things that others do not. Thus, they can become carriers of their congregation's grief and discomfort during anxious times.

Some of those who notice and feel the pain respond to anxiety and conflict within their congregation by drifting away from church commitment or moving to another congregation or denomination. But others are able to stay within their denominations of origin. Why would they take the potentially hazardous trek of exploring and critiquing the systems and behaviours that work against healing and transformation as followers of Jesus Christ? There may be many reasons for this, but one that I have noticed in my ecumenical travels is a deep desire to share this healing with 'my people', the people whose story we have lived and understand.

Accordingly, my research is grounded in the Lutheran Church of Australia (LCA).[10] While asking the question, 'What's going on *here*, among *my* people?', I note that factors affecting *all* mainline churches in Australia include:

- Societal anxiety, stemming from such complex problems as loneliness and climate change. Bowen's eighth concept, societal emotional process, suggests that there is a feedback loop between our wider society and its various building blocks.[11] This means that increased societal anxiety will automatically lead to increased anxiety within congregations.
- Worldview changes that are challenging previously assumed connections between identity, societal order and religious thought.[12]

---

10 The LCA is also known as the LCANZ, an informal but popular recognition of the fact that it includes New Zealand as well as Australia.
11 R. Robert Creech, *Family Systems and Congregational Life: A Map for Ministry* (Grand Rapids: Baker Academic, 2019), 27.
12 Philip Hughes, 'Australian Culture: Formative Influences and Major Components' in *Charting the Faith of Australians: Thirty Years in the Christian Research Association*, ed. Philip Hughes (Nunawading: Christian Research Association, 2016a), 33. Hughes describes the change in Australian culture as 'a change from seeing the world as a system, in which each individual had to abide by certain rules, to seeing the world as a maze individuals had to personally negotiate'.

- Declining attendance and increasing average age of members in mainline denominations.[13]
- Public mistrust, especially in response to clergy misconduct and the findings of the Royal Commission into Institutional Responses to Child Sexual Abuse.
- A shortage of pastors/ministers/priests.
- Ongoing conflict around how we read and understand the Bible, manifested most significantly within the LCA as the 'ordination debate' over whether both women and men may be ordained.
- Significant uncertainties and changes to Sunday worship patterns because of COVID-19, as well as the impact of COVID-19 on societal anxiety.[14] This factor emerged after the conclusion of my research.

Application of Family Systems Theory within congregations

Family Systems Theory (FST) was not the only option available for making sense of emotional dynamics between pastors and congregations. I chose FST first because I had already found it helpful for making sense of what was happening within communities in complex situations. Secondly, by concerning itself with groups as well as individuals, FST encompasses both psychological and sociological understandings; that is, it helps us understand more about our behaviour both as individuals and as groups.

Psychiatrist Murray Bowen (1913-1990) pioneered FST for his work within biological families. Rather than taking a linear, cause-and-effect approach to people with anxiety, Bowen recognised the complexity of family units, exploring how the 'presenting patient' might be an indicator of dysfunction *throughout* the family system. Bowen considered that we are not free agents, but interdependent; within a family system my behaviour plays a part in determining your behaviour. As anxiety increases, so does the prevalence of dysfunction. R. Robert Creech noted

---

13 Australian Bureau of Statistics reports on religious affiliation, e.g. https://www.abs.gov.au/media-centre/media-releases/2021-census-shows-changes-australias-religious-diversity while National Church Life Survey Research https://www.ncls.org.au/ offers research profiles to individual congregations.

14 The current National Church Life Surveys completed in 2016 and 2021 offer participating congregations pre- and post-COVID comparisons. McCrindle Research also leads research into the impact of COVID as well as the Australian spiritual landscape, e.g. https://mccrindle.com.au/app/uploads/reports/Future-of-the-Church-in-Australia-Report-2020.pdf.

that we '*unconsciously* monitor those around us and *automatically* react or respond without thinking, as anxiety makes its way around the system'.[15] This statement mirrors my own observations and experience of congregations going through an anxious period. Bowen developed and applied his theories in his psychiatric practice by observing his patient's family unit and asking whether the person in crisis might in fact be reflecting wider dysfunction within the family system.

A family systems approach prompts questions like:

- Is the person displaying aberrant behaviour the only one with a problem?
- Or might their behaviour reflect dysfunction throughout the family system?

Rabbi Friedman considered communities of faith to be a particular type of family. Drawing on his background as a family therapist, Friedman applied Bowen Family Systems Theory in faith communities.[16] Until 2006, the Alban Institute sponsored a significant body of applied research which demonstrated the usefulness of FST principles within congregations. More recently, Creech has drawn attention to ongoing developments in the field of family systems and congregational life.[17]

Rabbi Friedman highlighted the leader's responsibility to manage their own emotions and reactions, and thereby reduce anxiety within the family system. Whereas we often view leadership development as learning to do things, or to do them better, Friedman equally emphasised the leader's role in *ceasing* from doing the things that perpetuate dysfunction and anxiety. For example, Friedman suggested that leaders can exacerbate anxiety by taking members' concerns and complaints too seriously. Friedman proposed the following paradox: 'The seriousness with which families approach their problems can be more the cause of their difficulties than the effect of their problems. Efforts directed at the seriousness itself will often eliminate the problem'.[18] In regular family units, this is something that parents gradually learn and at which grandparents often excel!

Specific concepts within FST

Bowen's theory claims that the dual forces of togetherness and individuality need to be present and in balance to promote healthy growth. His

---

15 Creech, *Family Systems*, 15.
16 Friedman, *Generation to Generation*.
17 Creech, *Family Systems*.
18 Friedman, *Generation to Generation*, 50.

framework also identifies eight concepts, some negative and some positive, for family systems.[19] The concept most relevant to my research was differentiation of self, which is a positive attribute. Many of the negative dynamics Bowen describes are manifestations of poorly differentiated relationships.

What is meant by differentiation of self? A self-differentiated person can remain emotionally connected with others while aware and thoughtful about how they respond to others' behaviour. A well differentiated person can reduce the anxiety within a community by lovingly and calmly behaving in ways that are consistent with their own principles despite the anxiety surrounding them.[20] In contrast, a less well differentiated person might unknowingly behave in ways that perpetuate dysfunction while sincerely believing themselves to be caring for others in their community.

Within Bowen's framework, co-dependence is roughly the opposite of differentiation of self. Co-dependence indicates emotional fusion in relationships. In a co-dependent relationship, the togetherness force is too high and the individuality force too low. It is 'a relationship in which two or more people support or encourage each other's unhealthy habits'.[21] Marks et al. undertook research to define three distinct co-dependent factors which provided the basis for my analysis of interview data:

- *Self-sacrifice (neglecting one's needs to focus on meeting the needs of others).*
- *Interpersonal control (an entrenched belief in one's capacity to fix other people's problems and control their behaviours).*
- *Emotional suppression (the deliberate suppression, or limited conscious awareness, of one's emotions until they become overwhelming).*[22]

Parsons and Lees further help define co-dependence: 'it is important to distinguish co-dependent behaviour from healthy, normal communal function, which is termed "inter-dependence"'.[23]

---

19 Creech, *Family Systems*, 19-27. The concepts are emotional triangles, the scale of differentiation, family emotional process, multigenerational transmission, family projection, sibling position, emotional cut-off and societal emotional process.
20 Creech, *Family Systems*, 20-21.
21 Andrew M. Colman, *A Dictionary of Psychology* (Oxford: Oxford University Press, 2015).
22 Anthony Marks, Rebecca L. Blore, Donald W. Hine and Greg E. Dear, 'Development and Validation of a Revised Measure of Co-Dependency', *Australian Journal of Psychology* 64 (2012), 119, https://dx.doi.org/doi:10.1111/j.1742-9536.2011.00034.x.
23 George Parsons and Speed Leas, *Understanding your Congregation as a System: The Manual* (Bethesda: Alban Institute, 1993), 8.

The term co-dependence is not often used in faith communities. It is more commonly used in reference to families with substance dependencies: While it takes two to form a co-dependent relationship, there tend to be distinct roles such as 'addict' and 'enabler'. However, the following offered encouragement to continue this line of enquiry: 'Christian communities are at increased risk of becoming co-dependent because we accept everyone, seek to operate graciously and so inadvertently enable dysfunctional people to dominate congregational leadership'.[24]

Methodology
Practical theology

The term 'practical theology' is broad and can refer to either the methodology or specific methods or tools. Practical theology methodology focuses on the human experience as 'a place where the gospel is grounded, embodied, interpreted and lived out'.[25] Practical theology is designed to facilitate research within faith communities such as congregations.

Practical theology is multivocal and multidisciplinary, and therefore well positioned for interpreting and understanding the complexities of congregations and offering paths toward healing and recovery. A multidisciplinary approach which uses psychological and sociological theories alongside theological principles can help us understand our humanity and our communities, guiding us to the heart of what may be troubling us.

For Alastair Campbell, practical theology 'is concerned with the study of specific social structures and individual initiatives within which God's continuing work of renewal and restitution becomes manifest'.[26] Thus, Campbell focuses our attention on the transformational, communal aspects of doing theology.

This research design began with a belief that everyone does theology. The point was to listen to what a range of people are observing and experiencing about emotional dynamics within congregations, and the theological meaning they are making from what they observe. Helen Cameron's four voices model of doing practical theology, as expressed in Figure 1, provided the framework for this enquiry.

---

24 Kenneth Alan Moe and Alban Institute, *The Pastor's Survival Manual: 10 Perils in Parish Ministry and How to Handle Them* (Bethesda: Alban Institute, 1995), 51-58.
25 John Swinton and Harriet Mowat, *Practical Theology and Qualitative Research* (London: SCM Press, 2006), 5.
26 Alastair Campbell, 'The Nature of Practical Theology' in *The Blackwell Reader in Pastoral and Practical Theology*, eds. James Woodward and Stephen Pattison (Oxford: Blackwell Publishers, 2000), 84.

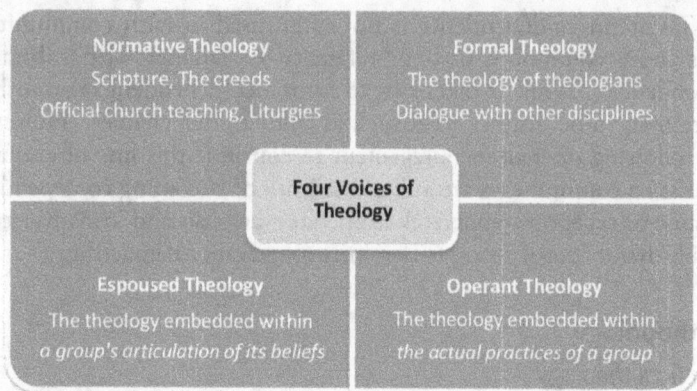

*Figure 1: Four voices of theology, as taught by Helen Cameron**

* Helen Cameron, Deborah Bhatti, Catherine Duce, James Sweeney and Clare Watkins, *Talking about God in Practice: Theological Action Research and Practical Theology* (London: SCM Press, 2010), 54.

The four voices process involves listening to the authoritative written texts of our faith traditions (Normative and Formal Theology) and what Christian faith communities say about what they believe (Espoused Theology) as well as observing how we behave (Operant Theology) and exploring the consistencies and inconsistencies between these voices.

Figure 2 represents the path I took from my observations and ideas to the outcomes of my research.

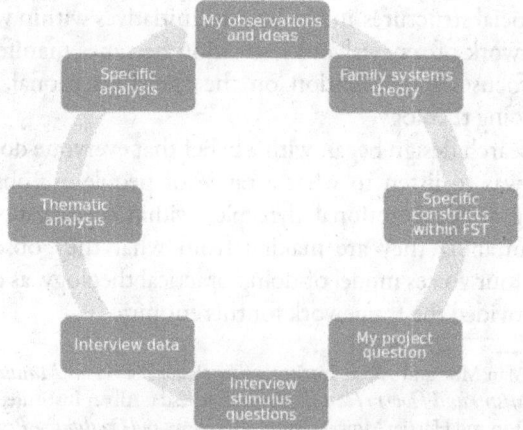

Figure 2: My research process

Returning now to the research question: 'To what extent can theories of differentiation and/or co-dependency be of use for understanding the pastor-congregation relationship in LCAQD congregations?'

The literature review indicated that the concept of differentiation of self might be key to understanding why congregations often work against their best (and stated) intentions. Following the practical theology process defined above, a critical review of the LCA's written expectations of the pastor-congregation relationship was conducted.

The first two relevant statements are from the LCA's Doctrinal Statements and Theological Opinions (DSTO), and the third document consulted was the LCA Letter of Call.[27] The DSTOs were drafted by theological experts[28] and subsequently adopted as the LCA's espoused theology. The first two documents indicate a side-by-side or reciprocal relationship between pastor and congregation, where each person takes responsibility for their own behaviour and their own contribution within the community, as follows:

'... the office of ministry does not give to those who bear it arbitrary power over Christians, nor does it deliver the ministers of the word up to the arbitrary directions and commands of men [sic]'[29] *and* '...the two ministries relate to each other through Christ.'[30]

In Bowen Family Systems terms, the expected relationship between pastors and congregations could be described as 'well-differentiated'.

In contrast, the LCA Letter of Call tends to use more active language for the pastor's role (e.g., 'guard and promote faithfully our spiritual welfare ... exercising spiritual oversight over us') and more passive language for the congregation's role (e.g., 'seek your counsel and aid for our spiritual welfare, cooperating in your endeavours'). This more hierarchical stance may promote a less-differentiated relationship, as it could be read to mean

---

27 The LCA Letter of Call (c2000) is a covenant used internally between pastors and congregations and is therefore not publicly available.
28 LCA members would generally consider that members of the Commission of Theology and Interchurch Relations (and its consultants) along with the bishops are its theological experts.
29 Commission on Theology and Inter-Church Relations, 'Theses on the Office of the Ministry', 1A, No VI (1950). This document was adopted by the LCA founding Convention of Synod 1966. https://www.lca.org.au/departments/commissions/cticr/
30 Commission on Theology and Inter-Church Relations, 'The Ministry of the People of God and the Public Ministry', 2D (1950). This document was adopted by the Commission for Theology and Inter-Church Relations (CTICR) 1992. https://www.lca.org.au/departments/commissions/cticr/

that the pastor is considered to hold responsibility toward something that is internal to congregation members, namely, the wellbeing of their souls.

The operant theology was investigated in consultation with a community that could be expected to share some of my insights and desires for transformation. The research was not so much a study of a congregation or congregations but of some people's perspectives on congregational life. The purposeful sample I chose comprised people whose work depended on them understanding how congregations 'tick', both organisationally and organically. They were skilled practitioners whose current (or recent) service (paid or voluntary) in the LCA means they are routinely called upon to provide consultative services in the areas of pastoral ministry or human services to pastors and congregations of the LCAQD.

My research paradigm was a blend of post-positivist and critical theory. The research was grounded in one district of the LCA. I limited the scope because it was a restricted exploratory study, and I wanted to minimise any confusing variables that might relate to geographical or cultural variations within the LCA.[31]

Interview planning and data collection

Through my career as a physiotherapist, I was experienced in analytical interviewing, but I was just beginning as a practical theology researcher. While I recognised that group dynamics and conversation would enrich the data I was able to gather, I was also working alone. Therefore, I conducted interviews with small groups of two or three rather than larger focus groups. This ensured that I could be present, responsive and able to hear all voices rather than being overwhelmed by the requirements of managing a larger group as well as listening and observing.

My interview questions defined the scope of my research as 'the emotional dynamics between pastors and congregations', and further focused the conversation by including definitions of and questions about differentiation of self and co-dependency. I designed the questions to be as spacious as possible to avoid leading the participants to simply agree with me. I wanted to know what participants were experiencing and observing. The questions are included in the appendix that follows this discussion. Ethical approval for this research was granted through the University of Divinity.

---

31 As it turned out, when participants were asked if any of their observations were specific to the Queensland District, they indicated that their observations were not Queensland-specific, but rather applied throughout the LCA.

Five interview participants were female and four were male. A further two were invited, but one of these did not respond and I was unable to schedule an interview for the other within my timeframe. Three participants were ordained LCA ministers, while four others had studied theology at a tertiary level. All were invited based on their experience of at least four LCAQD congregations.[32] Interviews were conducted over six weeks in small groups of two or three. One-to-one interviews were conducted when necessary, either because of the participant's preference or inability to attend their scheduled group. The risks identified and mitigated to the extent possible were loss of confidentiality, emotional triggering and reputational risk for the LCA or LCAQD.

The interviews used a neo-positive approach. I collected focused information while avoiding being too leading, leaving space for interviewees to determine the course of the conversation. Participants did not connect well with the concepts of differentiation of self or co-dependence, so I tended to emphasise the question: 'Imagine you are about to visit a congregation you haven't met before. Based on your previous experience, what signs of emotional dynamics, particularly in the pastor-congregation relationship, might you expect to see?' rather than the question about differentiation of self as the central piece of the interview. As the research progressed, I adopted the idea of a magic wand, saying for example:

> If you had a magic wand, where would you point your magic wand? You used the words 'stuck', and you are not the first group to use that... Where would you point that magic wand to get the church unstuck?

Because interview subjects were one step removed from the pastor-congregation interface, I discovered that I was collecting data at two levels. First, I gathered their expert observations of the pastor-congregation relationship and secondly, I made phenomenological observations of the narratives that my interview subjects were telling one another.

There were five interviews, each of 45 minutes to one hour, a total of 4 and a half hours. Participants chose not to prepare notes or diagrams ahead of the interview, but I took my own notes during the interviews. Analysis focused on interview transcripts as a more direct source of data than my interpretations of what was said.

---

[32] As the LCA is a small church and this is a sensitive topic, I have deliberately bundled information about participants in a summary form here to protect their privacy.

Results

Thematic analysis: narratives

First, all data referring to emotional dynamics within congregations, and particularly between pastors and congregation members, was extracted from the transcripts.

Interview transcripts were then coded with reference to Saldaña.[33] The first round of coding was thematic. A common pattern was that participants:

- Described a narrative of decline: numerically and behaviourally our church is not what it used to be.
- Provided observational data, as requested by the stimulus questions.
- Spontaneously analysed this data, looking for cause and effect and possible meanings.
- Reflected on possible solutions or ways back to who we once were.[34]

The spontaneous meaning-making (which occurred especially within group interviews) may have been because participants were:

- expert practitioners and therefore expected to be problem solvers;
- deeply committed to the LCA; and
- encouraged by the spaciousness of the interview process to develop a narrative either as individuals or as a small group.[35]

Specific analysis: emotional dynamics between pastors and congregations

Using the same coded data, emotional dynamics between pastors and congregations were investigated. Four unhealthy behavioural scenarios emerged:

- The theologically rigid pastor (i.e., in an authoritarian way) who controls and limits his congregation.
- Emotionally unhealthy congregation members whose loud voices have too much influence on decisions.

---

33 Johnny Saldaña, *The Coding Manual for Qualitative Researchers* (Los Angeles: Sage, 2015).

34 To obtain this data, I introduced a question to some interviews: 'If you had a magic wand where would you point it?' However, participants proffered solutions even without being asked this question.

35 It was a significant element of this research for me to observe and reflect on how groups use narratives for identity and meaning-making. I will return to the concept of group narratives in my suggestions for further research.

- Unrealistic community expectations of pastors which the pastor internalises as shame and depression.
- An attitude held by some congregations that if they get just the right pastor, he will fix their problems.

These final three mirrored my own observations discussed earlier in this paper.[36]

Specific analysis: co-dependent themes

The coding so far seemed to indicate some recognition of congregational family system dysfunction, even though participants did not connect with specific terminology such as differentiation of self and co-dependence. The interview data was then analysed for the presence of the co-dependent factors identified by Marks et al.

The data indicated interpersonal control and emotional suppression, but not self-sacrifice. Interestingly, participants observed these behaviours in *both* pastors and congregational leaders. Quoted examples of actual comments are italicised.

Interpersonal control exerted by **pastors**

- *'The pastor made sure that everything was done because it needed to be done his way because that's the way that he was taught how it should be done.'*
- *'They see themselves almost as a sort of fatherly, corrective, school-mastery type headmaster to stop chaos breaking out in the playground.'*

These comments seem to align more with how the LCA Letter of Call describes the role of pastor than with the DSTOs explored above.

Interpersonal control exerted by **congregational members**:

- *'The most unhealthy people end up dominating where we go and the choices we make as a community and the leadership that a pastor can have because the most unhealthy people are usually the noisiest.'*
- And the pretend quotation: *'... my family has been here since 1903, and we've always done it like this. My father gave the money for those pews ...'*

---

36 Note that I did not provide illustrative scenarios to avoid leading participants.

As the average age of congregation members increases, it can be challenging for leaders to find a good balance between caring for members by providing the familiar and the preferred, and caring by helping them to face the cost of change and growth.

Emotional suppression by **pastors**:

- *One participant commented that 'Very few have a real understanding of their own interior geography'.*
- *'The pastor says to himself: "I can't do that, but I feel like I need to; otherwise, I'm a failure".'*

Thus, participants described both deliberate suppression and limited conscious awareness of one's emotions.

Emotional suppression by **congregational members**:

- *'... dynamics between members: restricting [others], afraid to have honest conversations.'*

This comment suggests that when some members act in interpersonally controlling ways, others avoid conflict. Steinke proposes that Christian communities are more likely than other groups to avoid or suppress emotions: 'Christian communities allow this behaviour as we erroneously think that to confront it would not be "the Christian thing to do"'.[37]

Interpersonal control was the co-dependent factor most observed by participants. This research, therefore, suggests that pastors and lay leaders within the LCA consider themselves responsible for others' behaviour, and that they have the capacity to change others' behaviour. Because this interpersonal control dynamic flowed in two directions (they are each trying to improve the other), I considered the term 'enmeshed'[38] to be a more useful descriptor than co-dependence. An enmeshed community in Bowen's terms is one where the togetherness force is too high and the individuality force too low. Individuals within an enmeshed system will find it harder to think for themselves and more likely to react automatically to those around them.

---

37 Steinke, *Congregational leadership in anxious times*, 13.
38 This term was suggested by one study participant, possibly based on his experience using David and Karen Olson's Prepare-Enrich program.

Discussion

Within congregations, we find dedicated servants of God, both paid and volunteer. They generously share their gifts and time to serve their communities, giving 'above and beyond'. However, it is not unusual to hear behind-the-scenes narratives such as 'Of course it's X's way or the highway: he's a bit precious like that' or 'We really want to try something different, but this ministry is so important to Y that we don't have the heart to tell her'. Thus, we triangulate[39] one another into our discomfort rather than speaking with the person whose behaviour is offending or limiting us.

We perpetuate unhealthy dynamics when we avoid courageous conversations that might help us as individuals and communities to transform and grow, even while concerning ourselves overly with what others are doing. An enmeshed community may perpetuate this interpersonal control dynamic by providing a place of belonging for others who behave like them and being less likely to be inviting for well-differentiated people: 'We unconsciously seek the company of those with cultural factors similar to those of our own families'.[40]

Another way we control others within congregations is by passively resisting change and growth by not participating even while we vote in favour of the plan. And if people with new or different ideas do not give up and move on, family systems such as congregations have the option to scapegoat them, laying the blame for all problems on one person and expecting that when this person leaves the community that all the problems will be solved.

Scapegoating is the flipside of our idea that there is a perfect pastor who will solve all our congregation's problems. In one case, we are looking for the arrival of a person (the pastor) who will solve our problems and in the case of scapegoating it is the pastor or member's departure that we believe will solve our problems. The paradox is that as anxiety grows these things are more likely to happen, but at a time in history when we can least afford them!

As someone who would be a healer within her community, this presents quite a challenge. How does one encourage one's congregation to embrace better-differentiated behaviour without being interpersonally controlling? I can begin by examining my own tendencies to be interpersonally controlling; to ask how I might be focusing excessively on how others

---

39 A Bowen FST concept: Creech, *Family systems*, 19-20.
40 Chris Creech, *Toxic Church* (Ansley: Motherhood Printing, 2019), 62.

need to change their beliefs or behaviours, to the detriment of my own self-examination. Sometimes the best solution is to step away and take a break.

In this discussion, I proposed that anxious behaviours within congregations might help shine the light on issues that need addressing. Family systems theory offered a framework for understanding the ways that groups such as congregations act towards the status quo and against transformation. Specifically, the research question included the concepts of differentiation of self and co-dependence. Within this pilot study, the most significant marker was the dynamic of interpersonal control: the idea that pastors and other congregation members consider themselves to be responsible for others' behaviour, possibly to the detriment of attention to their own behaviour. While study participants connected with the idea of emotional dynamics between pastors and congregations, the concepts of differentiation of self and co-dependence did not gain traction. However, since this project concluded, I have presented this research on five occasions, and in each case family systems concepts provided tools for helping people unpack their lived experiences of congregations. There are, no doubt, other ways into this understanding and awareness besides the way I chose, but I am grateful to have seen my research bear fruit within my circles of influence.

Future research
Narratives of decline

Although beyond the scope of the current research question, all participants in this project happened to be from the same LCA 'tribe', namely those in favour of the ordination of women and men. They related a specific 'narrative of decline' where the LCA 'golden age' faded over time. Mayer argues that as we continually tell one another narratives of past times, our concept of what is true changes or develops. So, we can end up allowing narratives that are not completely factual to define ourselves and our possible futures.[41] Investigating and critiquing common LCA narratives of decline is an area for further research.

---

41 Wendy Mayer 'Religious conflict and the dark side of historical reasonings', in Adrian Brändli and Katharina Heyden, eds, *Claiming History in Religious Conflicts*, Bibliotheca Helvetica Romana 39 (Basel: Schwabe Verlag, 2021) 37-42.

Deeper longings

The final thematic element to the narratives developed by study participants was to offer solutions, a preferred future. Participants described their deeper longings as, firstly, a renewal of LCA identity as people who understand and live God's grace. For example:

- *'If I had a magic wand, it would be to give pastors and congregations so much assurance and confidence of their union with Christ that they could relate to one another without fear and become a genuine learning community together.'*

And, secondly, participants longed for a community that can love even in the face of disagreement. For example:

- *'To use M. Scott Peck's model of movement toward authentic community, where his last movement is authentic community: I stop trying to change and convert, I start to accept you for who you are ...'*

These comments suggest that while participants observe co-dependent behaviours between pastors and congregations, the behaviours did not appear to be a primary problem but rather secondary to an identity crisis within the LCA; as Lutherans, we are meant to be people who understand salvation by grace but we are a bit stuck in how we live it as communities (especially in the context of theological disagreement).

Questions of identity and community seem to be crying for attention at every turn. Perhaps you also have heard questions like this: Who are we when we no longer have an overflowing church and Sunday school? When our children no longer worship with us? Who are we when we disagree? Who are we when so many fail to return to Sunday worship after a pandemic? These questions reflect our anxiety. According to Family systems theory, they can also perpetuate it.

Therefore, the concepts of identity and community would also be worthy of further research.

Conclusion

While this paper has investigated how anxiety within a congregation can bring out the worst in us, anxious times also present opportunities for growth into the new things that God will do. Anxious times help us to let go of what no longer is or what we thought we had under control. We are invited to be patient and still during our 'unknowing', to recall our identity. We are created in God's image and for relationship, restored with God and with one another at the cross of Christ, and members of the church which in the power of the Holy Spirit continues to be healed and restored. As we look toward those beside us in the unknowing, we can remind one another of these things.

I knew from my work as a physiotherapist how important it can be for healing to hear someone's story and help them to tap into their natural resources and skills, and this research helped me to apply narrative processes within congregational groups as well. This project demonstrated for me both the power of narrative for group meaning making, as well as the importance of critiquing these narratives.

Chapter Thirteen

A possible response to the wicked problem of financing the Catholic Church in Australia after the sexual abuse crisis

Brendan Long

An economic model of the Catholic Church in Australia[1]

'Wicked problem' is a term applied to a situation that has the characteristics of a problem which increases in complexity with every elusive attempt to solve it.[2] The inherent dynamics of the problem seem to defy any clear solution. If we look at the financial situation of the Catholic Church in Australia we may have a textbook example of what a wicked problem means in a real world situation. Furthermore, the issue has added feature of being 'wicked' in both the normal and technical senses of the expression.

What does it mean to say that the financial dynamics of the Catholic Church in Australia, and in many other countries, constitute a wicked problem? First, it is wicked in a normal sense of the word. Sexual abuse of minors by a minority of clerical, religious and lay professionals in the Catholic Church has incurred unspeakable personal damage to victims whose rights for just compensation are manifest. What has happened is wicked defying description in words, a manifestation of pure evil, not just Augustine's *malus est privatio boni*,[3] not just an absence of good. It is more like what Rahner talks of in his notion of the *mysterium iniquitas*,[4] when the subject experiencing such guilt in the 'depths of

---

[1] An early draft of this paper was presented at the Australian Catholic Theological Association conference in June 2021 as well at the Association of Practical Theology in Oceania conference in December 2020.

[2] Horst W.J. Rittel and Melvin M. Webber, 'Dilemmas in a General Theory of Planning', *Policy Sciences*, 4, No. 2 (1973): 155-169.

[3] Augustine, *Enchiridion*, Chapter 11, *A select Library of the Nicene and Post-Nicene Fathers of the Christian Church*, Vol. III, ed. Philip Schaff, https://www.ccel.org/ccel/schaff/npnf103/npnf103.i.html.

[4] Karl Rahner, 'Guilt-Responsibility-Punishment Within the View of Catholic Theology', *Theological Investigations*, 6, 14 (Darton, Longman and Todd), 210.

its existence', through engaging in actions, horrendous actions, can constitute a definitive saying 'no' to God. For Rahner, a point can eventually be reached where the spiritual 'subject really is evil, and understands this evil as what he or she is and definitely want to be'.[5] This is ineffable evil, beyond adequate description in words, wicked beyond words. Rahner's more brutal notion of evil manifest in human behaviour is more likely to resonate with both public opinion and the seething sense of betrayal silently but sensibly radiating in the church pews.[6]

Still, the more technical, and less emotive, sense of the word 'wicked' as a problem also emerges in the response to the sexual abuse crisis. With increasing claims for compensation for victims, increased insurance costs associated with Church pastoral activity and those associated with market evaluation of potential common law actions, extraordinary regulatory compliance costs of meeting acceptable professional standards, training in child protection safeguards and instituting safe places of worship and pastoral practice, expenses are increasing and probably increasing increasingly.[7] On the revenue side of the ledger, the fiscal mechanics have been clear for many years. As the cohort of Mass-attending Catholics declines the revenue from parishioner contributions becomes a revenue base that decreases increasingly. Costs increasing increasingly, revenues decreasing increasingly: this is the essence of the wicked problem for Church business managers. COVID-19 has temporarily exacerbated the revenue problem and in so doing has highlighted it.

Theological research is not usually supported by approaches to build quantitative schemata of underlying fiscal dynamics of funding of pastoral practice. However, there is a case that it now should be. If the hypothesis in this paper is to be pursued with rigour, then a conceptual framework is required to analyse the problem, albeit an approach taken from fundamental, if somewhat rudimentary, economic analytical methods. This is attempted here. Problems of costs and revenue are well suited to graphical analysis. In Figure 1, the horizontal axis represents time and the vertical axis represents dollars, capturing revenue and costs of a

---

5 See Karl Rahner, :*Foundations of Christian Faith: An Introduction to the Idea of Christianity*, translated by William V. Dych (The Seabury Press; New York, 1978), 101.

6 Similarly, the comments of the late Cardinal Martini at a prayer breakfast in Australia some years ago resonated. When asked what should be the attitude to sexual abusers in the Church, he quoted the Gospel of Matthew: 'it would be better for them to have a large millstone hung around their neck and to be drowned in the depths of the sea (Matthew 18.6 NIV).

7 There is limited data publicly available to quantify these costs. Further research is required, ideally with the support of ecclesiastical institutions, to bring this data into the public domain. Only then can the theoretical claims presented in this analysis be supported or rejected on the basis of empirical evidence.

diocese. Revenue is decreasing at an increasing rate due to population dynamics of the Mass-attending cohort. This revenue effect is represented in the dotted line in Figure 1 which slopes down steeply over time. Costs have been increasing moderately in the past—increasing but not at an increasing rate. This is the solid line sloping upwards but not steeply. For the sake of the illustration let us say at some time in the past these curves intersected and the Church in aggregate more or less broke even, even if it probably required cross-subsidies from larger, richer archdioceses to poorer regional dioceses like the Broome Diocese. Nevertheless, in the past we could speak of a notional 'break-even point' in aggregate. The fiscal dynamics of costs increasing and revenue decreasing increasingly then created a situation of emerging deficits which were funded by asset sales, revenue from investments or borrowing. This is the area shaded black. The model of emerging deficits is arguably the fiscal situation of the Catholic Church in Australia in recent years. It does not consider the effect of COVID-19.

The hard mathematical logic of this emerging structural deficit in Church finances at an aggregate level is as unrelenting as the demographic trends that drive it. The revenue base is declining as the donating cohort diminishes while costs are only increasing. This is in itself a wicked problem.

Figure 1. A graphical model of pre-COVID aggregate Catholic Church financing

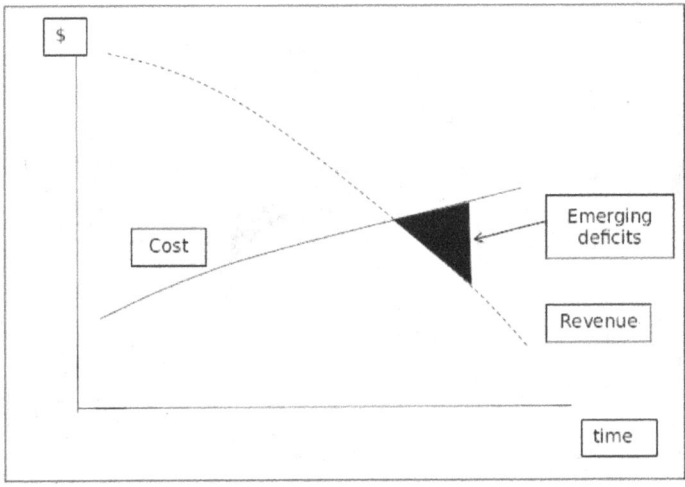

The impact of COVID-19 can be readily modelled. There was a decline in revenue in 2020–2021 from COVID-19. Given that the Catholic Church claimed status for the JobKeeper payment for professional church staff, this revenue decline from COVID-19 must have exceeded 15 per cent for church organisations as charities in the JobKeeper period.[8] The basic structure of the wicked problem remains with the COVID-19 effect being a revenue shock (a sharp short-term decline in revenue) that washes through over time.

The real argument presented is that this simple conceptual model probably fails to capture the truly wicked nature of the problem of Catholic Church financing in Australia and the starkness of the fiscal reality while capturing the long term demographic and consequent fiscal impact of declining Mass attendance. For the sake of illustration, let us ignore the COVID-19 effect as it will pass and is unlikely to fundamentally effect the fiscal dynamics which we are seeking to capture. Let us introduce another shock to the model. Let us assume an event or set of related events occur that alter the cost structure of the Catholic Church's operations significantly and permanently. A revenue shock like COVID-19 is a problem, but a short term one.[9] A permanent increase to the cost structure of the financial entity (the Church at diocesan level) is another thing entirely. In the graph below (Figure 2), the solid line, the cost curve, shifts upwards steeply with costs now increasing at an increasing rate from a selected point.

Figure 2. The fiscal impact on the Catholic Church of responding to the sexual abuse crisis

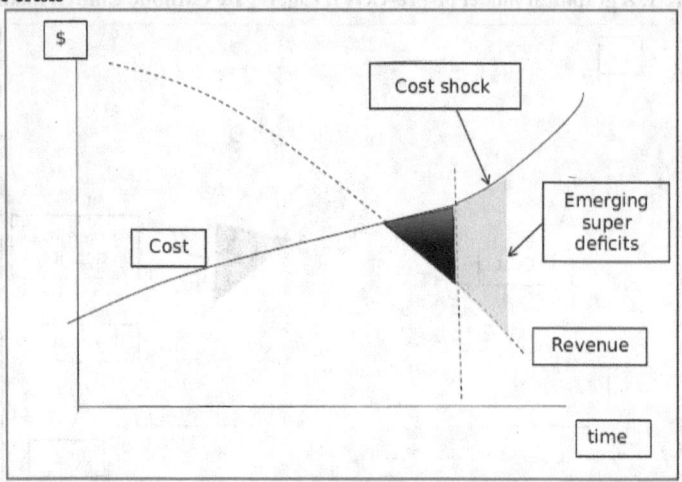

---

8 This 15% threshold was initially a requirement of access to the JobKeeper regime for not-for profit organisations.
9 It remains to be seen what the long-term effect of the pandemic on Mass attendance will be.

What event in the life of Catholic Church in Australia could constitute a fundamental enduring shift in the cost structure of its operations? The response to the sexual abuse crisis constitutes exactly this type of shock. The National Redress Scheme requires all participating institutions, including Catholic dioceses, to agree to honour payments to victims under an agreed statutory formula. These costs are not insignificant but are likely to constitute a fraction of the ultimate costs the Church must bear in its response to the sexual abuse crisis.

First, the statutory scheme faces a cap of only $150,000. Victims may come to the view that common law damages claims may exceed this threshold and proceed with civil litigation seeking higher damages payments. Participating institutions also agree to fund additional services of counselling and support which are costly. Very significant enduring costs are likely to be experienced through higher insurance premiums associated with professional services liability insurance. Costs of ensuring safe places of worship and pastoral activities require significant training costs and expensive new compliance regimes. Such costs are significant, unavoidable and enduring. It is argued that they will increase, and may increase at an increasing rate, for perhaps a decade as new claims for redress come to light and the full scope of the abuse crisis comes to be appreciated. Claims made to date may represent simply the tip of the iceberg.

Seen in fiscal terms, the threat to Catholic Church financing is pervasive and enduring. If, as proposed above, the Catholic Church in Australia was facing a wicked problem of reducing revenue and fiscal deficit before the impact of the sexual abuse crisis, then its advent in fiscal terms expands the impact of this situation dramatically. Potentially, the requisite fiscal response to the sexual abuse crisis, in the absence of some measure to increase Church revenue, could rise to a point where it could threaten to break the back of the Catholic Church's financial structure, forcing it into a future state of enduring super deficits, unsustainable financial stress that effectively threatens its continued operation as we understand it today, with consequent impacts on pastoral and liturgical Church life.

Of course, what is proposed here is simply a conceptual model and the fiscal dynamics hypothesised may not come to pass. However, the warning that I seek to make in this paper is that there is a genuinely wicked problem of church financing which has been potentially made radically worse by the future costs of financing compensation, child safety policies and other redress measures associated with dealing with the fiscal impact of adequately addressing historical sexual abuse in the Catholic Church in Australia.

Pope Francis' theological approach to economics

The stylised economic model can be considered within the context of a contemporary theology of economics. A range of approaches could be adopted. For example, the classical approach in Catholic Social Thought (CST) could be deployed. Here we see a consistent approach developed since *Rerum Novarum* (1891) of papal teaching which critiques narrow economistic approaches that reduce the human person to the level of an economic agent and seeks to see economics as serving the pursuit of the common good. It is a tradition that speaks to a preferential option for the poor, a sense of solidarity with the plight of all persons and human dignity that flows from work that provides the means to support a family.[10] Rather than produce a synthesis of this still-emerging critical theology of economics, this work narrows its focus on the unique and challenging perspective offered by Pope Francis on economic engagement, while it is also noted that Francis' thought assimilates much of the historical CST tradition and aligns with newer reflections. Pope Francis has demonstrated a keen interest in the ethics of economic praxis in his theological and pastoral statements, especially the Apostolic Exhortation *Evangelii Gaudium* and the encyclical *Laudato Si'*. A short discussion of the relevance of these statements to economics may provide the theological lens to analyse the wicked problem outlined above.[11]

Evangelium Gaudium

Pope Francis' first engagement on the question of economics is found in *Evangelii Gaudium*. True to its title, it is a wide-ranging statement of a

---

10 See Pope St John Paul II in *Laborem Excercens*, n. 7, and Pope Benedict in *Caritas et Veritate*, n. 45 at vatican.va. See also the summary in 'The Emerging Views of Pope Francis on Economics', *Faith and the Political in the Post Secular Age*, ed. Anthony Maher (Bayswater, Vic: Coventry Press, 2018).

11 This section relies on elements of a paper presented at the 2015 APTO conference in Canberra, subsequently published in Long, 'Emerging Views', 134-155. Brendan Long, 'What does Pope Francis' Emerging Approach to Economics Mean for Tax Policy in Australia?', *St Mark's Review*, 235, no. 1 (2016): 44-56, and Brendan Long, Jon Campbell and Carolyn Kelshaw, 'The Justice Lens on Taxation Policy in Australia', *St Mark's Review*, 235, no. 1 (2016): 94-106.

joyful and praise-filled vision of Christ's word of love for all. However, strong criticisms are made especially in the economic area. In fact, Francis' language on the influence of economic forces on marginalised persons, the poor, is strident and confronting, especially for the professional economist and theologian who engages with economics. Francis' call is made clear in a section in *Evangelii Gaudium* titled 'No to an economy of exclusion'. His message is that poverty is not just the result of a form of social exploitation or oppression which would flow from a typical Marxist perspective. His challenge is different. It is not social structures or class mechanisms that drive social exclusion, but an instinct in the human person to see themselves solely as consumers and ultimately to see other persons as consumer goods.

> Just as the commandment 'Thou shalt not kill' sets a clear limit in order to safeguard the value of human life, today we also have to say 'thou shalt not' to an economy of exclusion and inequality. Such an economy kills ... Human beings are themselves considered consumer goods to be used and then discarded. We have created a 'throw away' culture which is now spreading. It is no longer simply about exploitation and oppression, but something new.[12]

Who is being killed by the consumer culture that throws away things? It is living human beings who are killed—we kill others by treating them as mere objects of consumption in our participation in an economic system which makes people merely goods that can be discarded.

Francis' challenge to the consumerist society can be analysed through the twin lenses of the theologian and the economist. Starting with the theological lens, we can note that what Francis is appealing to is not a claim that we directly decide to harm, least of all kill, others by deciding individually to treat other persons as means to our personal ends. This would reduce all of us to monsters. Rather it seems he invokes the long tradition in Christian theological reflection which asserts that we as persons can be implicated unconsciously in processes which can be evil in that they lead to a degradation of others' dignity through complex and unforeseen processes. Francis' view could be seen as an application of the notion of original sin to economics, even though this is not stated explicitly.

In Catholic theology, original sin is, of course, not sin understood as bad acts. Original sin is only analogous to the notion of sin as evil choices,

---

12 Pope Francis, Evangelii Gaudium, n. 13. vatican.va

as Rahner outlines in his classic article 'Sin of Adam' in *Theological Investigations*.[13] Through original sin we are thrown into a broken world prior to the deployment of our personal moral faculty, our connation, and which we cannot escape without some sense of participation.[14] If such economic participation seems to create evil in the world, by treating persons as means in a consumerist society rather than as ends, the Gospel message is still a call to metanoia, a call to repentance even if the choice is not one of personal sin but of social participation in a process with evil consequences—sin in an analogous sense. For Francis, we seem to be inoculated or anaesthetised against realising this, so addicted have we become to the allure of the consumerist society.[15] The position is not new to Francis and is present in statements of Pope St Paul John II and Benedict XVI.[16]

Laudato Si'

In *Laudato Si'*, Francis is also highly critical in tone and content of contemporary economic institutions but also provides a strong positive message about the power of Christian spirituality to open a new way of approaching the complex discussion between theology and economics. This way appears to be an appeal to an economic asceticism that should be adopted for the sake of the common good.

Although the topic of *Laudato Si'* is climate change, a key focus is also a response to social exclusion:

> The social dimensions of global change include the effects of technological innovation on employment, social exclusion, an inequitable distribution and consumption of energy and other services, social breakdown, increased violence and a rise in new

---

13 Karl Rahner, 'Sin of Adam' *Theological Investigations*, Vol.11, Chapter 11 (New York: Seabury Press, 1974).
14 This author has sought to explore this notion of original sin in economics in published works (see for example Brendan Long, 'Adam Smith's Theodicy' in *Adam Smith as Theologian* ed. Paul Oslington (New York: Routledge, 2011) and Brendan Long, *Adam Smith and the Invisible Hand of God* (New York: Routledge, 2022).
15 Even in his recent encyclical, *Fratelli Tutti*, a positive message of the common life of all persons, Francis calls us to account for the fact that in the Parable of the Good Samaritan where Jesus tells of the person who helps the man hurt by the robber and left on the road to die, there is in us all something of the robber and something of the person who passes by leaving the hurt man to die (*Fratelli Tutti*, 69). Francis calls us to account for evil in our lives.
16 See Long, 'Emerging Views', 136-137 for a more detailed discussion.

forms of social aggression, drug trafficking, growing drug use by young people, and the loss of identity. These are signs that the growth of the past two centuries has not always led to an integral development and an improvement in the quality of life. Some of these signs are also symptomatic of real social decline, the silent rupture of the bonds of integration and social cohesion.[17]

What Francis seeks is a new economy which combats the dominant paradigm of consumption and production in market forces with a new approach which recognises that there are excesses in normal economic processes that erode the common good. It is a radical message. He calls for a certain economic asceticism, a charitable and faith-filled response to dial back the excesses of the market economy as they lead to environmental and social evils. He wants us to give away the throw-away culture that he sees present in consumerist society and calls for a change to personal consumption habits for the sake of the common good. He says strongly that less (in terms of personal consumption) can yield more—the common good.

> It is the conviction that 'less is more'. A constant flood of new consumer goods can baffle the heart and prevent us from cherishing each thing and each moment....Christian spirituality proposes a growth marked by moderation and the capacity to be happy with little.[18]

Drawing on the tradition of asceticism in Catholic spirituality, Francis calls in *Laudato Si'* for an economic asceticism in personal consumption decisions. Francis takes the spirituality of Saint Francis to show how joy is found in renunciation. Less is more from the spiritual perspective in matters economic.

Francis is making the strong claim that we should actually come to realise that in economic matters we actually harm ourselves spiritually when we allow ourselves to make economic concerns the primary focal points of our practical living—the economic 'more' is a spiritual 'less'.

Applying Francis' theology of economics to church financing in Australia

Francis' critical theological commentary on the prevailing economic paradigm does not mandate any specific response to our research. His innovative

---

17 Pope Francis, *Laudato Si'*, n. 46.
18 Pope Francis, *Laudato Si'*, n. 222.

contribution is to call for a personal and institutional economic asceticism. In essence, his moral theology of economics is a very simple one: in economic engagement, live according to the maxim that less is more. Francis claims that the throw-away culture of consumption involves interference with the pursuit of the common good in economic terms. Francis' answer is that, for the sake of the Kingdom of God, for the sake of the common good, we should choose to constrain the appetite we aggressively display for personal consumption, and institutions should also adopt the same approach. If less is more for the world, then less is also more for Church institutions that can show the way, as St Francis did by living his economic asceticism.

What does Francis' framework ask of us, the Catholic Church in Australia, in order to deal with our wicked church financing problem? The key point is that the assets of the Church, its most valuable income streams, are not to be clung to, not to be defended as a litigant in a court hearing over a property dispute. Rather, to the contrary, we should value it lowly, so as not to be just a consumer or producer in the economy, but price our assets and our services in a radically different way. In fact, we should value them lowly in a commercial sense, and price highly instead the spiritual asset of the faithful service of the common good as the product we genuinely market, our true offering to society. Francis seems almost to say that we as Church are better off without the wealthy assets and high income streams that they generate as these distract us from that true treasure—that more genuine wealth we have—the faith filled service of the poor and the marginalised. This 'pearl beyond price',[19] this is our real wealth, the treasure of faith and faithful service, the Kingdom of God.

It is a sort of kenotic moral theology of economics, focused on Christ's kenosis, his giving away of his life, finding ultimate value in the loss that life has brought to all. Less is more, in Christ's death infinitely more, our ultimate fulfilment of our human lives. And yet we so often do not imitate or live this kenosis Christology in our ecclesial real-world living. So much of the professional engagement of Church officials is devoted to the maintenance and defence of its property. It often seems to be the primary focus of Church activity at the corporate level. Francis wants to turn this perspective on its head, 'Let us smell like the sheep and live like the pauper';[20] that way we are closer to Jesus and more truly our

---

19 Matthew 13:45-46.
20 Homily of Pope Francis, Chrism Mass, Holy Thursday, 28 March 2013, https://www.vatican.va/content/francesco/en/homilies/2013/documents/papa-francesco_20130328_messa-crismale.html

true selves. I argue that Francis' theology of economics calls on the Church to freely, for spiritual reasons, be ready to let go of wealth and income if that will materially assist sufferers of child sexual abuse by the Church. If we are to turn around an economy of exclusion, an economy that kills, we as practical theologians need to do more than simply identify a problem that needs to be addressed.

Church institutions should reflect on their capacity to make an economic contribution to solving the wicked problem. It is open to Church institutions, including Public Juridic Persons (PJP),[21] to reflect on their capacities to deal with the wicked problems of church financing, exacerbated by costs of adequately dealing with the fiscal effects of sexual abuse in the Church. By doing so, Church bodies would be responding to Francis' call to direct economic processes towards a clear common good. There would be a giving away, a sense of valuing the economic gains of the institutions as being valued less than the spiritual good of giving to the marginalised. It would be a less is more approach. Freely choosing to direct a small quantum of financial resources from the corporate activities of the Church broadly defined, included PJPs, towards dealing with the wicked problem of church financing exacerbated by the financial implications of historical sexual abuse would be a powerful spiritual option.

It would be a grand statement that the ultimate goal of economic endeavour and, yes, by Church institutions, is to make the economic processes serve those most in need and, in so doing, not just say 'No' to an economy of exclusion but say 'Yes' to economics that directs financial resources to those whom they can serve most. It is argued here that if we take seriously Francis' theology of economics, and seek to apply it to the wicked problem of church financing in Australia, one option is for those elements of the Catholic Church which generate economic wealth, essentially school and hospital networks, to agree to set aside a modest element of their corporate gross revenue, say one per cent, to improve funding of compensation to victims of sexual abuse. But how can we do this?

The data question

The official Church that operates commercially at diocesan level is not a cashed-up merchant bank. Generally, bishops run the pastoral activities

---

21 A Public Juridic Person (PJP) is a legal entity under canon law that allows various Church ministries to function in the name of the Catholic Church while also usually exercising an independent form of governance.

of the Church on a shoestring. Staff are generally employed at sub-market wages and clerical and religious professionals are even cheaper labourers in the field. More wealthy archdioceses, the 'big three' in Australia, Sydney, Melbourne and Brisbane, appear to have large asset bases. However, these assets are not really liquid assets that can be commercially realised, as the more valuable land is often zoned by local councils for religious usage, the costs of maintenance of these assets is high without generating much revenue, and they are fully utilised in essential pastoral activities. No one is suggesting we could or should put St Mary's or St Patrick's Cathedrals on the market, probably not even the victims of sexual abuse. Even the 'big three' suffer the impact of the wicked problem outlined above, and rest of the 'official Church' just and only just manages to sort of make ends meet in church financing.

So where does the real wealth of the Catholic Church in Australia lie? Is there an income base capable of making a contribution to the problem of church financing, including a generous response to fiscal costs of Church sexual abuse? I approach the question as a professional economic revenue specialist and my answer is 'Yes', such an economic base for the Church in Australia manifestly exists. So where does it lie?

Economists do not usually measure wealth on the same terms that households do. A person or family measures wealth in terms of how much they own and how much they owe—their net realisable value. This is a point-in-time snapshot of the person's or household's net worth. Economics call this a 'stock' value, which, of course, with the exception of land assets, generally depreciates over time. The stock of physical assets in the unpublished balance sheets of dioceses are depreciating assets and are not readily realisable in the market. It is a similar situation for the Catholic Church in most international jurisdictions.

Economists, in contrast, measure wealth as the net present value of the income stream that can be generated from the stock of assets over their economic life—like the market value of the revenue a company can earn from its ongoing operations. The real economic value of the Church lies in the income streams that can be generated by the operative use of assets held. One of the unique aspects of the Catholic Church in Australia is that it operates an educational system that supports about 777,000 students in 1,715 schools in 2020.[22] It is a very large education system operated by dioceses and private 'non-systemic' educational institutions

---

22 National Catholic Education Commission, 2020 Annual Report, https://www.ncec.catholic.edu.au/docman/reports-1/annual-reports/628-2021-annual-report/file, 22.

often constructed as PJPs, and is the largest non-government education service provider in Australia. Similarly, religious orders created a private charitable hospital and health care network well before the state started to build the publicly funded health care system nearly a hundred years ago. These have been developed over time to form a large private and public hospital system of immense economic value. Aged care systems have also been developed by Catholic religious institutions. Catholic health and aged care now forms ten per cent of the overall hospital and aged care systems.[23]

These health and education systems generate enormous income streams. They are essentially permanent parts of the fabric of health, education and aged care service provision and the subsidies they enjoy are essentially a permanent part of public finance in Australia at least for the conceivable future. They are simply too large for governments to contemplate running the health, education and aged care systems without them. In legal terms, these institutions are not-for-profit institutions. The net revenue they generate is not taxed. Aged care generally runs at a loss or breaks even. Many systemic schools barely cover costs even with public subsidies. Catholic public hospitals are 'block funded' from grants at State level and operate like state-funded hospitals and are unlikely to generate significant fiscal surpluses.

Here we see a public policy and public theology research priority. The data on revenue from major Catholic education institutions, dioceses and public hospital networks is simply not available at sufficient levels of granularity for analysis. Financial reporting from Catholic educational institutions is not readily accessible in the public domain. Some financial data is available in annual reports of organisations that publish this data. Financial reporting through the ACNC[24] reporting framework is difficult to access as major institutions like dioceses are Basic Religious Charities and are exempt from formal reporting requirements. Some data is available on public hospital networks at State/Territory level but reporting is sporadic and inconsistent.

Here we suffer a want of financial transparency. It is important that this data is available on an annual basis under consistent reporting methodologies. It is an important task that could be done by Catholic university researchers with the assistance of agencies of the Australian Catholic Bishops Conference. If we are to follow Francis' call to make our economic activities as Church serve the common good, then we

---

23 https://www.cha.org.au/the-sector/.
24 Australian Charities and Not-for-profits Commission.

need to adopt a transparency model and move towards full financial disclosure of revenue by Catholic Church agencies and PJPs. If it is just and right for public companies to produce annual financial reports for shareholders, why should the Church not also follow this standard and report financial outcomes for its real shareholders, us, the Catholics in the pews, employees of Catholic organisations and those who access the services they provide. Let us live in the light.[25]

If we turn to the private hospital network, we find a richer source of data. IBISWorld publishes the revenue of Australia's top 500 private companies each year.[26] Table 1 shows the latest data from the IBISWorld Survey for Catholic health care agencies that, in terms of their private health care service delivery, are private companies, as well as being PJPs.

Table 1. Gross revenue from Catholic hospitals as private companies, 2020-21

Organisation	Revenue ($m)
St Vincent's	2,200
St John of God	1,853.8
Calvary	1,422.7
Mater/Mercy Partners	1,097.0
Mercy	860.6
Cabrini*	531
Catholic Healthcare	360.5
Total of key 7 Catholic Health/aged care providers	**7794.6**

* Surprisingly, the Cabrini hospital network is not included in the latest IBIS*World* listing. For Cabrini the 2019 data that was published is presented without indexation—an option for conservatism in the calculation.

So Catholic hospital networks, established as private companies, generate about $8bn a year in gross revenue. If these organisations contributed one per cent of their gross revenue to deal with the wicked problem of church financing, that would amount to $80m per annum. Here we have a readily identifiable source of data, an income stream of considerable value, more valuable in terms of gross revenue than many significant listed public companies on the Australian stock exchange.

---

25 John 3:21.
26 *IBISWorld, The Top 500 Private Companies 2020-21*, https://content.ibisworld.com/media/424pkppq/top-500-private-companies-australia.pdf.

From the NCEC Annual Report 2020, we can calculate that in 2019 the gross revenue of the Catholic education system in Australia was $13.7bn. Two other large Catholic institutions that are private companies are also included in the IBISWorld publication of revenue. These are the St Vincent de Paul Society with revenue of $782.4m per annum and the Australia Catholic University with revenue of $552.2m per annum. This total revenue base of hospitals, the St Vincent de Paul Society and the ACU constitutes about $9bn per annum (from private companies) and, if we add Catholic education (systemic and private), we come to a total revenue base of $22.7bn per annum.[27] It is a large potential revenue base and a one per cent voluntary contribution of these organisation to deal with the wicked problem of church financing exacerbated by historical sexual abuse would be in the order of $227m per annum—a large figure—a contribution of such magnitude that it could potentially deal with the wicked problem outlined in this paper.

These organisations could, if they chose, decide to make a fiscal contribution to deal with our wicked problem. They have the financial capacity to do this. So the reality is that we don't have in Australia the poor Church Francis wants. What we have is one part of the Church rapidly going broke and another very rich, in fiscal terms, something of a pantomime horse!

It is a curious problem but not one which Francis' critical lens cannot be applied to. If the proposition is correct that the effect of sexual abuse, combined with demographic trends, is creating emerging super deficits in church financing at diocesan level, and the health and education arms of the Church produce more revenue than many of the largest companies in Australia, then the corporate church activities must themselves embrace economic asceticism for the sake of the common good.

There is clearly one obvious barrier to this. A large component, maybe a majority, of these Church corporate revenues flow to foundations which have independence in canon law as PJPs and also are separately constituted legal entities under Australian law. So a bishop cannot just access these income streams to offset the fiscal costs of responding to sexual abuse. However, if Church organisations genuinely listen to the challenge Francis is making, they should want to contribute to such an arrangement. Why is this? Francis' call is for all Catholics to embrace economic asceticism for the sake of the Kingdom, not for an economic reason but as a spiritual discipline. Is not this spiritual discipline exactly

---

27 Such a calculation allows a rough estimate of the wealth of the economic assets of the Catholic Church in Australia which is $500bn.

the principle that the religious congregations that founded health and education services in Australia adopted, and upon which thy live as their key charism? Francis' call is but an articulation of the core foundational spirituality of these religious institutes. Further, the idea of a giving away to others is at the heart of this 'less is more' economy of compassion that Francis wants.

But who should pay?

So if we have identified an income base that is capable of making a contribution to the wicked problem of church financing exacerbated by the fiscal impact of justly dealing with sexual abuse claims, is there then a quick answer to be given—make these wealthy institutions pay! Why not, if they are the wealthy arm of the Catholic Church in Australia, as someone has to pay? There is here a complex question of moral theology and business ethics. If a major mining company created environmental costs from mining most would agree that they must meet the costs of environmental remediation. They owe a duty of care in law to the public and in theological terms they must be good stewards of what is entrusted to them.[28]

However, this is a rather lame analogy to apply to Church institutions like Catholic hospital networks. Such institutions generally have no direct accountability for sexual abuse which occurred outside their institutions. Perhaps a better analogy is the coal exporter who contributes to climate change or the electricity generator who burns coal to produce electricity. The company is not directly responsible for the global damage as a small part of a big problem but is implicated in the process. Catholic hospital and education networks are in some measure arguably implicated with sexual abuse costs as being part of a system that created these costs but their connection to the abuse is generally very weak, excepting of course for crimes by their direct employees or clerics and religious working in their institutions. So should the wealth generating elements of the Catholic corporation in Australia pay?

We need to look at what this would mean in economic terms. If we adopt the proposal of contributing one per cent of gross revenue to deal with the stated wicked problem, who would pay in the end? The costs would be passed on to the users of the services. School fees and private health insurance premiums would probably rise by about one per cent.

---

28 See, for example, 1 Peter 4:10.

So should those who pay to access these services be forced to pay for the crimes of paedophiles or to bail out religious institutions facing financial stress as a result of compensation for these crimes?

In terms of the former case, the answer is clearly 'No'—why should I who at one time had five children in fee-paying Catholic schools have to pay for these crimes? In terms of bailing out the Church financially, the question is complex. Should users of health and education services pay for the costs of maintaining a parish church and other pastoral activity? It is not obvious why they should be asked to, but it is not unreasonable that they could be, since there is no compulsion to use these services. It is a choice for providers of services to make or not make and a choice for users of those services to respond accordingly. What the ethics of the situation demands is that full information about these decisions is adequately disclosed—adoption of a model of transparency in financing decisions with users of services fully informed in the public arena.

It is here that the ball probably lies in ethical terms, both secular and theological. It would be wrong to force parents in systemic Catholic schools to pay for the extreme costs that a few paedophiles have caused. It would be wrong to force persons with private health insurance to pay higher premiums to pay for sexual abuse costs. That is because there is no causal nexus whatsoever between their choice to access the services and the costs created to the 'Catholic system' as a whole by paedophiles in its ranks. Catholic moral theology is not utilitarian ethics. The lack of any cooperation with the bad acts of sexual predators by users of education and health services suggests, a fortiori, that they bear no responsibility and in no way should be forced to pay for these costs through higher costs passed on to them through higher fees or higher insurance premiums.

There is another option. Providers of wealth generating services in the grand corporation of the Catholic Church in Australia, Catholic private/systemic schools and Catholic private hospitals, could choose to make the proposed one per cent contribution. This should be disclosed to the users of the services. Then they can decide whether to absorb that cost or take their money, their children, their business elsewhere. Why should the institutions do this and why should the users of their services accept it? It could be done as an act of altruism, of giving away, of an option for economic asceticism, out of a recognition that sometimes less is more in financial matters.

This is consistent with the moral theology of economics that Pope Francis presents. Catholic education and health service providers—the wealthier arm of the corporate division of the Catholic Church in

Australia broadly understood—could choose to make the one per cent revenue contribution without acknowledging any real moral accountability but do this for sake of the common good. That good is the better funding of support to victims and the support of pastoral activities really threatened by the fiscal impact of bad acts of offenders. It would be a free act of reconciling love, an act of genuine compassion. Not forced, not required, but freely given. Yes, it would have real fiscal costs and impacts on families and people who access private health services.

However, Francis says we should value the money less than the social good the forgoing of it brings. And there would be a real financial good for victims whose claims to recompense are manifest and who suffer still from an ecclesiastical institution that is fiscally constrained to meet these costs, as much as it now really wants to and really needs to. The wealthy part of 'mundus Catholicus' in Australia could freely choose to take up the burden, even though it has no obligation to, from a free act of agape love, to take the financial hit freely, as Francis calls us to live an economic life which directs economic resources away from excesses of personal 'consumption', valuing more highly the social good this financial costs brings, reflecting that more is sometimes less or better, that less economically can sometimes be more, ethically and spiritually.

A potential response to the wicked problem

This is what the wealth generating arm of the Catholic Church in Australia can do and should do. Dioceses are struggling to meet fiscal demands without dealing with the fiscal impact of historic sexual abuse financing costs. It is simple economics—revenue must sustain costs. The revenue generating arm of the Church must take the burden of meeting these costs as only such activities can. They are not legally required to do this in legislation of the Commonwealth, common law or canon law. But they can and they should.

The real theological question here is what is Church? The Catholic Church in Australia is like a set of separate silos on a big grain farm. Should each of these silos, independent financial operations organised under canon law, operate independently as private fiscal estates responsible only for their part of the grand business enterprise? Or should all these entities, dioceses and PJPs such as Catholic hospital networks or independent schools see themselves as part of the body of many parts? As St Paul says, all parts of the body serve the whole to make one unity—the Catholic People of God in Australia. Let all parts of the body serve the whole. Let not the hand and the arm work independently but all for the sake of the unity of the body. Or take John Donne, the metaphysical poet, who says that none of us is 'an island ... but a part of the continent, a part of the main', so that we when are looking at the dire fiscal implications of the Catholic Church in Australia, we, as one Church, should 'never send to know for whom the bell tolls'; we should know 'it tolls for thee', for us, for all Catholics.[29]

If the mission of the profitable arm of the Church's operations, defined in St Paul's analogy of the body or applying John Donne's analogy of the island and the continent, is genuinely motivated by the universal mission of the Church to serve the poor, then it seems to me that, at least in principle, there should be an openness to direct a small measure of the true wealth of the Church in Australia to be freely given away as an act of agape love, of economic asceticism, for the sake of those most needy in the Church, those harmed by us, the victims of child sexual abuse.

---

29 *Devotions Upon Emergent Occasions*, Meditation XVII, 1623.

Chapter Fourteen

Hearing God's voice: The role of revelatory experiences in ministry and mission among Australian Pentecostals

Tania Harris

Introduction

The revelatory experience, or in common parlance, 'hearing God's voice' is frequent in Pentecostal practice. Pentecostals speak of God 'talking' to them regularly and personally. A 2006 10-country survey indicated that Pentecostals are two to three more times likely than the average Christian to report that they have received a direct revelation from God.[1] The practice of revelatory experience has also been reported among Pentecostal and Charismatic groups in North America,[2] Asia[3] and Africa.[4] Studies in North America, the UK and Australia have found that these experiences arise in the form of dreams, visions, voices, sensory impressions and the like, and contain the possibility of new and previously unknown information. It has been suggested that they form a key component of Pentecostal spirituality.[5]

However, the experience that is so valued by Pentecostals is also known for its volatility. This is the particular burden of Pentecostal experience which is characterized by new and extra-biblical revelation.

---

[1] Paul Alexander, *Signs and Wonders: Why Pentecostalism Is the World's Fastest Growing Faith* (San Francisco: Jossey-Bass, 2009), 117.
[2] Margaret M. Poloma and John C. Green, *The Assemblies of God: Godly Love and the Revitalization of American Pentecostalism* (New York: NYU Press, 2010), 135.
[3] Dennis Lum, *The Practice of Prophecy: An Empirical-Theological Study of Pentecostals in Singapore* (Eugene: Wipf and Stock, 2018), 1.
[4] Allan Anderson, *An Introduction to Pentecostalism* (Cambridge: Cambridge University Press, 2004), 197.
[5] Daniel E. Albrecht, *Rites in the Spirit* (Sheffield: Sheffield Academic Press, 1999), 228; Sang-Whan Lee, 'Pentecostal Prophecy', *The Spirit and Church* 3 no. 1 (2001): 147–71.

These types of experiences are frequently associated with pastoral fallout and present a significant risk to the stability of church communities. Yet limited attention has been given to these problems in the Pentecostal academy and, indeed, to the experience itself.[6]

At the same time, the recent emphasis on the concept of *missio Dei* (the mission of God) in missiology and ecclesiology has served to reorient the focus of mission from the activity of the church to the activity of the 'missionary God'.[7] This shift has highlighted the role of the Spirit and given rise to the call for Pentecostal voices in the conversation. British scholar Andy Lord advocates for the integration of Pentecostal, Charismatic and Evangelical voices into a theology that transcends denominational identities for the purpose of mission. In this, he argues for engagement with practical realities.[8] This article represents a response to Lord's call, as it brings into dialogue missiological insights on the role of the Spirit with the findings of a 2020 PhD study among Australian Pentecostals as they reflect on their revelatory experiences.[9]

The discussion therefore fulfils a dual purpose that moves in both directions. The first is to engage the Trinitarian insights of *missio Dei* to the practice of Pentecostal revelatory experience. The second is to offer a Pentecostal voice to missiological discussions on the Spirit's role in the church. The discussion allows for renewed understandings about the role of revelatory experience in relation to *missio Dei* and helps to address some of the ministry problems brought about by Pentecostal revelatory experience. We begin with a description of the distinctive nature of the experience, including its associated ministry problems and neglect in the academy.

1. The Pentecostal revelatory experience

From the outset, it is necessary to define what is meant by the 'Pentecostal revelatory experience'. While Christianity has always maintained a

---

6 Tania M. Harris, 'The Place of Contemporary Revelatory Experiences in Pentecostal Theology', *Journal of the European Pentecostal Theological Association* 41, no. 2 (2021).
7 David J. Bosch, *Transforming Mission: Paradigm Shifts in Theology of Mission* (Maryknoll: Orbis, 1991).
8 Andy Lord, 'Spirit-Driven Gospel Communities of Transformation', *Mission Studies* 34 (2017): 180; Kevin Ward, 'The Needed Contribution of Charismatic and Pentecostal Christianity to Missional Theology and the Missional Church Movement', Presented at the Australian and New Zealand Association of Theological Schools Conference 2019.
9 Tania M. Harris, 'Towards a Theology of Pentecostal Revelatory Experience', PhD Thesis (Sydney, Alphacrucis College, 2020).

belief in a revelatory God, understandings about how that revelation is expressed varies widely among ecclesial traditions. For conservative streams of Evangelicalism, the experience is equated solely with the reading and exposition of Scripture by the Spirit's illumination.[10] Although these activities remain valid for the Pentecostal, when it comes to 'hearing God's voice', there is clear differentiation from them.[11]

1.1 The nature of Pentecostal revelatory experience

While it is difficult to make generalisations about the nature of revelatory experience across global Pentecostalism, sociologists and practical theologians in North America, the UK and Australia provide some insight. For Pentecostals (and Charismatics),[12] 'hearing God's voice' includes the possibility of direct contact with God by the Holy Spirit apart from Scripture or human intermediaries. God's 'voice' may be heard in the form of inspired experiences such as dreams, visions, voices and sensory impressions.[13] Fundamental to these expressions of 'hearing God's voice' is the element of revelation whereby God 'discloses' or 'unveils' something that was previously secret or unknown (1 Corinthians 14:26). Termed 'high-level' revelation by sociologists, Pentecostal encounters include the likelihood of previously unknown, future-oriented and extra-biblical information.[14] These inspired messages arise spontaneously apart from cognitive reflection.[15]

---

10 For example, Richard B. Gaffin, 'A Cessationist View', in *Are Miraculous Gifts for Today?*, ed. Wayne Grudem (Grand Rapids: Zondervan, 1996), 23–64.

11 Lee, 'Pentecostal Prophecy', 159-160.

12 The Charismatic church stream (typically those who affirm and practise spiritual gifts, but who are not affiliated with the Pentecostal church) generally shares the Pentecostal approach to revelatory experience. For British Charismatic Max Turner, there is no sharp line dividing them. The difference is 'one of degree and not of kind; one of emphasis, and not absolute' – distinctions exist only in terms of semantics, expectation and presentation, *The Holy Spirit and Spiritual Gifts* (Grand Rapids: Baker Academic, 2012), 339-345. Thus, in this paper, I speak of a 'Pentecostal-Charismatic' (P-C) approach to Spirit experience (also Douglas Oss, 'A Pentecostal/Charismatic View' in *Are Miraculous Gifts for Today?*, ed. Wayne Grudem (Grand Rapids: Zondervan, 1996), 238–83.

13 Mark J. Cartledge, 'Charismatic Prophecy: A Definition and Description', *Journal of Pentecostal Theology*, no. 5 (1994): 83-84; Margaret M. Poloma, *Main Street Mystics: The Toronto Blessing and Reviving Pentecostalism* (Walnut Creek: AltaMira Press, 2003); Harris, 'Towards a Theology', 214.

14 Cartledge 'Definition', 81; Lum, *Practice of Prophecy*, 67, 93, 212; Harris, 'Towards a Theology', 77-78, Charles Y. Glock and Rodney Stark, *Religion and Society in Tension* (Chicago: Rand McNally, 1965), 54-61.

15 Cartledge, 'Definition', 88; Lee, 'Pentecostal Prophecy'; 160, Lum, *Practice of Prophecy*, 92.

The Pentecostal revelatory experience is best understood in the context of its worldview, which sees contemporary Spirit-encounters as analogous to those of the New Testament church. For Pentecostals, the present experience of the Spirit is 'historically primitivist', in that it is based on the prophecy of Joel in Acts 2:16-17, the legitimising text for the events of the original Day of Pentecost.[16] Biblical and contemporary horizons are fused such that there is no phenomenological demarcation between biblical and contemporary experience. Thus, Pentecostals affirm the phenomena described in Acts (including glossolalia, healing, miracles, prophecy, dreams and visions) as repeatable and strive to emulate them in their own practice. These experiences are held to be phenomenologically equivalent to and even identical to those of the first century church.[17]

In my own research among Australian Pentecostals, this 'experientially continuous' approach to the biblical characters framed the expectation for contemporary revelatory experiences.[18] In keeping with typical Pentecostal practice, the biblical narratives (e.g. Acts 8:29, 10:9-13, 13:2, 16:9) were used as models for understanding the experience and provided concrete demonstrations of its outworking at every phase. Hence, revelatory messages were 'heard' in the same modes as the biblical experience (as dreams/visions and voices), understood to have the potential for epistemological reliability and, once tested as authentic, were seen to be authoritative over the intended audience and the circumstances to which they referred.[19]

1.2 The ministry problems of Pentecostal revelatory experience

Although valued for their contribution to spirituality, Pentecostal revelatory experiences are also characterised by volatility and disruption. A multiplicity of pastoral and sociological problems have been identified by scholars and popular leaders alike. Pentecostal scholar Matthias Wenk highlights the tendency of Pentecostals to sensationalise revelatory experiences and pursue them as 'personal oracles' and 'newly revealed insights' rather than for their 'biblical purpose'.[20] Popular Pentecostal preacher John Bevere observes that contemporary prophetic ministry panders to

---

16 Steven J. Land, *Pentecostal Spirituality: A Passion for the Kingdom* (Sheffield: Sheffield Academic Press, 1993), 72.
17 Anderson, *An Introduction*, 20; Land, *Pentecostal Spirituality*, 15.
18 Tania M. Harris, 'Where Pentecostalism and Evangelicalism Part Ways: Towards a Theology of Pentecostal Revelatory Experience Part 1', *Asian Journal of Pentecostal Studies* 23, no. 1 (2020): 30-31.
19 Harris, 'Towards a Theology', 212-213.
20 Matthias Wenk, 'What Is Prophetic about Prophecies: Inspiration or Critical Memory?', *Journal of Pentecostal Theology*, no. 26 (2017): 194-5.

personal agendas, human desires and 'idols of the heart' rather than to the 'biblical emphasis' of repentance and ministry.[21] He labels current prophetic ministry as a 'church-wide crisis' and details a torrid list of counterfeit prophecy's effects: 'broken marriages, dashed hopes, divided congregations, unrealizable promises, terrorized pastors, rebellion, despair, guilt and discouragement'.[22] North American pastor and scholar Michael Brown further notes rampant abuses, 'foolish gullibility' and a chronic lack of discernment. He also points to mercenary prophets who laud their gifts for financial gain and status.[23] The problems are serious and widespread, but not particularly novel. Oliver recounts the misuse and abuse of revelatory experience throughout its history.[24]

In addition to the pastoral issues, revelatory experiences pose a significant threat to institutional stability. Sociologists have long recognised the disruptive nature of revelatory experience, with those involving *new* revelation representing the greatest challenge.[25] German sociologist Max Weber was the first to describe this phenomenon. He showed that the charismatic experiences that are so vital to the establishment of new ministries later act to challenge bureaucratic structures, leading to disruption.[26] The core issue is the power-tussle between the voice of the institutional leadership and 'voice of God' as experienced by the individual. The Pentecostal concept of *all* having the capacity to hear from God (Acts 2:16,17) unwittingly invites conflict between leader and follower. As Coleman describes it, God's voice acts like a 'third person into the mix, bringing the constant threat of social cleavage'.[27] Glock and Stark further show that experiences known for their *commissioning* nature and new and previously unknown revelation run the highest risk of instability. As a result, these high-level revelatory experiences are actively discouraged by institutions as they grow.[28] Evidence of this Weberian

---

21 John Bevere, *Thus Saith the Lord?* (Lake Mary: Creation House, 1999), 59.
22 Bevere, *Thus Saith the Lord?*, 6.
23 Michael, L. Brown, *Playing with Holy Fire* (Lake Mary: Charisma House, 2018), 15-27, 29-34, 80-83.
24 Jeff Oliver, *Pentecost to the Present, Book 1: Early Prophetic and Spiritual Gifts Movements* (Newberry: Bridge-Logos, 2017), 97.
25 Margaret M. Poloma, *The Assemblies of God at the Crossroads: Charisma and Institutional Dilemmas* (Knoxville: University of Tennessee Press, 1989), 30, 70.
26 Max Weber, *The Theory of Social and Economic Organization*, trans. AM Henderson and Talcott Parsons (New York: The Free Press, 1947).
27 James S. Coleman, 'Social Cleavage and Social Change', *Journal of Social Issues*, no. XII (1956): 56.
28 Glock and Stark, *Religion and Society*, 60.

dynamic has been found in North American (Assemblies of God), South African and Australian Pentecostal churches.[29]

1.3 Neglect of theological reflection on revelatory experiences in the Pentecostal-Charismatic academy

In spite of the ubiquity of extra-biblical revelatory experience in Pentecostal practice, there is a surprising dearth of theological reflection on the topic in the academy. Instead, Pentecostal-Charismatic scholarship tends to focus on the gift of prophecy (requiring an intermediary) in the public service rather than the direct universal experience in private settings.[30] This neglect in the Pentecostal-Charismatic academy extends to the field of missiology. Even though the previous two decades have seen a substantial increase in attention to the Spirit's role by Pentecostal scholars in mission,[31] these works generally reflect the Pentecostal emphasis on the sign of glossolalia and the Spirit's empowerment for mission as the central feature of the Spirit's outpouring, with Acts 1:8 as the primary text.[32] The frequency of Spirit revelatory experiences within Pentecostalism is regularly acknowledged, but not elaborated upon.

This may in part be due to accepted understandings about Acts 2:16,17 where the Spirit's role is seen to refer primarily to vocational mission rather than revelation. So, for Pentecostal Roger Stronstad, the New Covenant status of believers as 'prophets' is equated with inspired preaching— 'everyone who preaches the good news about Jesus is a prophet'.[33] John Penney is even more emphatic about the Spirit's role at Pentecost: 'The Spirit of prophecy in Luke, then, is not to be understood as a universal capacity for receipt and delivery of revelations,

---

29 Poloma, *Crossroads*, Poloma & Green, *Godly Love*; Matthew S. Clark, 'An Investigation into the Nature of a Viable Pentecostal Hermeneutic' (Ph.D. thesis, South Africa, University of Pretoria, 1997), 218; Angelo U. Cettolin, *Spirit, Freedom and Power* (Eugene: Wipf and Stock, 2016), 76, 97-98.
30 Harris, 'Place of Experiences'.
31 Veli-Matti Kärkkäinen notes the significant contribution of Pentecostal scholarship, 'The Pentecostal Understanding of Mission', in *Pentecostal Mission and Global Christianity*, ed. Wonsuk Ma, Veli-Matti Kärkkäinen and J Kwabena Asamoah-Gyadu (Eugene: Wipf & Stock, 2014).
32 For example, Land, *Pentecostal Spirituality*,60; Kärkkäinen, 'Pentecostal Understanding', Julie C. Ma and Wonsuk Ma, *Mission in the Spirit: Towards a Pentecostal/Charismatic Missiology* (Oxford: Regnum, 2010).
33 Roger Stronstad, 'The Rebirth of Prophecy: Trajectories from Moses to Jesus and His Followers', *Journal of Biblical & Pneumatological Research* 5 (2013): 14; also Kärkkäinen, 'Pentecostal Understanding', 34.

but of participation in a prophetic community in which missionary proclamation is the paramount activity'.[34]

This omission of reflection on extra-biblical experiences in the academy has had grave consequences for its practice in Pentecostalism. What is lacking is a clear theological framework by which to conceive the function of revelatory experience, so that associated ministry problems can only be addressed. A missiological perspective provides a needful contribution to this framework.

2. Methodology: a study in three Pentecostal churches

My PhD study investigated the theology and practice of revelatory experience among Australian Pentecostals. It drew on the tools and theories of practical theology to reflect biblically and empirically on the contemporary revelatory experience. Specifically, the study employed Mark Cartledge's dialectic model[35] Jeff Astley's concept of 'ordinary theology'[37] and David Martin's work on 'rescripting'.[38]

Cartledge's model draws on the concept of 'dialectic', which is based on the notion of dialogue and is modelled on the interaction between creature and Creator through the response of faith. A Pentecostal-Charismatic perspective highlights the pneumatological dimension in this process as the Spirit works to lead humanity into truth. His model reflects the pastoral cycle that begins with the experience in question and is followed by theological reflection and engagement with the broader conversation. The 'conversation' involves both the 'lifeworld' of the subjects as well as the broader theological 'system' they are a part of. This allows for each voice to interrogate the other in a way than enables movement towards renewal and transformation of both.[39]

Cartledge's methodology employs the testimonies and theological reflections of individuals as the primary source of data. He points to the work of Astley who seeks to place value on the theology and theologising

---

34 John M. Penney, 'The Testing of New Testament Prophecy', *Journal of Pentecostal Theology* 10 (1997): 58.
35 Mark J. Cartledge, Mark J. Cartledge, 'Practical Theology and Charismatic Spirituality: Dialectics in the Spirit', *Journal of Pentecostal Theology* 10, no. 2 (2002): 93–109. and his use of testimonies,[36] (Farnham: Ashgate, 2010).
37 Jeff Astley, *Ordinary Theology* (Aldershot: Ashgate, 2002).
38 David Martin, 'Undermining Old Paradigms: Rescripting Pentecostal Accounts', *PentecoStudies: Online Journal for the Interdisciplinary Study of Pentecostal and Charismatic Movements* 5, no. 1 (2006): 18–38.
39 Cartledge, 'Dialectics', 93–109.

of 'ordinary' Christians living out their faith in everyday settings. This 'God talk', which Astley argues is often ignored by the academic elite, is distinct from doctrine and dogma and includes the 'content, patterns and processes of people's articulation of their own theological understandings'.[40] The value of ordinary theology is that it takes place in personal learning contexts as individuals reflect on their experience and work out answers to their own theological questions.[41] Astley shows that their insights should be incorporated into the theological discussion.

Cartledge parallels Astley's ordinary theology with sociologist David Martin's concept of 'rescription'. In this understanding, ordinary theology forms a kind of script, and scholarly engagement with the script forms a process of 'rescripting'. This approach allows the insights of personal stories to be brought into dialogue with the academic voices of various theological traditions (as well as the insights of social science). The process thus allows for any dissonance between the script and the academy to be articulated and then properly addressed against the 'script' of Scripture and the various theologies available. From there, recommendations can be made for praxis.

The study employed qualitative tools to investigate the theology and practice of a sample of Australian Pentecostals. Qualitative methods were chosen as they allow the experiences and reflections of individuals to be examined in detail. They are particularly suited for examining the 'why' behind the 'what' – in this case the theology behind the narrative. Practical theologians Swinton and Mowat show that qualitative research is best suited to discovering 'ideographic knowledge'. This type of knowledge differs from 'nomothetic' knowledge that is 'falsifiable, replicable and generalizable' and gained through the scientific method.[42] In contrast, ideographic knowledge is discovered in the examination of unique and non-replicable experiences. The goal of qualitative research is not objectivity as much as deeper understanding through a rich and thick exploration of particular situations.

This approach recognises that two individuals will not experience the same event in the same way and there are thus limits to generalisation and transferability. However, there remains a degree of shared experience that resonates across different contexts. Qualitative research seeks to identify the issues that extend beyond the specifics of individual situations. Hence

---

40 Astley, *Ordinary Theology*, 53, 56.
41 Astley, *Ordinary Theology*, 159.
42 John Swinton and Harriet Mowat, *Practical Theology and Qualitative Research* (SCM. Kindle Electronic Edition: 2006), Loc. 839-974.

it draws on the language of *themes* and *patterns* and relates them to wider systems of theological knowledge.[43]

In the study, data was gathered from a representative sample from three local Pentecostal churches in Sydney over a period of six months. The primary criterion for selection of the three churches was that they were all Pentecostal in name and affiliation. This was to maximise the likelihood that participants would hold to a position of phenomenological equivalency and that high-level revelatory experiences would be present for investigation. The churches were further selected for their ability to represent different styles and expressions of the contemporary Australian Pentecostal movement; in this case, an independent church with revivalist expression, a classical Pentecostal church[44] and a Pentecostal church with 'seeker-sensitive' tendencies.[45] Although this sample is too small to represent the theology and practice of wider Pentecostalism in Australia, it enables the possibility of exploring the themes common to revelatory experience.

In-depth semi-structured interviews were the primary method used to examine the ordinary theology and practice of revelatory experiences in the study. The study involved 54 semi-structured individual interviews and 7 focus groups. In total, 162 revelatory experiences from a representative sample of 89 individuals were investigated. Swinton and Mowat show that in research pertaining to 'ideographic' knowledge, more importance is placed on the nature of the sample than the size of the sample.[46] In this project, it was estimated that a sample of 50 individuals would provide sufficient revelatory experiences with the element of extra-biblical and previously unknown information to address the focus of the project. The sample was also intended to ensure a good spread of subjects across age-groups, genders, educational backgrounds and levels of Christian affiliation so that common patterns could be identified.

---

43 Swinton and Mowat, *Practical Theology and Qualitative Research*, Loc.
44 Amos Yong shows how the designation 'classical' arose in the 1970s in response to the Charismatic movement in mainline Protestant and Catholic denominations and refers to churches and denominations which have their origins in the USA during the 1910s and 20s. The central feature is glossolalia as the initial evidence of the baptism of the Holy Spirit. Amos Yong, *Discerning the Spirit(s)* (Sheffield: Sheffield Academic Press, 2000), 151.
45 This term was coined to describe the strategy of the influential Willow Creek Church in Chicago as they designed their services to appeal to the visitor or 'seeker' as a form of evangelism. Gregory A. Pritchard, *Willow Creek Seeker Services: Evaluating a New Way of Doing Church* (Grand Rapids: Baker Books, 1996).
46 Swinton and Mowat, *Practical Theology and Qualitative Research*, Loc.

Questions covered the hearing, recognising and response phases of revelatory experience: 'Tell me a time you heard God's voice', 'How did you know it was God?' and, 'What happened as a result of the experience?' Afterwards, each interview was recorded, transcribed and coded using NVIVO software. A summary of the findings relating to the function and outcomes of revelatory experience follows.

3. Findings: the function of revelatory experience

The data revealed clear understandings about how revelatory experiences functioned for interviewees. Six outcomes were apparent.

The primary function of revelatory experiences for respondents was to *build a 'personal' relationship with God*. Two-way communication (speaking and hearing) was seen as integral to this process. Experiences were understood to reflect God's inclination towards friendship and intimacy in ways that were analogous to human relationships. Since prayer involved the sharing of personal concerns and petitions towards God, it was unsurprising that God would respond in kind. The personal nature of subject matter (family, career, health, finances, lifestyle and the like) reflected understandings about a God who was interested in everyday concerns and actively desired to be involved in an individual's life.

This experiential process was sometimes contrasted with learning via the Scriptures, with the key distinction being the *personalised* nature of the messages:

> I mean you have the Scriptures—and they're awesome, but for me, if I didn't have it [hearing God's voice], I'd be very lost. It makes it personal; it brings you face to face with those encounters, it changes you.

Thus, revelatory experiences allowed for a generic knowledge of God's nature to be applied to personal contexts. Doctrines such as the love and omnipresence of God were actualised in individual settings.

A second outcome of revelatory experience was to provide a vehicle for *experiencing the felt presence of God* in specific and tangible ways. As such, it functioned as an apologetic: 'I know God is real'. This was particularly the case in instances involving revelation of previously unknown information. Respondents understood that as a sovereign and transcendent deity, God was able to disclose information from beyond the confines of human intelligence and the material realm. Such experiences induced a sense of wonderment and facilitated the development of affections towards God.

Thirdly, revelatory experiences functioned pragmatically to *provide care and protection*. This included emotional and physical concerns. For example, 'God spoke' to protect individuals from car accidents, domestic abuse, fire in the home, an impending lawsuit and suicide. Some experiences related to the healing of physical ailments including the correction of a misread x-ray that circumvented brain surgery, diagnosis of a serious vitamin deficiency and the healing of arthritis in a pianist's hands. The revelation of previously unknown information often equipped the person to deal with the matter at hand. There were also several experiences that produced hope for future provision, including finances, housing and relationships. Such experiences reinforced facets of God's nature to the individual.

Fourthly, revelatory experience initiated a *process of personal transformation*. The experience acted as a change agent, providing the impetus for personal growth and behavioural changes that resulted in betterment of life. As one interviewee described it, 'It's not the information he has given me that is as important as the process of my changing to accommodate what that will look like'. Areas of focus included healing from emotional wounds such as abuse, divorce and childhood trauma as well as the development of self-esteem, body image and leadership ability. The experience also involved aspects of moral change, including the forgiveness of others, development of generosity, how to be a better marriage partner and the removal of corrupting influences. In turn, this led to the restoration of positive human relationships and the removal of negative ones. Experiences often deeply affected the recipient and contributed to their transformational impact. A small number of experiences were reported to have a disciplinary function. These were understood in the context of a loving relationship and seen as a necessary curtailment of poor attitudes and decisions. Experiences frequently called for a denial of personal desires and surrender to divine ways.

A fifth outcome of revelatory experience was to *reveal God's plan* for the person's life. In a significant number of cases, revelatory experiences provided a form of personal guidance that resulted in radical shifts in careers or geographic locations. In cases where experiences involved the fulfilment of predictive information, participants felt a sense of affirmation and confirmation for their decision.

Finally, a significant number of experiences acted to mobilise respondents to *church and mission-related activity*. These included instructions related to church attendance, volunteering and active service with local welfare services and visitation, calls to vocational ministry, intercessory prayer and evangelism as well as cross-cultural mission. Often the experience led to major life change, including the call to an unknown tribe in China, foster children, work with the homeless, minister on trips to India, plant a church, evangelise strangers, enter pastoral ministry and commence outreach courses. The experience also prompted intercession for the (often previously unknown) needs of friends, family and international leaders. Once discerned to be from God, respondents treated their experiences as authoritative. Thus, the revelation acted to challenge, equip and mobilise individuals to pray, serve and evangelise. Individuals correlated the Spirit's work in their own lives to the biblical experiences (such as Paul's 'Macedonian call' (Acts 16), mobilising them towards the same mission.

4. Analysis in dialogue with missiologist Craig Van Gelder

This analysis brings the ordinary theology of Pentecostals in the sample relating to the *role* of revelatory experience into dialogue with missiological thinking. Themes and patterns from the ordinary theology of participants are rescripted in conjunction with understandings of *missio Dei*.

I have selected the voice of missiologist Craig Van Gelder[47] to engage the testimonial data. Even though Van Gelder lies outside the Pentecostal tradition and does not necessarily share the Pentecostal view of extra-biblical revelatory experience, his work provides an appropriate vehicle for analysis because it aligns well with the Pentecostal approach to the biblical text. Van Gelder examines the role of the church in mission based on a particular reading of *Spirit-led activities* in the New Testament accounts. This approach reflects the Pentecostal hermeneutic and their expectation for experiential continuity with the biblical characters. It also aligns with the Pentecostal focus on the narratives and their literal and pragmatic connections with the activities of the early church.[48] Like Van Gelder, Pentecostals are concerned with *practical* outcomes.

---

47 Craig Van Gelder, *The Ministry of the Missional Church: A Community Led by the Spirit* (Grand Rapids: Baker Books, 2007).
48 Keith Warrington, *Pentecostal Theology: A Theology of Encounter* (London: T&T Clark, 2008), 191.

4.1 The work of Craig Van Gelder

Together with a chorus of missiologists, Craig Van Gelder argues that the contemporary church should be by its nature missional. The church is created and led by the Spirit to fulfil *missio Dei*. Since the Spirit is already doing the work of 'changing lives and transforming communities', the task of the church then becomes to *facilitate* that work under the Spirit's leadership. This involves careful discernment and response to what the Spirit is *already doing*. Thus, church leadership should be focused on 'discerning the Spirit's leading and discovering ways to implement ministry in their particular context in light of that leading'.[49] For Van Gelder, this is described largely as the examination of Scripture in light of the church's respective confessional traditions and history.

Van Gelder notes that if the church is to participate in God's mission in the world, it must first understand the ministry of the Spirit. Careful attention to the Spirit's work in Scripture provides the framework for understanding this participation. To that end, Van Gelder draws on a survey of Spirit-led activities in Acts and the epistles to define the nature of the Spirit's ministry.[50] This provides a template for discerning the work of the Spirit in the contemporary church. Five dimensions are included: 1. Create a new type of reconciled community with one identity in Christ (Galatians 3:28); 2. Empower leadership to guide the community (Acts 6; 1 Corinthians 12:28); 3. Lead into sanctified living consistent with a new nature in Christ (Romans 8:2-14; Galatians 5:25); 4. Lead into active ministry for the sake of others in the church and for the world based on gifting (Ephesians 4:7-8; 1 Corinthians 12:7); and 5. Lead into the world to unmask principalities and powers so that these powers come to know the wisdom of God (Ephesians 6:12, 3:10).

Van Gelder shows how the leading of the Spirit engages the local context within which it is located. As the Spirit's mission is 'embedded in a particular context', there can be 'no one size fits all' in terms of church programs or models.[51] Emphasis is therefore placed on discerning the particular workings of the Spirit in the local church and its community.

Further, Van Gelder examines how the Spirit's ministry leads to growth and development in the church. He proposes that this aspect is so prominent in Acts that it should be seen as the 'lens' through which the work of the Spirit is understood. He also notes that Spirit-led growth

---

49 Van Gelder, *Missional Church*, 19.
50 Van Gelder, *Missional Church*, 41.
51 Van Gelder, *Missional Church*, 63-67.

often came through 'conflict, disruption, interruption and surprise'.[52] The voice of the Spirit is seen to agitate, challenge and redirect rather than merely confirm, with the immediate consequences bringing undesirable results at first.

4.2 Rescripting ordinary theology

The rescription process allows for differences and similarities to be identified between the voices of the academy and the 'ordinary theology' of study participants. Three themes from the data are highlighted here for rescription with Van Gelder: 1. The ministry and missional outcomes of revelatory experience; 2. The lack of a missional framework for the discernment of revelatory experience; 3. A missiological solution to the sociological problem of institutional instability.

4.2.1 The ministry and missional outcomes of revelatory experience

Clear correlations can be seen between Van Gelder's understanding of the Spirit's work and the study data. To varying degrees, all of Van Gelder's five categories for Spirit-led ministry were evidenced in the testimonies. Revelatory experiences helped to build relationships in the life of the church. They provided the impetus for sanctified living and transformation into Christlikeness. They comprised calls to ministry at lay and vocational levels. They precipitated outreach and missional activities within the church and community. As individuals heard, discerned and co-operated with the Spirit, they experienced the work of God among them. The data clearly supports Van Gelder's supposition that the Spirit is already doing the work of 'changing lives and transforming communities'.[53]

The ministry and missional outcomes of revelatory experience in the study can be further delineated in two ways. The first aspect relates to *motivation* for ministry and mission and is highlighted in Van Gelder's third dimension of sanctification into Christ's nature. The data showed that a prominent function of revelatory experience was to bring about personal transformation. Areas of healing, self-esteem, forgiveness, generosity and relationship-building were all prominent. The Spirit's revelatory work was seen actively ministering to individual lives.

---

52 Van Gelder, *Missional Church*, 158.
53 Van Gelder, *Missional Church*, 151.

Here, the experience provided the trigger for new moral behaviours as individuals were asked to forgive when they were reluctant to, reconcile with those they disagreed with and be generous when they did not want to be. However, this 'new nature' was not entirely directed to the self. Revelatory experiences frequently reflected an orientation towards others. The Spirit spoke to call attention to the needs of the wider community and provided the impetus for respondents to engage in outreach, service and mission. Emotions were often involved as the revelatory experience stirred compassion and a sense of urgency. These affections motivated participants to partner with the divine mission in new ways. Hence the divine-human relationship formed the context for missional outreach.

The second aspect of missional outcomes in the study related to *directions and strategies*, reflecting Van Gelder's fourth dimension – *lead into active ministry based on gifting*. Here, the Spirit provided participants with specific instructions to minister to others in new contexts and ways. This enabled contextualisation to occur. As Van Gelder observes, while the mission may not change, the manner in which it is done will.[54] In keeping with similar studies,[55] divine directions led participants into a range of missional activities such as intercessory prayer, visitation, giving and work in needy communities. Divine instructions led participants to a range of places, from the local gym and the next-door neighbour to remote locations overseas.

For respondents, revelatory experiences were to be obeyed because they were held to be divinely authoritative—even when the prospect invoked a level of trepidation. One of the intriguing aspects of the experience was the 'otherness' of 'God's voice'. Phrases such as 'It was not something I would say or think', 'It was so random' and 'It had never entered my mind' were used repeatedly in testimonies. Several interviewees reflected on how their experiences took them beyond their normal lifestyles and inclinations but found that this is what 'they were born for'. One interviewee would not have considered the possibility of fostering a child due to her single status. Another reflected on the Spirit's leading into children's ministry, 'It's funny because I continually wanted to fight it. It wasn't something I wanted to do ... I never felt convicted to do kids. But

---

54 Van Gelder, *Missional Church*, 151.
55 In the American Assemblies of God: Poloma & Green, *Godly Love*, 120,141; in North American Episcopalian churches: Ralph W. Hood Jr, *Handbook of Religious Experience* (Birmingham: Religious Education Press, 1995), 176, and in Britain: William K. Kay, *Pentecostals in Britain* (Carlisle: Paternoster, 2000).

then I thought, 'Wow, I really walked into my hub here!'" In other words, participants would not have contemplated such mission-related actions without the revelatory experience, yet later found this to be consistent with their 'gifting'.

In many cases, the element of previously unknown information was essential in providing strategies that could not be humanly devised (for example, the location for a church in an unfamiliar city, the existence of an obscure tribe in China and the secret sex crimes of a North Korean dictator). Pentecostal scholar Crinisor Stefan frames this new revelation in terms of Jesus' promise to his disciples: the Spirit would speak both *retrospectively* to remind them of the truths established by Jesus (and now recorded for us in Scripture) (John 14:26) and prospectively to guide them into what is 'yet to come' (John 16:13-14).[56] The function of previously-unknown or future-oriented revelation then was to apply the 'established truths' of Jesus' mission to the new contexts as 'things to come'.[57] This provided new and innovative approaches to mission as well as opening up networks and resources that were previously inaccessible.

The missional outcome of revelatory experience in relation to mission is aptly illustrated by Rowena's testimony. As a beginning actor and committed Christian, she questioned her place in an industry that was at times morally challenging and isolating. After praying for wisdom, she received a vision in which she saw herself standing on a high cliff, looking out to sea. The night was dark but lit by a full moon. Suddenly, the ocean seemed to shift. Waves of water rolled back to expose what was beneath. Strewn across the ocean floor were countless numbers of fish bones and carcasses. Rowena was struck with a deep sense of conviction: 'These are all the fish that nobody went to catch'.

Rowena's experience led her to see the entertainment industry as her mission field and an affirmation of her career choice. Imbued with a sense of divine purpose, she was able to view the challenges of her work as an opportunity to 'shine God's light'. The revelatory experience not only provided motivation for service but reinforced the specific location for her involvement in *missio Dei*.

As in Van Gelder's work on the Spirit's role in the early church, the Spirit in contemporary revelatory experience can be seen facilitating *missio Dei*. The study data indicated the potential for high-level revelatory

---

[56] Crinisor Stefan, 'The Paraclete and Prophecy in the Johannine Community', *Pneuma: The Journal of the Society for Pentecostal Studies*, 27 no. 2 (2005): 273.
[57] This is in contrast with the evangelical tendency to interpret John 16:13 as illumination on *past* issues. For example, Turner, *Holy Spirit*, 82.

experiences to provide *motivation* and *strategy* for mission. In this way, Spirit encounters led to new directions that precipitated growth in the manner of the early church.

At the same time, the data is in contrast with Van Gelder's work which places emphasis on the development of certain skills, aptitudes and organisational leadership to facilitate the Spirit's work in mission. For Van Gelder, 'reading the context' and developing aptitude for change are held to be essential.[58] In contrast, the study participants' role centred more on *submission* to the revelatory experience as the Spirit took the lead in initiating and strategising, particular in the initial stages. In this way, the concept of *missio Dei*, with the triune God as primary acting subject, was reinforced. This did not negate human involvement entirely—respondents continued to be actively engaged in the process through obedience and co-operation. However, the process appeared to arise more on divine than human initiative.

4.2.2 The lack of a missional framework for the discernment of revelatory experience

The missional framework advocated by Van Gelder enables contemporary revelatory experiences to be conceptualised by the ministry of Jesus.[59] At a practical level, this shapes expectations for the function of the Spirit's revelatory work. As noted, Van Gelder emphasises the work of *discernment* in the church as a core need.

While the ministry and missional outcomes of revelatory experience were evident in the testimonial data, respondents often lacked a missional framework for their discernment. Experiences were more likely to be conceived in terms of divine affections and in response to personal needs, rather than the broader scope of Christ's ministry. This lack of a theological framework may contribute to the misguided penchant for 'personal oracles' sought 'for their own sake' observed by Wenk.[60] Tyra.[61] expresses a similar concern and calls for prophetic experiences to find their place in the church's mission.

The lack of a missional framework in the ordinary theology of study participants is reflected in the Pentecostal- Charismatic literature which generally fails to make the link between the universally accessible

---

58 Van Gelder, *Missional Church*, 63-67.
59 Van Gelder, *Missional Church*, 38.
60 Wenk, 'What Is Prophetic about Prophecies,' 194-5.
61 Gary Tyra, *The Holy Spirit in Mission* (Downers Grove: IVP, 2011).

revelatory experience and Christ's ongoing mission..[62] The experience is usually seen through the lens of prophecy elucidated in the epistles and is rarely associated with private revelation demonstrated most clearly in Acts..[63] This has had the effect of disconnecting the practice of hearing God's voice from Christ's mission. For example, respondents in the study readily referred to the rubric of 'encouragement, edification and comfort' (1 Corinthians 14:3) to describe their experience. Though helpful, this perspective does not reflect the Spirit's work as an extension of Christ in the same way as the narratives. As Stronstad has shown in relation to Luke and Acts, Christ and the Spirit have the same function..[64] As Van Gelder notes, the Spirit's activity should be viewed through a Christocentric lens as the Spirit acts to *continue* the ministry of Jesus (John 16:7).

Even while Van Gelder does not conceive 'what the Spirit is saying' in terms of revelatory experience, his missiological framework provides the theological grammar for Pentecostals to reflect on their experiences in light of their wider purpose. Revelatory claims could be judged by their fruit in producing outcomes related to Christ's ministry and mission. This in turn would mitigate against any penchant for personal agendas and act to minimise pastoral damage, as well as provide a corrective for the rise of 'mercenary prophets' and 'celebrity mega-prophets' whose identity is based on the Old Covenant prophets rather than on Christ.[65] An approach that links Spirit activity to Jesus reorients the focus from personal needs to missional service.

4.2.3 A missiological solution to the sociological problem of instability

The third theme evident in the data was a potential solution for the problem of social instability wrought by revelatory experience. The findings concurred with other sociological studies that show a correlation between revelatory experience and instability. In the study, this was particularly present in 'Church C', where concerns about the risk of

---

62 The link between Jesus' ministry and the Spirit is often made in Pentecostal hermeneutics (For example, Jackie David Johns and Cheryl Bridges-Johns, 'Yielding to the Spirit: A Pentecostal Approach to Group Bible Study', *Journal of Pentecostal Theology* I (1992): 114, but is rarely applied to direct revelatory experience (For example, Paul K. King, 'Discerning Dreams', *The Pneuma Review* (blog), 2020.
63 Harris, 'Place of Experiences'.
64 Roger Stronstad, *Spirit, Scripture and Theology: A Pentecostal Perspective* (Baguio City, APTS, 1995), 174-177.
65 Masiiwa Ragies Gunda, 'Prediction and Power: Prophets and Prophecy in the Old Testament and Zimbabwean Christianity', *Exchange* 41 (2012): 335-51.

dissension were apparent. Instances of individuals defying leadership decisions were cited as a cause for breakage and fallout from both sides. Social instability was also a product of poor discernment. Where a process of testing was neglected, claims to revelatory experience brought confusion, poor decision-making and conflict. This highlighted the need for appropriate training in discernment. However, once discerned, even 'authentic' experiences revealed potential for disruption since 'God's voice' acted to challenge pre-existing attitudes, mindsets and behaviours and led them in new directions. As one interviewee describes it; 'God's continually challenging us. We're in our comfort zones and it's like "I don't want to do that". But he's challenging us, because he knows it's better for us'. It was the recognition of a voice 'other' than their own that triggered change and often led to institutional disruption.

A missional framework provides a theological solution to this sociological problem. As Van Gelder shows, the Spirit's activity was the key to its expansion of the early church, yet this inevitably involved disruption. The onset of change is 'inherent in what it means to be human' and 'what it means to be Christian'.[66] Hence, if the church is to produce growth, it should *anticipate* change. From a theological perspective, the sociological driver of 'institutional stability' cannot be the goal. A missional framework embraces the change wrought by revelatory experience and then provides a mechanism within the community to channel it into divine purpose. Indeed, this approach was evident in 'Church A', where the risk of revelatory experience was acknowledged by senior leadership, yet *welcomed* in spite of it as *evidence of the Spirit's work*. This perspective equipped them to manage and minimise any fallout arising from the experience.

Conclusion

The value of practical theology is seen in providing a vehicle by which the voices of praxis and the academy can be brought together. In this case, the dialogue allows the Spirit's role in the *missio Dei* to provide an instructive contribution to the theological understandings and practical outworkings of revelatory experience in the Pentecostal church. A missiological framework enables extra-biblical Spirit experiences to be seen as the work of the triune God who has demonstrated the nature of divine ministry and mission in Jesus and continues this work via the Spirit today. As the Spirit spoke in the early church to call, develop and send the biblical characters in pursuit of Jesus' cause, so the Spirit motivates and directs mission activity in contemporary settings. This

---

66 Van Gelder, *Missional Church*, 155.

framework provides the appropriate language and guidelines for the function and outcomes of the revelatory experience within the greater ministry and mission of the church. This in turn assists in minimising the pastoral damage and sociological instability of the experience and enables it to be harnessed for kingdom purposes. At the same time, the discussion allows the dynamic of Pentecostal revelatory experience with its distinctive emphasis on new revelation to be highlighted in the missiological conversation.